Confidence, credibility and macroeconomic policy

The results of macroeconomic policy are often frustratingly unpredictable. One of the major reasons for this is the importance of confidence and expectations in economic affairs. For a government's economic policies to succeed they must gain and maintain economic credibility, which many governments are finding increasingly difficult. *Confidence, Credibility and Macroeconomic Policy* explores this interaction between fiscal and monetary stabilisation, confidence and expectations, and the credibility of the government's financial policies.

The volume is divided into three parts. Part I begins with an overview of the interrelationship between fiscal policy, credibility and inflation and presents two original, experimental studies that explore the effects of macroeconomic policies on expectations. Part II focuses on empirical research and presents historical as well as contemporary evidence on the importance of public confidence and expectations to the success of fiscal and monetary policy. Part III covers the definition and functions of consumer confidence as it is measured today. It includes an overview of its role in the 1990s along with theoretical frameworks that explicitly incorporate confidence in macroeconomic stabilisation. *Confidence, Credibility and Macroeconomic Policy* will be an invaluable guide for all those interested in macroeconomic policy.

Richard Burdekin is Associate Professor of Economics at Claremont McKenna College and Claremont Graduate School. **Farrokh Langdana** is Associate Professor of Economics and Finance at Rutgers School of Management.

Confidence, credibility and macroeconomic policy

Past, present, future

Richard C.K. Burdekin and
Farrokh K. Langdana

Routledge
Taylor & Francis Group
LONDON AND NEW YORK

First published 1995
by Routledge
2 Park Square, Milton Park, Abingdon, Oxfordshire OX14 4RN

Simultaneously published in the USA and Canada
by Routledge
711 Third Avenue, New York, NY 10017

First issued in paperback 2014

Routledge is an imprint of the Taylor and Francis Group, an informa business

Typeset in Garamond by
J&L Composition Ltd, Filey, North Yorkshire

British Library Cataloguing in Publication Data
A catalogue record for this book is available from the British Library

Library of Congress Cataloguing in Publication Data
Burdekin, Richard C. K. (Richard Charles Keighley). 1958–
Confidence, credibility, and macroeconomic policy: past, present, future/by Richard C. K. Burdekin and Farrokh K. Langdana.
p. cm.
Includes bibliographical references and index.
1. Economic stabilization. 2. Uncertainty. 3. Monetary policy. 4. Fiscal policy. I. Langdana, Farrokh K. II. Title.
HB3732.B87 1994
339.5—dc20 94–33820

ISBN 978-1-138-86580-8 (pbk)
ISBN 978-0-415-10278-0 (hbk)

The chief cause of the evil is a want of confidence. The greater part of it could be removed almost in an instant if confidence could return, touch all industries with her magic wand, and make them continue their production, and their demand for the wares of others.

(Alfred Marshall, 1879)

It is not necessary, apparently, that you should *justify* public confidence, but you have to *get* that confidence, whether justified or not. Finance seems extraordinarily like medicine in some respects.

(Udney Yule, 1927)

To
Yanjie, Eileen and Emma
RCKB

To
My dear wife Mary
FKL

Contents

Figures

Tables

Foreword

This book preaches the virtue of securing macroeconomic policy credibility.

It has been my pleasure to be able to demonstrate that the theory works in practice. Fresh from the experience of being New Zealand's Minister of Finance from 1990–1993, I can also confirm the authors' view that macroeconomic credibility and the confidence in that policy setting is hard won and easily lost.

New Zealand is a classic case study of the damage that discredited macro policies can do, just as we can demonstrate the worth of restoring macroeconomic credibility.

Reversing the trend of some two decades when budget deficits were the norm, New Zealand has managed to balance its books in the 1993/94 financial year, with a string of surpluses forecast to follow.

Our growth rate is currently one of the highest in the OECD (some 5 per cent) and our inflation rate one of the lowest (some 1.3 per cent). Economic confidence is at high levels with the number of new jobs rising and the recorded rate of unemployment falling.

The credible conduct of macroeconomic policy has played a very significant part in securing this turnaround. The New Zealand experience demonstrates that there are three vital elements to the achievement and maintenance of policy credibility: the quality of the policy setting; the commitment and the consistency with which the policies are pursued; and the perceived sustainability of the approach.

Our macroeconomic policy setting has been such a success because New Zealand's fiscal and monetary policies have been in harmony rather than in conflict and because the integrity of the conduct of fiscal and monetary policy is guaranteed by a tailor-made legislative framework.

Historically the New Zealand experience (writ large on a global scale) has seen fiscal policy at odds with monetary policy and vice versa. So often a determination to dedicate monetary policy to the achievement of price stability has been torpedoed by fiscal laxity. There are plenty of shameful (and expensive) episodes of monetary policy, under political instruction, being required to bail out poor fiscal policy. When monetary and fiscal policy are at war, interest and exchange rates tend to get caught in the crossfire with the economy an inevitable casualty.

Restoring the balance between fiscal and monetary policy is the crucial first step to macroeconomic credibility. Cementing in that credibility is the next step. New Zealand has chosen two pioneering pieces of legislation to guarantee a sound and successful framework for the conduct of monetary and fiscal policy.

The Reserve Bank Act 1989 legislates for a truly independent central bank, mandated to conduct monetary policy in a fashion that achieves and maintains price stability. Price stability is defined by a policy targets agreement as ranging between 0–2 per cent.

Stripped of political influence and stripped of the pretence that monetary policy can do other than achieve price stability, the Bank is free to pursue a singular and unequivocal policy objective which it does with distinction. It is the monetary policy setting for all seasons, proving itself in both recession and recovery.

The companion measure – the Fiscal Responsibility Act 1994 – seeks to achieve a similar credibility for the fiscal policy setting. The fiscal responsibility code has a very heavy emphasis on transparency. New Zealand is the first sovereign state in the world to subject itself to comprehensive accrual accounting. Combined with the availability of high quality financial information, the frequent and full disclosure of the fiscal position acts as a natural check and balance against bad fiscal behaviour.

Transparency itself isn't enough. The legislation goes further and identifies the characteristics of responsible fiscal policy and enshrines those in a set of legislative principles that will guide the conduct of fiscal policy. A government is free to self-select the specific fiscal targets (in that sense this is not a Gramm-Rudman model), but must do so in a fashion that is consistent with the legislative principles.

The five chosen principles are the following.

(a) Reducing total Crown debt to prudent levels so as to provide a buffer against factors that may impact adversely on the level of total Crown debt in the future, by ensuring that, until such levels have been achieved, the total operating expenses of the Crown in each financial year are less than its total operating revenues in the same finance year;

> The first principle acknowledges that, currently, New Zealand's debt levels are too high and should be lowered significantly in order to reduce the economy's vulnerability to adverse factors. This should be achieved by running surpluses on the operating balance.

(b) Once prudent levels of Crown debt have been achieved, maintaining these levels by ensuring that, on average, over a reasonable period of time, the total operating expenses of the Crown do not exceed its total operating revenues;

> The second principle implies that once debt has been reduced it should not (in general) be increased. In particular, a government should not borrow to 'pay for the groceries'. This principle is a medium to long term one. In the short term, cyclical factors may well result in temporary, and desirable, deviations from balance.

(c) Achieving and maintaining levels of Crown net worth that provide a buffer against factors that may impact adversely on the Crown's net worth in the future;

> The third principle recognises that there are a wider range of factors relevant to the fiscal position than a focus solely on debt would reveal. For example, the Crown's balance sheet includes a significant exposure to public service pension liabilities that are not caught within the usual definitions of public debt. More generally, it is not just the level of debt which is important but also the assets which are backing it. As for the debt principles, the focus on Crown net worth also reflects the thought that, over time, governments should prepare for eventualities that may not be reflected in the current balance sheet. For example, an aging population may imply impending increments to health and retirement income support.

(d) Managing prudently the fiscal risks facing the Crown;

> The fourth principle also acknowledges vulnerability issues and requires that governments should actively manage the risks

inherent in its assets, liabilities and off-balance sheet items such as guarantees.

(e) Pursuing policies that are consistent with a reasonable degree of predictability about the level and stability of tax rates for future years;

The fifth principle reflects the importance of stability in tax and expenditure levels for private sector planning and hence growth.

Recent editorial opinion supportive of this measure has been very encouraging. To quote:

'No one should quibble with any of this. It is all part of dealing openly with the public about the public's money, and would be a useful spur to keeping governments honest.'

The Fiscal Responsibility Act's strength 'is that it sets a very effective and public tripwire. If future governments wish to change direction and abandon a successful economic policy for narrowly political reasons, they will be required to declare their hand openly. They will also have to set out the reasons – and the likely fiscal consequences – for maximum political and public debate.'

The two monetary and fiscal statutes together constitute a legislative framework that promotes sound, credible policy and that acts as a bulwark against policy stances that would compromise the credibility of the policy setting.

The nicest thing about all of this is that Farrokh and Richard prove macroeconomic credibility works in theory and New Zealand proves that it works in practice!

Hon. Ruth Richardson,
Minister of Finance, New Zealand, 1990–93

Acknowledgements

We have benefited greatly from the assistance rendered by a large number of individuals, without whose help this volume would not have been possible. Professor Giles Mellon, in particular, has contributed immensely to the last two chapters of the book, and we are most grateful for his assistance and cooperation.

We are indebted to the Honourable Ruth Richardson, New Zealand's Minister of Finance from 1990 to 1993 and former Chairman of the New Zealand Parliament's Finance and Expenditure Committee, who has kindly contributed the foreword to this volume.

We are very grateful to Robert J. Barro for his encouragement and assistance in our experimental testing of his revival of Ricardian equivalence, and to Robert E. Lucas Jr., for his suggestions and intuition regarding our experimental verification of his universally well-known 'islands' model. We also thank Alan Blinder and William Baumol for their comments pertaining to the theoretical chapters on consumer confidence and stabilisation theory.

Our colleagues at Claremont and at Rutgers School of Management have been most helpful, and we are most grateful to Deans Anthony Fucaloro, George Benson, Ivan Brick and Rosa Oppenheim. We also wish to express our appreciation to Professors Sven Arndt, King Banaian, Paul Burkett, Michael Crew, Carter Daniel, Lawrence Fisher, Cheryl Holsey, Mike Kuehlwein, Steve Lewarne, Pierre Siklos and Tom Willett, and the anonymous referee of Routledge, for their assistance in various chapters of this book. Ida Huang, Edward Cooper and Greg Michels provided invaluable help with the graphs.

Financial assistance was generously provided by the Research Resources Committee of Rutgers School of Management and by a Claremont McKenna College summer research grant.

We acknowledge the infinite patience and tolerance of our wives Yanjie Burdekin and Mary Langdana, and Richard Burdekin also owes much to his in-laws, Delong Feng and Shuqin Shi, for keeping the children at bay while this volume was finished.

And finally, we are indeed grateful to our editors at Routledge, Alan Jarvis and Alison Kirk, who have been very encouraging and most kind in allowing us additional time in which we could extend and update the material in this book.

Introduction

As the United States, Canada, Japan, and the economies of Western Europe struggle to emerge from their respective recessions of the early 1990s with varying degrees of success, many of the emerging Eastern European republics are still grappling with additional problems such as runaway budget deficits and rampant monetisation. This money creation has, in turn, led to increases in inflation which range in magnitude from double-digit inflation to hyperinflation proportions in the former Soviet Republics, and the former Yugoslavia. Difficulties in charting a new course for monetary and fiscal policy are further compounded by the disturbing macroeconomic observation that successful fiscal or monetary policies for one country might sometimes prove unworkable for another. Or, even more confounding, a successful fiscal/monetary mix for one economy at a particular point in time will not necessarily work later on, even when applied to the same economy where these policies had borne fruit in the past!

One reason for the apparent unpredictability of macroeconomic policy is that it is conducted in an environment of individuals whose expectations are themselves functions of the past successes and failures of these macroeconomic policies. Individuals remember the consequences (both good and bad) of past policies, and use this information efficiently ('rationally') to form expectations of the results of these same polices in the future.[1] However, in doing so, they might indulge in hedging behaviour that could nullify policies that had previously proved effective for that government.

For example, mounting budget deficits due to profligate government spending in country A (which, hitherto was a balanced-budget economy) could necessitate a large increase in monetary growth in period 1 to monetise most of the deficit.[2] This might result in a temporary decrease in interest rates and an increase in GDP growth, only to be followed (inevitably) by future inflation (period 4 onwards, for example) which would, eventually, make its citizens worse off. The economy (period 4 onwards) would, in fact, tend to be characterised by net lower real GDP growth and a higher residual rate of inflation. Furthermore, national real wealth balances would deteriorate as the 'inflation tax' would sharply reduce the real value of household savings and incomes.

If the monetary authority of this country A were induced to increase money growth again in, say, period 10 – perhaps due to budget deficits burgeoning further out of control – individuals would use the information from periods 1–9 rationally, and form expectations of the consequences of renewed monetisation. They would, in all likelihood, rapidly contract for higher wages in anticipation of higher prices (in period 10). Moreover, as individuals seek to avoid the ongoing inflation tax by reducing their real money balances, further impetus is given to the inflationary spiral as the existing money stock is turned over faster and faster.

Expectations and public confidence, as influenced by the macroeconomic history of an economy, might account for sharp differences in inflation rates between two countries A and B even when the increases in the deficits (for example) in the same periods are identical. Country A could be in the 'Brazil or Russia' class whereas country B could be in the 'New Zealand or US' class, with the credibility of their respective monetary and fiscal policies being significantly different.[3] Citizens of the former draw on past information and experience (of low monetary credibility and discipline) to immediately associate any increases in deficits with automatic monetisation and, hence, rapid inflation, and indulge in hedging behaviour – wage indexation and so forth – which further adds to the inflationary pressure. Citizens of the latter class who form expectations in similar fashion using their information efficiently do not, however, indulge in hedging behaviour to the same extent because their country's macroeconomic policies have relatively greater credibility bred largely by greater monetary and fiscal discipline in the past.

At the same time, as shown in Chapter 4's account of the American Civil War, events that reduce the government's prospects for redeeming its debt issues out of future taxes will hurt bond sales today. Confidence that the deficits will not be inflated away is certainly likely to be critical in determining individuals' willingness to continue purchasing government bonds. Moreover, to the extent that stronger bond demand makes it feasible for the government to avoid financing the deficit with money creation, expectations of lower inflation could themselves become self-fulfilling. Conversely, when confidence is lacking, as appears to be the case in, say, Russia today, lack of demand for bond issues helps ensure the inflationary consequences of money finance.

This backdrop makes macroeconomic policy forecasting as difficult as the task of predicting expectations. As opposed to the field of engineering or the pure sciences where 'policy' is conducted in environments comprised of invariant Laws of Nature, macroeconomic policy is conducted in environments comprised of individuals that incorporate the past, present and expected future consequences of fiscal and monetary policies in decisions made in the present. Furthermore, as new information becomes available, individuals constantly update their information sets in forming expectations on the credibility and efficacy of current and future policies.

Therefore, the explicit inclusion of concepts and factors such as 'consumer confidence', 'expectations' and the 'credibility' of fiscal and monetary policies in the design and implementation of macroeconomic stabilisation are imperative not only for their theoretical and academic relevance, but also for their very real world policy implications. Macroeconomic theorists who do not explicitly account for these confidence and expectational factors and fiscal/monetary policy makers who simply choose to mimic successful macroeconomic policies of other countries (whose macroeconomic histories might be different and whose policies might have different degrees of credibility) run grave risks of retarding economic growth and damaging credibility in their own economies.

The objective of this book is to explore and present the role of the confidence factors in the effective design, analysis and implementation of the fiscal/monetary policy mix by presenting the results of experimental, empirical and theoretical research.

We distinguish between 'confidence' (which is used synonymously with 'sentiment') and 'expectations'. Expectations are, following the rational forecasting rules suggested by Muth (1961), defined as the mathematical conditional forecasts of future policy and macroeconomic activity based on the efficient use of all available information (in current and past time periods). 'Confidence' or 'sentiment' is harder to pin down mathematically, incorporating more broad-based, and idiosyncratic, influences such as the nature of previous policy regimes – the potential importance of which was discussed above – and agents' perceptions as to whether today's deviations in policy will be sustained in the future. Interestingly, the experiments and case studies in this book suggest that, up to a point, confidence in the restoration of a past non-inflationary regime can play a critical role in the public's willingness to hold the government's debt instruments (even in cases that eventually end in default and/or hyperinflation).

The overall 'credibility' of proposed (or current) macroeconomic policies is determined by households who (i) form rational expectations using all available information efficiently, and (ii) combine these expectations with more idiosyncratic information on the nature of the policy regime in determining their degree of 'confidence' in the efficacy of the proposed policies.

This book is divided into three parts, each containing three chapters. Chapter 1 attempts to set the stage for the rest of the book by providing a general perspective on the role played by the fiscal policy regime and confidence factors in determining the extent to which expansionary fiscal policy will feed into higher inflation rates. Chapters 2 and 3 present macroeconomic experiments designed to verify some of the cornerstone theories of macroeconomic policy, and to determine how agents react to controlled changes in the monetary and fiscal environment. Here we test the actual changes in expectations and behaviour of 'producers' and 'households' who respond to changes in fiscal and monetary policies in an experimental setting designed to mimic the macroeconomy.

Chapter 2 experimentally tests the theoretical fiscal propositions discussed in Chapter 1, with a particular emphasis on the influence of expectations on household behaviour when the fiscal regime shifts from tax-backed temporary deficits to a policy based on continuous bond financing.[4] In addition, the long-term credibility of bond financing is examined in this chapter. Chapter 3 begins with a brief overview of the interaction of monetary stabilisation policy with confidence factors and presents an experiment designed to test the influence of changing expectations on producer output behaviour in regimes characterised by increasing as well as decreasing attempts at monetary stabilisation.[5] In addition, this chapter experimentally explores the importance of monetary credibility – or absence thereof – for national output.

Part II is comprised of Chapters 4–6, which present the results of empirical research exploring the effect of the confidence factors.

Chapters 4 and 5 explore the roles of confidence, expectations and credibility in the historical high-inflation episodes experienced in America during the Civil War of 1861–1865 (Chapter 4) and Germany after the First World War (Chapter 5). These high-inflation periods highlight the importance of confidence factors in influencing the consequences of the fiscal and monetary policies pursued. We then examine the recent experience in Europe under the European Monetary System and present empirical tests of whether or not exchange rate pegging brought about any change in private sector behaviour in the post-1979 period.

Finally, Part III (Chapters 8–10) offers an overview of the definition, measurement and possible theoretical and empirical role of 'consumer confidence' in today's macroeconomy. The final two chapters provide theoretical frameworks that explicitly incorporate endogenised consumer confidence terms and describe possible avenues for research and policy making that attempts to exploit the interactions of confidence with macroeconomic stabilisation.

In writing this book, we have endeavoured to present our research in a manner that would benefit a wide range of readers. Our theoretical, experimental and empirical results are accompanied by reviews of the economic theories underlying them, and by explanations stressing the economic intuition. This book will cater to analysts, research economists, policy makers and students possessing an intermediate level of macroeconomic theory.

The volume is an extension of our previous books which present a rigorous, yet intuitive, policy-oriented approach to macroeconomic research. The first book *Sustaining Budget Deficits in Open Economies* (Routledge, 1990), explored the ability of governments to continually bond-finance large budget deficits with capital inflows, while the second book, *Budget Deficits and Economic Performance* (Routledge, 1992) described the interactive effects of deficits on domestic and foreign fiscal and monetary policies. The present volume extends this literature by analysing the effectiveness of macroeconomic stabilisation policies against a backdrop of confidence factors, which are likely to continue to play an important role in policy making in the future.

We hope that you find this book both interesting and timely.

Part I

Credibility in practice and in experimental testing

Chapter 1

Fiscal policy, credibility and inflation

The critical role of confidence factors*

> A Government can live for a long time, even the German Government or the Russian Government, by printing paper money. . . . It is the form of taxation which the public find hardest to evade and even the weakest Government can enforce, when it can enforce nothing else. Of this character have been the progressive and catastrophic inflations practiced in Central and Eastern Europe, as distinguished from the limited and oscillatory inflations experienced for example in Great Britain and the United States.
>
> (John Maynard Keynes, 1924)[1]

> [A]n effective prohibition of creating new money to cover deficits of the government or state enterprises, and . . . a guarantee to redeem rubles for gold at a price above the current market rate . . . is technically feasible. . . . And it could even be effective if anyone believed it. Yet the trouble with this, or any other plan relying on Russia's politicians and central bankers, is that it would be quite difficult to establish credibility and trust.
>
> (Alan Reynolds, 1993)[2]

INTRODUCTION AND OVERVIEW

Keynes' (1924) characterisation of inflationary deficit finance in Central and Eastern Europe seems remarkably applicable to the problems facing countries like Russia, the Ukraine and the former Yugoslavia in the early 1990s. During both the hyperinflations of the 1920s and those of the 1990s, resort to inflation finance led to a flight from the currency as the public sought to unload the depreciating currency to minimise their exposure to the inflation tax. The

European hyperinflations of the 1920s were ended by drastic fiscal reform and stabilisation of the exchange value of the currency (Sargent, 1993, chapter 3). Reynolds (1993) points out, however, that such reforms cannot succeed in Russia today unless the government is able to gain the confidence of the public. If the public expects the government eventually to revert to the money-financing policies that have characterised the early post-Soviet era in Russia, then inflationary expectations will remain high and so will the actual inflation rate.

As evidenced by such inflationary episodes as the American War of Independence, the American Civil War and the French Revolution, the ultimate effects of money-financed deficits were seemingly well-established even before the twentieth century (see Burdekin and Langdana, 1992, chapter 3; Tallman, 1993). In reviewing the interrelationship between the fiscal policy regime and confidence factors in the inflation process, it may, therefore, be appropriate first to consider why governments have continued to resort to inflation finance in the first place. The alternatives to money financing are either to reduce the deficit by cutting spending or raising taxes or else to finance the deficit by bond issuance. This latter option is exemplified by the 1979–1993 US experience, which shows that it is possible to run substantial budget deficits with only single digit

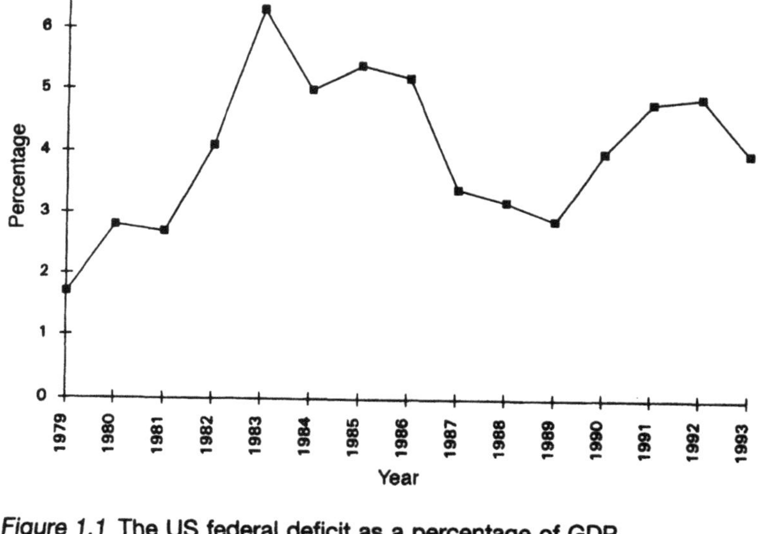

Figure 1.1 The US federal deficit as a percentage of GDP

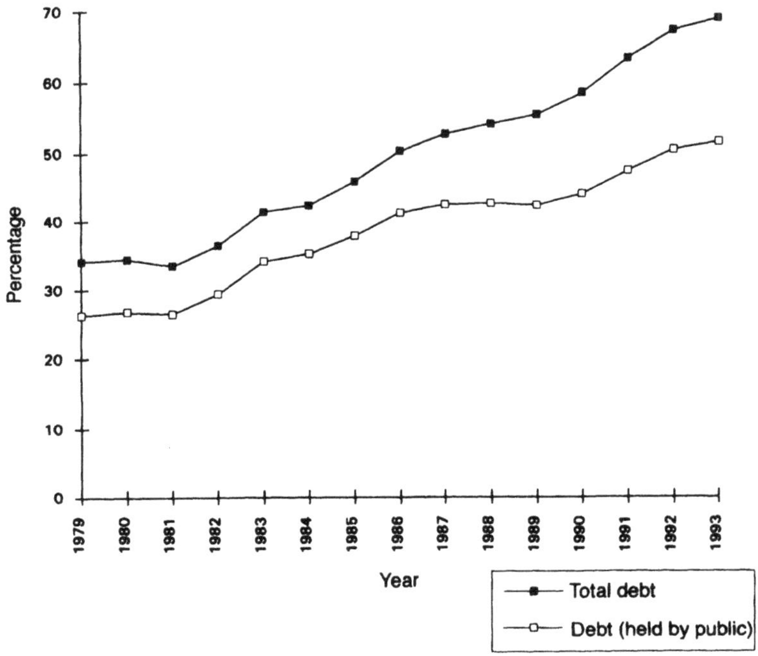

Figure 1.2 **US federal debt as a percentage of GDP**

inflation provided that there is a ready market for the government's bonds.

The ratio of total federal debt to gross domestic product (GDP) in the United States reached 69.1 per cent in 1993 and the deficit/GDP ratio was more than 4 per cent. The debt/GDP ratio has, in fact, been continuously rising since 1981 and the 2.7 per cent deficit/GDP ratio in 1981 remains the low point for the post-1979 period (see Figures 1.1 and 1.2). Nevertheless, the perception of the US dollar as a 'safe haven' has continued to encourage foreigners, particularly the Japanese, to purchase a significant portion of the debt. Despite the explosive debt growth since the end of the 1970s (Figure 1.3), the share of the publicly-held debt accounted for by foreigners has declined only slightly from 22 per cent in December 1979 to 20 per cent in September 1993 (see Figure 1.4).[3]

The US situation contrasts sharply with developments in countries like Russia, where the lack of developed financial markets

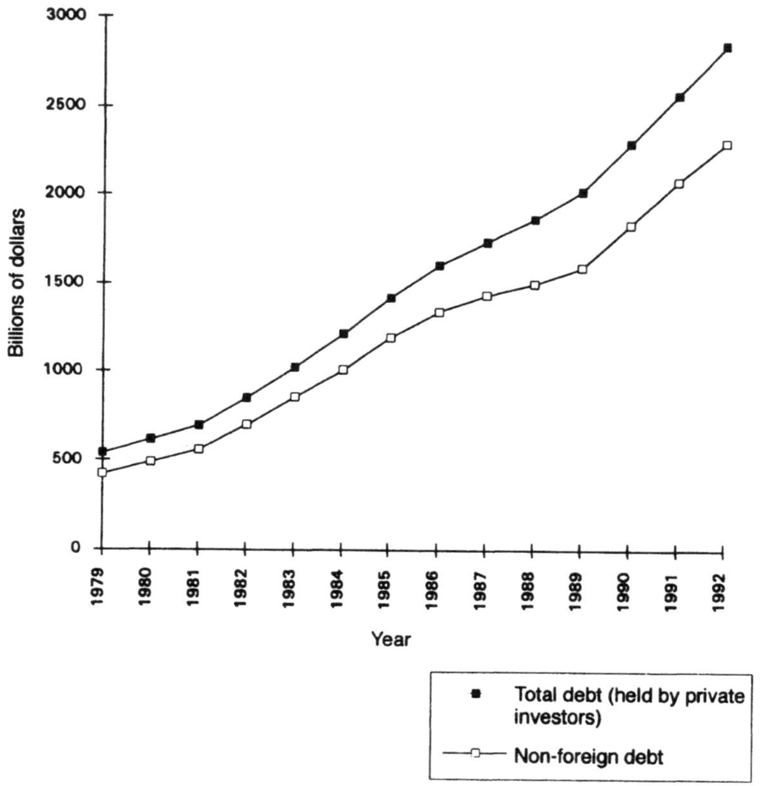

Figure 1.3 Total US public debt held by private investors vs. non-foreign holdings

compounds the (justifiable) lack of confidence in the stability of the rouble, thereby severely limiting the market for Russian bonds. Indeed, while Russia's monetary base rose from 1,450 billion roubles in December 1992 to 7,450 billion in September 1993, government bonds outstanding increased only from 15 billion to 20 billion over this same period – and in September 1993 government bonds accounted for less than one tenth of 1 per cent of Russia's 25,300 billion M-3 money supply measure (Lewarne, 1995, table 2). Central bank credit creation accounted for 40 per cent of Russia's GDP in 1992. While there has been some progress in establishing a nascent market for short-term treasury bills since 1993, even the greatly expanded June 1994 auctions could not bring government treasury bills outstanding to more than 3 per cent of the anticipated $35.7 billion deficit (Rosett, 1994, p. A10).

Whatever the actual state of a government's finances, the critical issue remains the perceptions of that government's future prospects of balancing its budget or at least of avoiding the necessity of repudiating its monetary and debt obligations through inflation. A recent example of the importance of expectations and confidence factors is given by Slovakia's experience after its 'divorce' from the Czech Republic. Despite inheriting the near-balanced budget pursued in 1991 and 1992 by the now-defunct Czechoslovak Federation, the Slovak koruna was already exchanging at a discount relative to the Czech koruna in early 1993 (*PlanEcon Report*, 1993e). This reflected the fact that the loss of the transfers previously received from the Czechs, and perceived structural problems hampering the Slovak economy's international competitiveness, fuelled expectations of future deficits – even though the actual Slovak deficit, at that time, remained quite low.[4]

There are also many earlier historical examples of the role played by confidence factors in influencing a currency's exchange value. Consider the US experience with the non-convertible 'greenback'

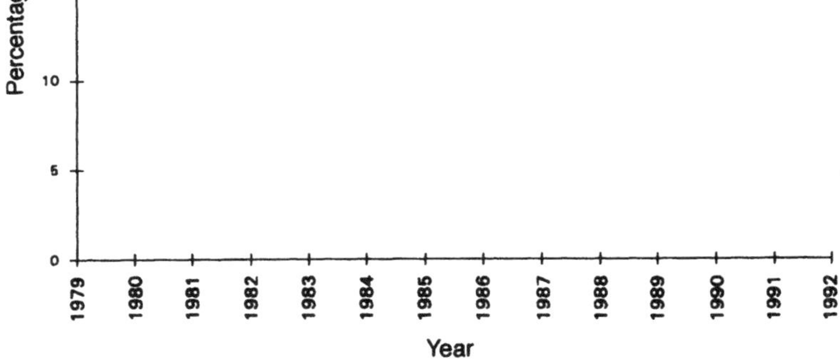

Figure 1.4 The percentage of US public debt securities owned by foreign and international subscribers

legal tender notes issued in the midst of the 1861–1865 Civil War. The greenbacks were authorised at a time of financial crisis whereby the banks had suspended specie payments at the end of 1861 and the government, facing rapidly mounting war expenditures, was already in arrears. On 8 January 1862, Congressman Elbridge G. Spaulding wrote of the need for 'at least $100,000,000 during the next three months, or the Government must stop payment' (Mitchell, 1903, p. 47). Although some bankers urged that the government rely on bond financing rather than money financing, it was feared that this 'might depress the price of bonds to the point of bankrupting the owners of earlier issues' (see Hammond, 1961, p. 7). Notwithstanding the government's promise that the greenbacks would eventually be redeemed in gold, the greenback quickly depreciated to an average of 62.3 per cent of par in February 1863. At the greenback's low point on 11 July 1864 the currency had declined to 35.09 per cent of its par value in terms of gold (Mitchell, 1903, pp. 423–424).

Declines in the greenback's gold exchange value were often linked with Confederate military successes that decreased the North's prospects of redeeming the notes at par (Mitchell, 1903, Chapter III; Calomiris, 1988b; Guinnane *et al.*, 1993). Similar, but inverse, fluctuations in the price of gold were evident in the South (Schwab, 1901, chapter IX). Distant as these events may seem now, they should remind us that under a fiat money system, money and bond issues are backed only by the public's confidence in the government's ability to redeem its debt obligations without resorting to the inflation tax. Rapid declines in the exchange value of the Russian rouble following the 1994 resignations of pro-reformers Fyodorov and Gaidar provide an example of how today's markets, like those of the past, react to events that are thought to increase the likelihood that the government will resort to inflation finance.

Lack of faith in a government's fiscal soundness has not only severely limited the scope for its bond issuance but also led to rejection of the national currency itself in many instances. During the German hyperinflation of the 1920s, for example, foreign bank notes increasingly took the place of the domestic currency as instruments of payment. In their anxiety to unload the rapidly depreciating mark, some German merchants even mistakenly accepted Confederate dollars at the prevailing US dollar exchange rate (*The Numismatist*, 1920). A number of Russians were apparently victimised in the same way in the midst of the chaotic monetary conditions of 1921 (*The Numismatist*, 1921). While there is no sign of Confederate currency re-emerging in post-Soviet Russia, it is evident that the rouble is also being increasingly shunned by the Russian public today. As early as November 1992, the estimated value of the US dollars circulating in Russia stood in excess of $10 billion (C. Goldberg, 1992).

The German government of 1923 had made a number of increasingly desperate attempts to combat the use of foreign exchange, culminating in the Decree of 7 September 1923, that permitted government agents to 'seize foreign currencies wherever they were to be found . . . People's houses and cafés were searched, letters opened, bill-brokers' transactions scrutinized' (D'Abernon, 1927, p. 20). Notwithstanding these activities, the real value of the foreign bank notes held in Germany at the end of 1923 was still estimated at around 1,200 million gold marks – while total Reichsbank notes in circulation at that time were equivalent to only about 497 million gold marks (Young, 1925, pp. 402, 529).[5] In contemporary Russia, concerns with the flight from the rouble have once more led to government attempts to interfere with the domestic circulation of foreign currency. Indeed, the use of the US dollar for transactions purposes was outlawed by the Russian government in 1994.

Even when a government takes concrete steps to put its finances in order, this has not always been enough to eliminate inflation. There is the question of whether or not the public is confident that the new-found fiscal and monetary restraint is sustainable. Participants in the experiments described in Chapters 2 and 3 evidence considerable concern on this score, and the postwar Latin American experience is itself replete with cases where even drastic fiscal tightening has not prevented inflation from remaining at double digit levels. Notably, public reluctance to hold the new Bolivian currency after that country's 1985 stabilisation was instrumental in keeping inflation at the 20 per cent level. In contrast to the experiences of Germany and other European countries after the termination of the 1920s hyperinflations, Bolivian real money balances remained below the pre-hyperinflation levels because of 'a general mistrust in Bolivian political institutions and in the stability of property rights' (Bernholz, 1988b, p. 766).

THEORETICAL PERSPECTIVES ON DEFICIT FINANCE

As a way of framing the issues involved, it is useful to consider the relationship between deficits and issuance of bonds and currency that is required under the government's intertemporal budget constraint. In order to remain solvent, governments must raise sufficient revenue from current debt and money issue to cover today's budget deficit plus interest payments and principal payments due on past debt issue. If the government continues to run deficits, the rising debt burden can be offset, for a time, by 'rolling over' the debt and issuing new debt to pay off the old debt. However, if there is no prospect of the government levying future taxes or cutting spending to reverse the progressive build up of debt, this rolling over of the debt must eventually be regarded as a non-sustainable Ponzi scheme.[6] At this point, no one will be willing to hold the government's debt, leaving monetisation of the debt (money finance) as the only remaining option.[7]

The government's dynamic budget constraint can be expressed as follows:

$$P_t(G_t - T_t) + D_{t-1} = D_t + M_t \quad (1)$$

where P_t is the price level, G_t is real government spending, T_t is real tax revenue, D_t is current debt issuance, D_{t-1} is the cost of servicing past debt issue, and M_t is current base money issuance.

While the form of this budget constraint is uncontroversial, the sustainability issue is not. At what point will domestic and foreign individuals refuse to hold government bonds, and render the deficits non-sustainable by forcing the government to monetise the debt – that is, to inflate it away? The answer to this question will vary from case to case, depending upon public perceptions of the government's willingness and/or ability to avoid resorting to the money financing option. Or, alternatively stated, the answer is a function of the credibility of the fiscal and monetary authorities' commitment to combat inflation-inducing monetisation of the debt. Nevertheless, we can safely say that, unless the public believes that current debt will eventually be redeemed out of future taxes, then bond issuance has inflationary effects today because of money issue expected in the future (see Langdana, 1990, chapters 11–15; Sargent, 1993, chapter 2; and Chapter 2 of this volume).[8]

There are instances, such as cases of war-induced temporary deficits, where confidence in the government's ability to redeem its obligations through future taxes and/or cuts in government spending has made reliance on bond financing feasible on a massive scale in the short run.[9] Following the outbreak of the Second World War, for example, the US debt/GDP ratio grew from 53.1 per cent in 1940 to a peak of 127.5 per cent in 1946 while the deficit/GDP ratio peaked at 31.1 per cent in 1943 before moving into surplus in 1947 (*Economic Report of the President*, 1994, table B-79). From June 1942 until the end of the war in mid-1945, the annualised growth rates of the public debt and the monetary base averaged 50 per cent and 20 per cent, respectively (Toma, 1991, p. 472). Nevertheless, the Federal Reserve and Treasury were able to keep the yield on 25-year Treasury bonds below 2.5 per cent over this period.

Toma (1991) calculates that the public would rationally purchase the US war bonds at the 2.5 per cent interest rate ceiling provided that there were expectations of a sufficiently high level of postwar tax financing.[10] For example, if the war duration expected in 1942 is set equal to the actual value of 3 years, all expenditures and interest payments would have to be financed from future taxes in order for the 2.5 per cent interest rate to be sustainable. This would imply zero postwar growth in the monetary base, which in reality did grow at only 1.7 per cent between 1945 and 1949 (see Toma, 1991, p. 475). Given the prior US record of temporary wartime deficits that had been repaid out of future taxes (Trehan and Walsh, 1988; Jones and Joulfaian, 1991), expectations that such a strategy would be followed after the Second World War may have been reasonable at the time.

The US situation can be compared to those of the Southern Confederacy of 1861–1865 and Germany during the First World War. In each case, difficulties in marketing the government's bond issues went hand in hand with the state's declining military and financial situation. The Confederacy was unable to successfully float any major loans subsequent to the $50 million loan approved by Congress on 16 May 1861. Even the cotton-backed £3 million Erlanger loan (equivalent to approximately $15 million) offered in Europe in March 1863 apparently had to be supported by government purchases amounting to nearly £1.4 million in order to keep the bonds from falling below par during April 1863 (see Bigelow, 1888, p. 187).[11] In First World War Germany, the government attempted to offset the declining demand for war bonds by placing restrictions on new private stock and bond issues. Indeed, by August 1918, 'the Reichsbank felt compelled to instruct its branches to discourage the sale of war bonds unless an economic need to do so could be demonstrated' (Feldman, 1993, p. 49).

While we address the trends in debt issues and real money balances in Civil War America and post-First World War Germany in Chapters 4 and 5, the losses experienced by Confederate and

German bondholders are, of course, part of the historical record. Confederate bonds became essentially worthless after 1865 (although transactions, at nominal values, were recorded as late as 1882).[12] Meanwhile, in Germany, at the time of the November 1923 stabilisation, 1,000 billion paper marks exchanged for a single pre-war gold mark (Sargent, 1993, p. 50). The prevailing sentiment in the United States at the time of the Second World War, however, may have been reflected in the sanguine assessment offered by Katona (1942, pp. 132–133):

> A Government would commit an irresponsible act if it induced people to save and buy war bonds and at the same time believed that inflation could not be averted and therefore expected to repay the bonds later with money of a lesser purchasing power. The only Government morally justified in issuing appeals for the purchase of war bonds is one which does everything in its power to prevent depreciation of the country's currency and is convinced of its ability to carry out this task successfully. Therefore large-scale purchasing of war bonds by the public makes it absolutely necessary for the Government to pursue an anti-inflationary policy with the greatest possible vigor.

In light of the subsequent more rapid growth of the monetary base, and the government's well-documented failure to engineer the postwar surpluses required to finance the wartime debt and money issues through future taxes, any attempt at repeating a World-War-II-type financing operation would likely be doomed to failure today. Indeed, the almost unbroken succession of US federal government budget deficits in the post-1960 period has not only called into question the government's ability to restore fiscal balance but cast doubt on its very solvency.

Hakkio and Rush (1991), for example, find that US government revenues and expenditures are not co-integrated over the 1964–1988 period. That is to say, no long-run equilibrium relationship between the two variables exists over the sample period (see Granger, 1986). This failure of US revenue and spending flows to converge implies that, if these same policies are continued, the debt to GDP ratio must rise without limit as 'the government is bubble-financing its expenditures, in which old debt that matures is financed by issuing new debt' (Hakkio and Rush, 1991, p. 431).

Hoover and Sheffrin (1992), in testing for causation between federal taxes and federal spending in the postwar period, obtain further evidence that the link between these two processes breaks down during the 1960s. After the late 1960s, taxes and spending appear to move independently of each other and neither variable is found to have a causal effect on the other. Such results suggest that the present US situation may, in the long run, be no more sustainable than the unfavourable fiscal imbalances currently faced by Russia and the less fortunate emerging market economies of Central and Eastern Europe.[13]

DOES FISCAL STRINGENCY ALWAYS ELIMINATE INFLATION?

Where financial markets are well-developed the correlation between moderate deficits and inflation is often quite loose, despite strong evidence that large deficits and inflation generally do go hand in hand. For today's developing countries, however, Table 1.1 shows that the average fiscal deficit in low inflation countries between 1983 and 1989 was 1.3 per cent of GNP; while for the high inflation countries the average level was 7.5 per cent of GNP.[14] Table 1.2 shows that, of the eleven major postwar stabilisation programmes documented by Végh (1992, pp. 670–691), there is no example of a sustained inflation decline that was not accompanied by a reduction in the government's budget deficit. Moreover, in those instances where the inflation rate renewed its upward climb, this was again

Table 1.1 Deficits, debt and inflation in developing countries, 1983–1989

	Low inflation countries	*High inflation countries*
Debt/GNP	39.5	45.9
Debt service/GNP	7.3	5.8
Budget deficit/GNP	1.3	7.5
Annual money growth	12.0	187.8

Source: Dornbusch *et al.* 1990, p. 34

Notes: The sample includes 88 net-debtor developing countries. All numbers are weighted averages over the period calculated with GDP weights. Countries with less than 6% annual (CPI) inflation were classified as low inflation countries, while countries with more than 15% annual inflation were considered high inflation countries

Table 1.2 Budget deficits and inflation rates during eleven postwar stabilization attempts

Argentina (1967:1–1970:2)			*Argentina (1979:1–1981:1)*			*Argentina (1985:2–1986:3)*		
Year/ quarter	*Inflation rate*	*Budget deficit/ GDP*	*Year/ quarter*	*Inflation rate*	*Budget deficit/ GDP*	*Year/ quarter*	*Inflation rate*	*Budget deficit GDP*
1966:1	29.2		1978:1	196.3		1984:1	508.6	11.0
1966:2	22.6		1978:2	185.1		1984:2	650.7	9.3
1966:3	16.0		1978:3	126.3		1984:3	827.4	6.9
1966:4	48.4	4.6	1978:4	166.9	3.2	1984:4	810.0	9.3
1967:1	21.8		1979:1	204.3		1985:1	1,004.4	10.1
1967:2	24.3		1979:2	138.4		1985:2	1,687.8	6.5
1967:3	39.2		1979:3	169.5		1985:3	258.5	3.0
1967:4	34.7	1.9	1979:4	96.7	2.7	1985:4	31.6	2.0
1968:1	10.8		1980:1	97.1		1986:1	40.4	4.7
1968:2	−1.4		1980:2	98.2		1986:2	63.9	2.2
1968:3	3.4		1980:3	73.2		1986:3	113.0	1.5
1968:4	27.4	2.1	1980:4	87.6	3.6	1986:4	107.2	8.7
1969:1	1.8		1981:1	71.6		1987:1	113.9	5.1
1969:2	−0.9		1981:2	129.8		1987:2	88.9	5.7
1969:3	6.7		1981:3	177.2		1987:3	215.7	8.1
1969:4	23.8	1.6	1981:4	125.0	8.1	1987:4	336.1	5.9
1970:1	6.0		1982:1	161.8		1988:1	179.9	9.3
1970:2	11.7		1982:2	71.3		1988:2	480.0	5.1
1970:3	14.4		1982:3	324.5		1988:3	954.8	3.5
1970:4	51.6	1.7	1982:4	342.6	7.2	1988:4	220.2	6.1
1971:1	42.8							
1971:2	23.7							
1971:3	43.7							
1971:4	38.5	4.3						
1972:1	98.1							
1972:2	58.6							
1972:3	47.0							
1972:4	64.4	5.2						

Bolivia (1985:3–)			Brazil (1964:2–1968:3)			Brazil (1986:1–1986:4)		
Year/ quarter	Inflation rate	Budget deficit/ GDP	Year/ quarter	Inflation rate	Budget deficit/ GDP	Year/ quarter	Inflation rate	Budget deficit GDP
1984:1	682.5		1963:1	73.4		1984:1	195.3	
1984:2	4,518.3		1963:2	85.5		1984:2	190.2	
1984:3	407.0		1963:3	78.7		1984:3	216.9	
1984:4	7,860.6	29.4	1963:4	92.4	4.2	1984:4	214.8	5.8
1985:1	123,729.9		1964:1	128.5		1985:1	273.6	
1985:2	4,217.9		1964:2	89.2		1985:2	170.8	
1985:3	38,803.3		1964:3	67.3		1985:3	258.0	
1985:4	508.6	10.1	1964:4	62.8	3.2	1985:4	246.4	13.0
1986:1	498.8		1965:1	99.0		1986:1	419.6	
1986:2	38.4		1965:2	67.9		1986:2	36.4	
1986:3	27.3		1965:3	30.6		1986:3	9.0	
1986:4	10.3	3.4	1965:4	25.0	1.6	1986:4	26.1	14.5
1987:1	16.7		1966:1	51.8		1987:1	268.1	
1987:2	11.0		1966:2	53.0		1987:2	862.5	
1987:3	3.1		1966:3	38.6		1987:3	347.6	
1987:4	12.1	7.7	1966:4	24.1	1.1	1987:4	262.5	14.4
1988:1	6.4		1967:1	34.8				
1988:2	34.7		1967:2	34.1				
1988:3	33.3		1967:3	20.1				
1988:4	12.3	6.5	1967:4	13.6	1.7			
1989:1	8.1		1968:1	20.9				
1989:2	4.9		1968:2	28.7				
1989:3	16.7		1968:3	25.0				
1989:4	33.8	5.1	1968:4	19.0	1.2			
1990:1	12.5		1969:1	22.0				
1990:2	6.4		1969:2	20.1				
1990:3	19.2		1969:3	25.3				
1990:4	33.1	3.3	1969:4	28.5	0.6			
			1970:1	16.8				
			1970:2	18.4				
			1970:3	28.6				
			1970:4	23.9	0.4			

Table 1.2 (Continued)

Chile (1978:1–1982:2)			*Israel (1985:3–)*			*Mexico (1988:1–)*	
Year/ quarter	*Inflation rate*	*Budget deficit/ GDP*	*Year/ quarter*	*Inflation rate*	*Budget deficit/ GDP*	*Year/ quarter*	*Inflation rate*
1977:1	90.4		1984:1	334.2		1987:1	139.1
1977:2	74.7		1984:2	447.8		1987:2	142.7
1977:3	53.5		1984:3	426.5		1987:3	143.3
1977:4	49.9	1.1	1984:4	710.9	13.0	1987:4	169.5
1978:1	33.0		1985:1	180.7		1988:1	272.3
1978:2	34.7		1985:2	365.8		1988:2	54.3
1978:3	33.4		1985:3	375.4		1988:3	19.4
1978:4	27.2	0.2	1985:4	40.7	2.8	1988:4	12.9
1979:1	25.4		1986:1	5.2		1989:1	24.6
1979:2	34.6		1986:2	29.2		1989:2	17.2
1979:3	51.8		1986:3	12.6		1989:3	13.7
1979:4	41.1	−4.9	1986:4	29.0	−0.7	1989:4	19.6
1980:1	29.5		1987:1	22.5		1990:1	46.0
1980:2	33.3		1987:2	18.0		1990:2	23.6
1980:3	28.1		1987:3	9.3		1990:3	24.3
1980:4	34.4	−5.5	1987:4	17.5	3.3	1990:4	25.8
1981:1	18.4		1988:1	17.7		1991:1	32.7
1981:2	11.7		1988:2	21.8		1991:2	15.3
1981:3	9.3		1988:3	7.3		1991:3	11.4
1981:4	6.7	−2.4	1988:4	22.0	8.1	1991:4	19.6
1982:1	2.9		1989:1	30.7			
1982:2	−0.8		1989:2	19.2			
1982:3	26.1		1989:3	12.8			
1982:4	55.8	2.3	1989:4	19.4	3.9		
1983:1	18.7		1990:1	12.6			
1983:2	25.4		1990:2	21.1			
1983:3	26.8		1990:3	19.0			
1983:4	26.5	2.6	1990:4	20.0	4.4		

Source: Végh 1992

	Uruguay (1968:2–1971:4)			Uruguay (1978:4–1982:4)		
Budget deficit/ GDP	*Year/ quarter*	*Inflation rate*	*Budget deficit/ GDP*	*Year/ quarter*	*Inflation rate*	*Budget deficit/ GDP*
	1967:1	119.3		1978:1	23.7	
	1967:2	61.8		1978:2	52.5	
	1967:3	191.1		1978:3	47.6	
−1.8	1967:4	130.9	3.0	1978:4	49.4	0.8
	1968:1	268.5		1979:1	68.9	
	1968:2	105.7		1979:2	73.2	
	1968:3	46.8		1979:3	90.0	
3.6	1968:4	5.3	1.7	1979:4	86.9	−0.2
	1969:1	16.6		1980:1	66.7	
	1969:2	19.6		1980:2	41.8	
	1969:3	10.9		1980:3	57.4	
1.7	1969:4	14.8	2.5	1980:4	34.6	−0.2
	1970:1	19.7		1981:1	25.1	
	1970:2	18.1		1981:2	29.7	
	1970:3	11.5		1981:3	40.4	
−2.3	1970:4	19.9	1.3	1981:4	25.2	1.4
	1971:1	27.4		1982:1	7.7	
	1971:2	19.0		1982:2	11.4	
	1971:3	28.3		1982:3	22.7	
−3.3	1971:4	60.6	5.8	1982:4	18.8	9.0
	1972:1	90.1		1983:1	139.6	
	1972:2	124.4		1983:2	31.6	
	1972:3	59.4		1983:3	36.0	
	1972:4	130.6	2.6	1983:4	47.2	3.9
	1973:1	160.3				
	1973:2	33.4				
	1973:3	134.0				
	1973:4	38.0	1.4			

always accompanied by a similar renewed increase in the budget deficit.

All three Argentinean stabilisation programmes and both of the Uruguayan programmes ended amidst a combination of rising budget deficits and rising inflation. The second Brazilian stabilisation programme (the Cruzado plan) did lower inflation temporarily, but the budget deficit was not reduced and within a year the inflation rate rose above the 246 per cent rate registered just prior to the implementation of the programme. Of the more successful stabilisation programmes, the 1985 Bolivian stabilisation brought inflation down from 38,803.3 per cent in the third quarter of 1985 to double digit rates in 1986. This occurred in conjunction with a sharp decline in the budget deficit from 29.4 per cent of GDP at the end of 1984, to 10.1 per cent at the end of 1985, and to 3.4 per cent in 1986. The 1985 Israeli stabilisation reveals a pattern similar to the Bolivian case – with the deficit being reduced from 13 per cent of GDP in 1984 to 2.8 per cent of GDP at the end of 1985. Other cases in which a sustained decline in the deficit was accompanied by a sustained decline in inflation are those of the first Brazilian stabilisation programme of February 1964–March 1968, and the Chilean and Mexican stabilisations.

While the Latin American experiences with high inflation do suggest that fiscal restraint is a prerequisite for a successful stabilisation package, the postwar evidence still leaves some troubling questions, however. Why, for example, did inflation in Chile and Uruguay decline so slowly following the enactment of 1978 stabilisation programmes that produced both budgetary surpluses and real exchange rate appreciation? Also, why, at the end of 1970, was Brazilian inflation still above 20 per cent despite a budget deficit of only 0.4 per cent of GDP and six years of fiscal stringency that had produced an average deficit of only 1.1 per cent of GDP? Furthermore, why did none of the eleven stabilisations detailed in Table 1.2 keep inflation at a single digit level for more than a quarter or two?

The repeated failure of the Latin American countries to eliminate inflation stands in sharp contrast to the post-First World War hyperinflations where, in each case, the implementation of the stabilisation programme reduced inflation to single digit levels and kept it there. Are these different results explained by the fact that most Latin American stabilisations occurred before the country entered hyperinflation? The Bolivian experience suggests otherwise. The monthly inflation rate of 57.6 per cent for the year preceding Bolivia's October 1985 stabilisation is higher than the inflation observed in post-First World War Austria and Hungary. Nevertheless, while in Austria and Hungary inflation quickly declined to monthly rates of 0.4 per cent and 0.2 per cent, respectively, Bolivian inflation continued at a monthly rate of 5.7 per cent in the year following the stabilisation (see Végh, 1992, p. 637).

In comparing the Bolivian case to earlier experiences with hyper-inflation, Bernholz (1988b) points out that, after the 1985 currency reform, the Bolivian real money supply in 1987 still had not risen beyond 60 per cent of its 1967 value. By contrast, in the post-First World War hyperinflations, the decline in the real money supply during the inflationary period was followed by a return to normal, pre-inflation levels. Bernholz (1988b, p. 767) argues that

> if the real stock of national money had grown to 100% instead of 60% or 70% because of more confident expectations concerning long-term stability, then the remaining inflation would have been wiped out as in the German and Austrian cases of the early 1920s.

The persistently lower level of real money balances may not be surprising given the postwar experience with inflation and political instability in Bolivia. Whereas Germany and Austria had enjoyed price stability and had been on the gold standard prior to the outbreak of the First World War, Bolivia had faced rising inflation since the late 1960s and the office of Bolivian President had been a revolving door with an average tenure of less than one year (Bernholz, 1988b). In the light of findings that countries with higher degrees of political instability have a greater tendency to resort to financing government spending through printing money (Edwards and Tabellini, 1991; Roubini, 1991; Soellner, 1991; Cukierman *et al.*, 1992), it may indeed have been rational for Bolivians to show a lack of confidence in the sustainability of the 1985 reform.

The postwar era is certainly replete with failed stabilisation programmes in Latin America. One explanation for this may be found in distributional conflict that arises as different groups push for tax breaks or social expenditures that increase their share of national income. While the potential importance of this phenomenon is by no means limited to Latin America (see Burdekin and Burkett, 1992, 1995), the problems posed by distributional conflict in this case have been reinforced by adverse external factors such as the debt crisis and declining primary product prices (Pazos, 1990). Thus, the government's ability to sustain its fiscal reforms may be in question to a much greater extent than was true after the hyperinflations of the 1920s.[15] A further concern, as emphasised by Kiguel and Liviatan (1991, p. 229), is that

> it is well-known that governments can use inflation (or devaluation) to achieve non-fiscal objectives, such as a reduction in the real wage or a real depreciation. Since inflation has been used to fulfill these functions in the past (especially in Brazil, to erode the real wage), the fiscal adjustment will not be enough to overcome these difficulties.

Naturally, repeated failures to stabilise can only further weaken public confidence in the government's will, and ability, to stick to its disinflationary policies. Nevertheless, Fernández (1991, p. 143) points out that governments may learn from these past failures and recognise that a 'change in the populist approach of basing stabilisation on deficit-ridden income policies is a necessary condition for price stability'. Recently, there have been growing indications of a genuine break with the populist policies of the past. Mexico was able to maintain the disinflation begun in 1988 and brought inflation down to single digit levels in June 1993 for the first time in two decades. Even Argentina, previously the scene of some of the worst inflationary problems, has implemented major fiscal reform and privatisation measures and also has committed to a fixed exchange rate with the US dollar under the convertibility law implemented on 1 April 1991 (see Hanke *et al.*, 1993, p. 73).[16]

ESTABLISHING CREDIBILITY FOR THE DISINFLATION PROCESS

As discussed above, restrictive fiscal and monetary policy has not always been successful in disinflating the economies of Latin America. So long as fears of renewed inflation remain, upward pressure on wage claims and downward pressure on the demand for real money balances is likely to persist. On the other hand, if the government's commitment to the disinflation is seen as credible and sustainable in the eyes of the public, a rapid termination of the inflation is theoretically possible as money growth rates, expected inflation rates and wage claims all decline together and demand for real money balances rises to a level consistent with a stable price environment. The abrupt ends of the post-First World War hyperinflations provide at least some hope that such a sequence of events might be attainable in practice.

Sargent's (1993, chapter 3) account of the post-First World War stabilisations emphasises the importance of combining fiscal reform with monetary reform and the establishment of an independent central bank. On the fiscal side, the government must evidence a sustainable commitment to moving the budget into balance. While the Latin American stabilisation episodes discussed above show many instances of temporary deficit reduction, in most cases the government was unable to maintain the new austerity programmes. One reason for this may have been the fact that there was really nothing constraining the government's ability to return to the deficit spending policies that had led to inflation in the first place. Assuming the public is aware of this, it would hardly be surprising if there were stickiness in inflationary expectations and wage claims and continued economising on real money balances. This point is, in fact, well illustrated by the results of the monetary 'experiment' conducted in Chapter 3, where participants simply refused to believe in the 'newly disciplined' central bank that was introduced after a prior high inflation sequence.

One way of restraining the government's scope for resorting to deficit finance is to cut off its access to the printing press. The importance of this is illustrated, for example, in the ending of the German hyperinflation in 1923. Webb (1992, p. 236) argues that, while the government's November 1923 promise to balance the budget did not have much initial credibility, the hard news of fiscal reform came the following month when 'the Finance Ministry petitioned the Rentenbank for further credit, but the bank denied the request'. Drastic fiscal tightening was undertaken at that time and, while the government's tax revenues covered only 1 per cent of its expenditures in October 1923, 100 per cent of the expenditures were tax financed by March 1924 (D'Abernon, 1927, pp. 31–32).

The importance of combining monetary reform with fiscal reform receives eloquent expression in the Honourable Ruth Richardson's foreword to this volume. In New Zealand, the firm mandate for price stability that was provided by the Reserve Bank of New Zealand Act 1989 has been followed by the Fiscal Responsibility Act 1994. The 1994 Act lays down a series of principles that will guide the course of fiscal policy, the first principle being that of running budgetary surpluses to pay off debt built up by loose fiscal policies in the past. Deficit reduction began, in fact, in the 1980s as the budget deficit was reduced from nearly 7 per cent of GDP in 1984 to around 2 per cent of GDP in 1989 (see Wells, 1990, p. 58). As pointed out in the foreword, budgetary balance was subsequently achieved in the 1993/1994 fiscal year. Inflation, meanwhile, has remained within the 0–2 per cent target range since late 1991.

Even though the spike in real interest rates and unemployment figures following the initial implementation of the 1989 Act suggested that there was to be no instant credibility for the anti-inflationary policies, the New Zealand government's perseverance now certainly seems to be paying off. Recent financial and labour market behaviour has been consistent with the inflation targets becoming credible to market participants (Fischer, 1993; Svensson, 1993). Ten-year real interest rates, for example, fell by nearly 4 percentage points between the end of 1990 and November 1993 (Reserve Bank of New Zealand, 1993, p. 16). Survey results suggest that, as of October 1993, expectations of inflation 4 and 7 years ahead stood at only 1.5 per cent and 1.6 per cent, respectively (Reserve Bank of New Zealand, 1993, p. 11).

While not so far approaching the near 0 per cent inflation record achieved under the New Zealand reforms, a number of Latin American countries have also undergone sweeping institutional changes in the last few years. In Latin America, a key problem has been that, with monetary policy remaining under firm government control, the government was free to expand the deficit without any concern as to whether the central bank would consent to finance this deficit. Indeed, just as distributive conflicts may lead to added pressures on the government purse, the lack of an independent monetary policy maker probably made it too easy for the government to accede to these demands through deficit spending (Burdekin and Laney, 1988; Burdekin and Langdana, 1992, chapter 7).[17]

In the 1990s, however, both Chile and Mexico introduced legislation making their central banks statutorily independent of government. Dornbusch and Fischer (1993, p. 17) characterise this institutional reform in Chile as 'the final step in assuring that a disinflation process was locked in'. The central bank's legal charter includes responsibility for monetary stability without any requirement for the bank to pursue the potentially conflicting goals of growth and full employment. In Mexico, the constitutional amendment passed by the Mexican Congress in June 1993 follows the US example in providing for staggered terms for the central bank's board so that no one president can readily 'stack the deck' in his or her favour (see also Hall, 1993).

Significantly, Mexico, like Chile, had moved its budget into surplus prior to implementing the legislation creating the independent central bank. An important reason why monetary autonomy has been so rare amongst less developed countries is that, in the absence of any significant market for government bonds, a commitment to an independent central bank is tantamount to a commitment to a balanced budget.[18] Meaningful monetary autonomy remains unattainable, for example, in Russia which has experienced deficits estimated at 11.3 per cent of GDP in 1991 and 15 per cent of GDP in 1992 coupled with 160.6 per cent inflation in 1991 and 2,525.2 per cent inflation in 1992. While, in 1994, the Russian government reached an agreement with the International Monetary Fund (IMF) to get the deficit/GDP ratio below 10 per cent; its ability to achieve this goal seemed problematic at best.

Nevertheless, many of the other emerging Central and Eastern European economies have now passed legislation that makes their central banks statutorily independent of government. The central banks of Bulgaria, the Czech Republic, Hungary, Slovakia and Slovenia all have limits on lending to the government (Siklos, 1994; Hochreiter, 1995). These central banks also have legislated price and/or exchange rate objectives, as does the Polish central bank. In spite of statutory provisions for central bank policy independence, the effective degree of central bank autonomy is, however, called into question both by uncertainty as to how the respective statutes will be interpreted in practice and, in many cases, by continuing pressures for deficit finance. While the Czech Republic has so far been relatively successful in bringing its budget into balance, demands for credits to finance government budget deficits and to assist loss-making state enterprises have, for example, led parliament to over-rule the legislated limits on fiscal financing in Bulgaria and Hungary (Hochreiter, 1995).

Table 1.3 provides 1991 and 1992 budget deficit and inflation data for the members of the former Czechoslovak Federation (the Czech Republic and Slovakia) together with Hungary, Poland and three members of the former Soviet Union – Estonia, Russia and the Ukraine.[19] The relatively strong fiscal position enjoyed in 1991 and 1992 in the former Czechoslovakia can be compared to the bigger deficits in Hungary and Poland that were equal to 7 per cent and 8

Table 1.3 Central and Eastern European deficit and inflation data

	Budget deficit/GDP		*Inflation rate*	
	1991	*1992*	*1991*	*1992*
Czech Republic	1.0	1.0	52.0	12.7
Estonia	−4.9	−1.5	N/A	N/A
Hungary	5.0	7.0	33.8	21.8
Poland	5.0	8.0	60.3	44.5
Russia	11.3	15.0	160.6	2,525.2
Slovakia	1.0	1.0	58.2	9.1
Ukraine	14.4	33.3	N/A	N/A

Sources: Bofinger 1993, p. 4 for the Czechoslovakian, Hungarian and Polish budget deficit data; Goldberg *et al.* 1993, p. 28 for the 1991 Russian and Ukrainian budget deficit data; Lewarne 1993, p. 27 for the Estonian budget deficit data; Gáspár 1993, p. 2 for estimates of the 1992 Russian and Ukrainian budget deficits; *PlanEcon Report* 1993a–e for the inflation data

Notes: The budget deficit data for the Czech Republic and Slovakia reflect the fiscal position of the Czechoslovak Federation that was dissolved at the beginning of 1993

The 1992 Russian deficit data and the 1992 Ukrainian deficit data are estimates

The inflation data refer to the percentage change in the retail price index, except for Russia where the new consumer price index is used

per cent of GDP, respectively, in 1992. These two countries also experienced higher inflation rates of 21.8 per cent and 44.5 per cent in 1992. In 1993, while the Slovak budget position deteriorated and its deficit was expected to exceed 6 per cent of GDP, the Czech Republic's strong fiscal position continued – and the fiscal budget moved into surplus during the first five months of 1993, accompanied by a monthly inflation rate as low as 0.5 per cent a month (*PlanEcon Report*, 1993f). In Hungary, meanwhile, the projected 1993 deficit of 6.4–6.7 per cent of GDP (*PlanEcon Report*, 1993g) suggested only a marginal gain from the 1992 ratio of 7.0 per cent.

Among the three members of the former Soviet Union included in Table 1.3, the severe fiscal problems experienced in Russia and the Ukraine can be compared with the budgetary surpluses enjoyed by Estonia in both 1991 and 1992.[20] Estonia has, in fact, combined fiscal tightening through tax hikes and reduced subsidies with monetary reform that places strict limits on the conduct of monetary policy. The new national currency, the kroon, was pegged to the Deutsche mark on 20 June 1992 under a 'currency board' arrangement (see Buyske, 1993). The amount of money outstanding under the currency board cannot exceed the board's reserves of foreign currency and other hard assets so long as the system is in place. The government's access to central bank credit was eliminated under this monetary reform.

The credibility gains associated with these reforms may help explain the rapid drop in Estonia's inflation rate from near 1000 per cent at the beginning of 1992 to an estimated annual rate of 33 per cent in 1993. Moreover, the IMF's prediction of 6 per cent output growth in 1994, if realised, would likely make Estonia the fastest growing economy in Europe for that year (Bivens, 1994). This does not necessarily imply that Russia should emulate Estonia's currency board arrangements for monetary policy, however. While maintaining a fixed exchange value for the rouble against, say, the US dollar, would indeed force Russia to refrain from her recent inflationary policies (Hanke *et al.* 1993), a strict exchange rate target of this kind would be infeasible in the short run owing to the presence of large deficits that can only be financed by money creation (Reynolds, 1993).[21]

In essence the problem is two-fold. First, the deficit has to be reduced to a sustainable level that does not require resort to money finance.[22] Second, the public has to be convinced of the permanence of this deficit reduction programme. While the use of a currency board or gold (Reynolds, 1993) would limit the government's ability to renege on its stabilisation programme, basing monetary policy upon either an exchange rate or a gold plank raises the danger of producing costly, and undesirable, outcomes that may actually force abandonment of the stabilisation measures. For example, a rise in the adopted foreign currency would force the currency board to follow restrictive domestic policy to maintain the fixed exchange rate, perhaps with the effect of causing painful, and unnecessary, output losses. A recent example of this problem is given by the breakdown of the pegged exchange rate system of the European Union following the continued appreciation of the Deutsche mark.

In short, just as too much discretion may be dangerous, too little discretion may put the government in an untenable situation. Indeed, in the European case, the countries that held on to the Deutsche mark peg until 1993 suffered considerable real costs in the preceding years but in the end could not support an exchange rate rule that had become so inconsistent with domestic economic conditions. If such strains made the exchange rate peg impossible for even the major Western European nations to maintain, how could an even more rigid variant of this policy be expected to work in less developed countries like Russia? A better answer surely would be to rely upon institutional constraints on expansionary policy.

In this regard, the evidence suggests that establishing a central bank with an effective degree of independence from government is an attractive option (on this point see, Burdekin and Langdana, 1992, chapter 4; Banaian *et al.*, 1995; Burdekin *et al.*, 1995). Certainly, the movements in this direction in both Central and Eastern Europe and in Latin America may indeed provide a means of 'locking in' the reforms already undertaken in many of these countries. This is not to say that an exchange rate peg cannot be effective under certain conditions (e.g. Estonia). However, an exchange rate peg can only be credible if the peg itself is sustainable and consistent with the economic fundamentals – conditions that were palpably absent in the recent operation of the European Monetary System.

CONCLUSIONS AND IMPLICATIONS

The importance of expectations, and of public confidence in the government, cannot be stressed too much. As discussed above, even drastic fiscal restraint often failed to put an end to the inflation process in Latin America. In Bolivia, for example, public reluctance to hold the new currency appears to have been instrumental in the fact that inflation – although greatly reduced – remained stubbornly at around the 20 per cent level after the 1985 stabilisation and currency reform. By contrast, where public perceptions are more favourable, the US experience has shown that a government can run large, and perhaps non-sustainable budget deficits without inducing any short-run inflationary pressure.

However, in recent years, the formerly high deficit countries of Latin America and the previously fiscally sound United States seem to have been heading in opposite directions. At the same time, movements towards greater central bank independence have taken place in Latin America, Europe and New Zealand while, in the United States, the Federal Reserve has been faced with increasing threats to its existing degree of autonomy. An interesting topic for study is whether these trends, if they continue, will provoke accompanying adjustments in private sector behaviour – as reflected, for example, in money demand and bond demand – in the United States *vis-à-vis* these other nations. The analysis undertaken in this book suggests that such adjustments might indeed occur, with potentially serious consequences for the relative standing of the United States.

In the following two chapters, we use actual experiments to illustrate how changes in the monetary and fiscal environment cause agents to update and revise their expectations, thereby changing their macroeconomic behaviour. We then use historical case studies in Chapters 4 and 5 to illustrate the process by which loss of monetary and/or fiscal discipline has eroded credibility and led to a flight from money and bonds in past inflationary episodes. Chapter 6 examines the extent to which credibility and public confidence have been affected by the operation of the European Monetary System in the 1980s. Finally, Chapters 7–9 focus on the role of 'consumer confidence' in today's macroeconomy and suggest ways of explicitly incorporating this confidence factor in macroeconomic stabilisation policy.

Chapter 2

Bond-financed deficits, taxation and expectations

An experimental test of the Ricardian equivalence theorem*

> No nation ought to be without a debt.
> A national debt is a national blessing.
>
> (Thomas Paine, 1776)

> Let us have the courage to stop borrowing to meet continuing deficits.
> Stop the deficits.
>
> (Franklin D. Roosevelt, 1932)

How do household expectations change when the government abruptly switches from taxation to bond sales to attempt to finance its large budget deficits? What effect does a prolonged reliance on bond financing have on the long-term credibility of such a deficit financing policy? The present chapter employs macro-experimentation techniques to test the actual behaviour of individual 'households' set in an artificial economy that shifts from taxation to a policy of long-term bond financing to meet its fiscal imbalances. The focus of this chapter will be the effects of fiscal policy on household expectations and long-term credibility – the experimental effects of monetary policy on the confidence factors will be presented in the following chapter.

Barro's (1974) revival of the Ricardian equivalence theorem has significantly influenced the course of subsequent macroeconomic research, due primarily to the relevance of its fiscal policy implications.[1] In its simplest and most intuitive form, Ricardian equivalence is said to exist if households do not consider holdings of government bonds to be net wealth, as they would according to standard Keynesian theory.[2] On the contrary, Ricardian households equate bond-financed budget deficits to 'inevitable' future tax increases deemed necessary to service and retire the government debt. Since the present value of anticipated future taxes just offsets the bond-financed government expenditures, government bonds do not constitute an increase in net wealth, and hence, taxation is considered equivalent to budget deficits.[3]

In addition, a rise in the national budget deficit – a fall in net public savings – is matched by an increase in private savings by Ricardian households, in anticipation of the future tax increases.[4] This increase in the supply of credit due to the increase in private savings offsets the increase in the demand for credit stemming from bond-financed deficits, leaving interest rates uncorrelated with deficit spending.[5]

This has enormous implications for fiscal policy. A decrease in taxes financed by an increase in government bond issuance, for example, would have no effect on aggregate demand in a Ricardian world. Debt issuance in lieu of taxation would leave private consumption, output, inflation and interest rates unchanged, thereby rendering taxation 'equivalent' to debt issuance. The conventional Keynesian results of deficits being positively correlated with consumption, prices, interest rates and national output, would not be generated here.

Barro (1974) demonstrated that Ricardian equivalence holds if individuals are maximising agents who have (i) the ability to optimise intertemporally, (ii) can perfectly foresee future tax increases, (iii) face perfect capital markets, and (iv) are perfectly linked to future generations ('infinitely lived') by means of intergenerational bequests or 'transfers'.

Ricardian households are assumed to be altruistic in that they genuinely care about the welfare of their descendants who will bear the brunt of the future tax liabilities. This sentiment prompts the current generation to discount the future liabilities fully and hence save more 'today' to leave an intergenerational transfer (bequest) to their descendants. This transfer effectively results in households being 'infinitely lived' – their altruism causes them to plan with an infinite horizon even though they have finite lives. This crucial assumption of an operative intergenerational transfer precludes the possibility of the positive net wealth effect of a bond-financed tax cut (and the attendant aggregate demand effects) that would follow if taxes were increased following the death of a ('finitely-lived') debt-purchasing individual (or household). Theoretical and empirical evidence supporting the equivalence theorem can be found in Barro

(1974, 1978a), Tanner (1979), Seater and Mariano (1985), Kormendi and Meguire (1990) and Evans (1985, 1987, 1991).[6]

However, Barro's (1974) assumptions have, to large extent, fuelled those critics who have rejected the entire theory outright, primarily on the grounds of absence of realism. A significant number of studies such as Feldstein (1982), Blinder and Deaton (1985), Reid (1985), and Modigliani and Sterling (1990) find evidence conflicting with Ricardian equivalence. Some excellent summaries of this large and growing body of literature can be found in Sweeney (1988), Bernheim (1989), and Thornton (1990).

Poterba and Summers (1987) have attributed the continuance of the vigorous debate (pertaining to the validity of Ricardian equivalence and the consequences of deficit spending) primarily to the fact that 'history has provided few satisfactory experiments for assessing the Ricardian equivalence proposition' (cited by Cadsby and Frank, 1991, p. 645). Indeed, while empirical and theoretical tests for and against the existence of Ricardian equivalence abound, experimental tests exploring household consumption and savings patterns and the nature of interest rate bidding on government debt are conspicuous largely by their absence.[7]

A pioneering attempt to contribute to the ongoing debate by implementing experimentation techniques was made by Cadsby and Frank (1991). Their experiment was conducted in the context of an overlapping generations model that made allowances for learning. Cadsby and Frank experimentally tested the validity of the major assumptions crucial to the existence of Ricardian equivalence, namely, (i) the ability of individuals to solve intertemporal optimisation problems, and (ii) the nature of the planning horizon faced by individuals, and its implication for bequests to successive generations.

Both these assumptions have been fraught with macroeconomic controversy. For example, Keynesian theory would predict that the individual's ability to solve intertemporal problems was 'not very good' while Ricardians and neoclassical economists would find it 'perfect' (Cadsby and Frank, 1991, p. 646). Similarly, neoclassical economists would believe that individuals employ finite planning horizons which end at their deaths, while Ricardians would claim that individuals have operational intergenerational bequest motives and infinite planning horizons. Cadsby and Frank examined both expansionary as well as contractionary fiscal policies with a particular focus on the intergenerational bequest outcomes which they found to conform closely with the predictions of Ricardian theory, after allowing for learning.

The present experiment differs from Cadsby and Frank in that the focus here is primarily on the experimental determination of the macroeconomic aspects of the Ricardian equivalence theorem. In particular, this experiment attempts to contribute to the ongoing debate by determining the effects on 'national' interest rates, savings and consumption when the fiscal regime shifts unexpectedly from taxation to bond-financed deficits. In addition, the present experiment explores interest rate behaviour following the regime shift as the fiscal authority continues to maintain large bond-financed budget deficits.

The important question is whether individuals who absorb this additional government debt will essentially behave like Ricardians à la Barro? Will they anticipate taxes on future generations with the purchase of government debt? If so, will they, with mounting concern over the welfare of their descendants, increase current savings to bequest funds to their kin who will bear the brunt of the future tax increases deemed necessary to service (or retire) the debt? Will these increased savings result in a dampening effect on interest rates and hence prevent the crowding out of private investment that is claimed to plague government spending in a traditional Keynesian economy? And perhaps, most important, how will households react to a continuous stream of government debt issuance following the regime shift from taxes to bond financing? The experimental determination of answers to these questions forms the central focus of this present experiment.

MODEL DESCRIPTION

A closed economy is comprised of a debt-issuing 'government' and households who are assumed to be concerned about the present value of anticipated real taxes that might be imposed on their descendants.[8] For convenience, taxes are assumed to be lump sum as in Barro (1984).

We make the following simplifications. The monetary authority lies dormant – the price level (P) and the nominal money stock remain constant. The deficits, therefore, have to be financed by bond sales as monetisation is not an option here. There are no transfer payments in any time period, and the government expenditures G_t in any period t, are exogenously given. B_t is the government debt issued in time period t, with the initial condition, $B_0 = 0$.

The intertemporal budget constraint is given by:

$$G_t + R_{t-1}B_{t-1}/P = T_t/P + (B_t - B_{t-1})/P. \quad (1)$$

Here R_t is the nominal interest rate, and T_t represents nominal tax revenues in period t. The left-hand-side of (1) represents the primary government spending G_t and the interest payments on the previous period's debt that have to be financed, $R_{t-1}B_{t-1}/P$. The right-hand-side represents real tax revenues T_t/P and real revenue obtained from bond sales in the current period, $(B_t - B_{t-1})/P$. (If there were no government debt issuance, the real government expenditures would be financed solely by real tax revenues, T_t/P.) In this economy, the level of current and expected government spending stays fixed; $G_t - G_{t-1} = 0$, at all times.

In time period t the government enacts a tax cut, and incurs a deficit of D_t along the lines of Barro (1984). Therefore, debt sales in period t are necessary to finance the deficit are $B_t=D_t$. Since taxes decline by T_t in period t, the current disposable income of households increases by T_t.

If the government then decides to balance its budget from period $(t + 1)$ onwards, it must raise taxes in period $(t + 1)$ by just enough to service the principal and interest payments on debt B_t issued in period t. Therefore, taxes will have to be raised by $B_t(1 + R_t)$ dollars in period $(t + 1)$.

The crucial issue here is the determination of household behaviour in period t when disposable income rises. In this simple case, the net change in the present value of aggregate real taxes is:

$$[-T_t + T_t(1 + R_t)/(1 + R_t)].(1/P) = 0. \quad (2)$$

Since there is no net aggregate effect of real taxes, the government's bond-financed deficit in period t has no aggregate wealth effect and hence does not affect household consumption and aggregate demand. Therefore, the deficit of D_t is viewed as equivalent to a current aggregate tax of T_t. Here, the tax cuts in period t are exactly sufficient to allow households the necessary funds to meet the higher taxes in the following period. The equivalence results continue to hold when the model is extended to the more realistic case in which the government issues debt in period t but never pays off the principal.[9]

Furthermore, and perhaps most crucial to this experiment, Ricardian households will increase their period t savings in order to meet future tax obligations on themselves, or to leave bequests to their descendants on whom the tax burden might fall. This savings-induced increase in period t loanable funds offsets the increased demand in government borrowing to leave interest rates, and hence capital investment, unaffected. Hence, there is no 'crowding out' of capital investment and no burden of the public debt along the lines of traditional Keynesian theory.

EXPERIMENT DESIGN

The experimental methodology is similar to that of Langdana (1994) where the Lucas (1973) 'islands' model of international output–inflation tradeoffs was experimentally tested with test market participants.[10] The present chapter employs an adaptation of the original Barro (1974) model that has been simplified to allow experimentation, while still preserving its theoretical integrity.

Participants in this experiment were MBA students in the core macroeconomics class at Rutgers School of Management, and the sample size was thirty-eight students. These students were the 'households' of Barro's economy who were to absorb government debt. They had no prior knowledge of Ricardian equivalence, nor the results to be expected – the experiment was conducted long before the concept of Ricardian equivalence was covered in class.

At the beginning of each time period, the government/treasury, which was represented by the experiment director, would announce the additional income Y_t of each household along with the lump-sum taxes. The income was held constant for all twenty-three periods to preclude any possible Keynesian multiplier effects associated with deficit spending.[11]

The experiment began with period 1 household income (Y_1) equal to \$500, and with the government/treasury issuing debt in addition to the \$30 lump-sum household tax T_1 to meet its obligations. The sale of 'government debt' to the students (households) was designed to mimic the auctioning process for US Treasury bonds.

In period 1 the government intended to obtain \$380 in revenues from bond sales (an average of \$10 per household), and throughout the experiment, the bonds were sold in ten equal denominations, for experimental convenience.[12] The students were required to submit individual interest rate 'bids' to purchase the government bonds at the beginning of each period, immediately following the announcement of the additional income, Y_t, the lump-sum taxes, T_t, and the denomination of the ten government bonds to be auctioned, B_t.[13]

The students were not allowed to discuss their personal bids with others – this was repeatedly stressed throughout the experiment. The ten students with the lowest interest rate bids – the 'winners' of the auction – were then sold the ten government bonds in individual denominations of $38 face value in period 1, with the interest rate being the average of the ten lowest bids.[14] Again, this was designed to replicate the 'non-competitive tender' bidding process at US Treasury auctions where the bond purchaser agrees to accept a return representing a weighted average of the successful bids.

In this economy, bond holdings were the only source of interest. The national income Y_t is represented by:

$$Y_t = C_t + TS_t + T_t. \tag{3}$$

Here C_t is the household consumption, and TS_t represents total household savings in period t, which are further divided into:

$$TS_t = B_t + S_t. \tag{4}$$

The two components comprising total household savings TS_t are (i) the interest bearing component comprised of government bond purchases, B_t, and (ii) the non-interest bearing component, S_t, which will be denoted simply as private 'savings' throughout this experiment S_t is purely for precautionary purposes to meet future exigencies on present or on future generations.[15]

The students were urged (in the written instructions in the Appendix, and verbally, during the experiment) to treat the income as 'real' and to make their consumption, savings and bond-purchasing decisions as judiciously as possible. The respondents had to record their individual period-by-period choices for C_t and S_t, along with their bond holdings B_t and their interest rate bids, and submit this information at the end of the experiment.

To summarise, for each period t, the additional income Y_t, lump-sum taxes T_t, and government bond sales B_t were exogenously given, while average savings S_t – obtained by computing a simple arithmetic average of the individual decisions – and the average interest rate on debt in period t, R_t, were endogenously obtained by experimentation.

Finally, the students had to participate in a short post-experiment survey to provide the experiment director with the personal intuition underlying the individual savings, consumption and interest rate decisions – especially in the critical periods following the unexpected change in fiscal policy from taxation to bond financing.[16]

The reward system was non-monetary and identical to that implemented in Langdana (1994). The experiment was conducted as part of an in-class learning exercise in macroeconomic theory, to be followed (upon completion) by a rigorous discussion of the theoretical aspects and policy implications of Ricardian equivalence. Attendance at all the bidding sessions (usually held at the end of class), completion of the survey and full compliance of all the instructions and rules was ensured by allocating a (small) portion of the course grade to the experiment.

The experiment was divided into twenty-three time periods, and three phases; phase 1 covered periods 1–6, phase 2 covered periods 7–15 and phase 3 covered periods 16–23.[17] The students were unaware of the duration of the experiment or the existence of the three phases.

Phase 1 was characterised by randomly increasing government bond sales from an average of $10 per household in period 1 to $20 in period 6. In addition, a lump-sum tax of $30 per period was imposed on each household in phase 1. Since 10 bonds were auctioned in equal denominations in every period, bonds were of individual face value of $38 in period 1, increasing to a face value of $76 in period 6. Phase 1 was primarily designed to compare the effects of similar increases in government borrowing in a regime with zero taxes, later in the experiment (phase 3).

Phase 2 (periods 7–15) was designed to be a steady state where the additional bond sales remained constant at an average of $20 per household, and the income as well as the lump-sum tax remained unchanged.

Phase 3 (periods 16–23) was begun by an unexpected fiscal 'regime shift' from taxes to bond-financed deficit spending, following an 'election' at the end of period 15.[18] Taxes fell to zero in period 16 and bond financing increased by a factor of 2.5, from $20 to $50 per household. To ensure that total government revenues remained at period 15 levels, the bonds were individually denominated in amounts of $190. The experimentally observed changes in interest rates and average savings from periods 15 to 16 were crucial in determining if households considered taxes to be equivalent to bond financing. Debt issuance then continued at the new elevated level in the economy with zero taxes, from periods 16–23, with policy makers pursuing a policy of continuously bond-financed deficits.

'Infinitely-lived' generations, crucial to Ricardian equivalence, were experimentally designed as follows. At the beginning of the experiment it was announced that the principal and interest on government debt was to be paid in the following semester. Furthermore, following period 16, the households were informed that 'elections' would again be held in the period following the completion of the experiment and before the commencement of the following semester. This was designed to inject an element of uncertainty regarding the longevity of the dramatic tax cuts experienced since period 16.

Therefore, current generations were made to 'meet themselves' in the following semester when the principal and interest payments were to be made in an environment of uncertain tax policy. This experimental construct attempted to replicate the theoretical 'infinitely-lived' generations deemed necessary for the operational intergenerational transfers of Barro's Ricardian equivalence theorem.

Now that the households were experimentally allowed the mechanism as well as the motivation to be infinitely lived, the crucial question was whether they would, in fact, display Ricardian tendencies on being given a bond-financed tax cut? And if so, would they continue to exhibit Ricardian behaviour when the fiscal authority embarked on a policy of continuously bond-financed deficits? The results of the experiment are discussed next.

RESULTS

The average values of the interest rates R_t and savings S_t are presented in Table 2.1 and the time paths of bond sales, average interest rate bids, and household savings as a percentage of income (for all three phases) are presented in Figures 2.1–2.3.

With household income fixed at \$500, as government borrowing increases in addition to the \$30 in household taxes, we obtain the following results for phase 1 (periods 1–6). The average interest rate increases from period 1 to period 6 by 43.12 per cent ($R_1 = 5.31$ to $R_6 = 7.60$) as presented in Table 2.1 and the time path in Figure 2.2. This interest rate increase accompanies a 100 per cent increase in total government borrowing, from \$380 in period 1 to \$760 in period 6. Average household savings, expressed as a percentage of income, fall from $S_1=15.53$ to $S_6=8.39$, a decline of 46 per cent in phase 1 (Figure 2.3).[19]

These are the traditional Keynesian results that phase 1 was designed to replicate – increased demand for government borrowing drives up interest rates in an economy with a fixed national

Table 2.1 Debt, interest rate bids and savings

	Period	B_t[a]	R_t[b]	S_t[c]
Phase 1 (T_t = 30; Y_t = 500)				
	1	38	5.31	15.53
	2	38	5.33	14.99
	3	41.8	5.49	15.03
	4	45.6	5.83	13.61
	5	57	6.48	12.20
	6	76	7.60	8.39
Phase 2 (T_t = 30; Y_t = 500)				
	7	76	7.65	8.53
	8	76	7.70	8.63
	9	76	7.74	8.82
	10	76	7.87	9.29
	11	76	7.99	9.76
	12	76	8.14	10.13
	13	76	8.20	9.11
	14	76	8.31	9.37
	15	76	8.42	9.37
Phase 3 (T_t = 0; Y_t = 500)				
	16	190	8.57	10.01
	17	190	8.53	11.30
	18	190	8.55	11.30
	19	190	8.57	11.32
	20	190	8.90	11.33
	21	190	9.66	11.35
	22	190	9.73	11.34
	23	190	9.82	11.34

[a] Represents the individual denomination of government debt in every period
[b] Average interest rate on government debt in every period
[c] Private savings expressed as a percentage of income Y_t

income. This rise in interest rates is held accountable for 'crowding out' private capital investments.[20] Here, according to proponents of 'crowding out', households who might want to indulge in private capital investment with their pool of savings S_t, might now be precluded from doing so ('crowded out'), due to the higher interest rates stemming from increased government borrowing.

Phase 2 was designed to create a steady state with increases in total government borrowing held at $760 per period, taxes fixed at

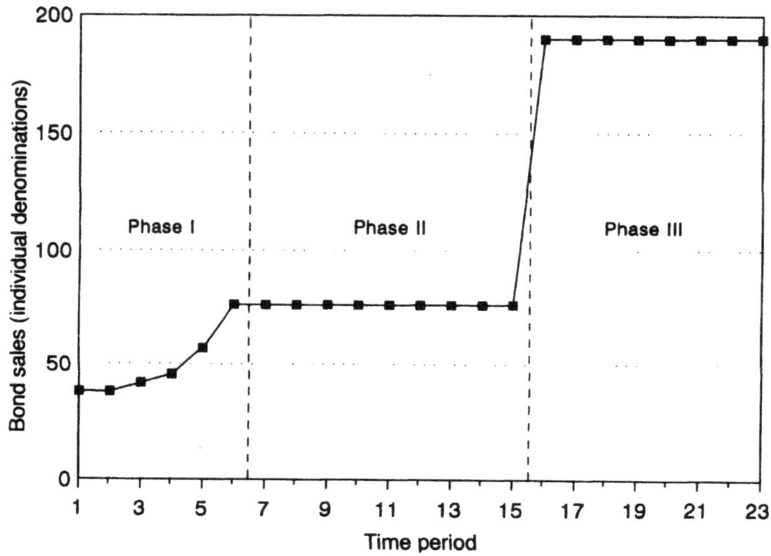

Figure 2.1 Bond sales time path

\$30 and income fixed at \$500 per household, from periods 7 to 15. This phase was designed to 'lull' households into some permanent spending and consumption patterns, prior to the unexpected shift in tax policy in phase 3.

The results indicate a gradual, yet relatively minor, increase in interest rates from period 7 to period 15: $R_7 = 7.65$ increases to $R_{15} = 8.42$, an increase of 10 per cent during phase 2. This upward 'drift' in interest rates will have special significance when compared with the results of phase 3.

The fiscal regime changes unexpectedly in phase 3, with lump-sum taxes falling to the polar case of zero, and total government borrowing increasing to \$1,900 to maintain the national level of government revenues obtained in phase 2 (\$1,140 in total tax revenues and \$760 in bond sales).

In period 16 – crucial for determining whether households behave in a Ricardian fashion – interest rates are found to increase from $R_{15} = 8.42$ to $R_{16} = 8.57$, an increase of only 1.80 per cent, in spite of a 150 per cent increase in government borrowing. This contrasts significantly with the 43 per cent increase in interest rates in phase

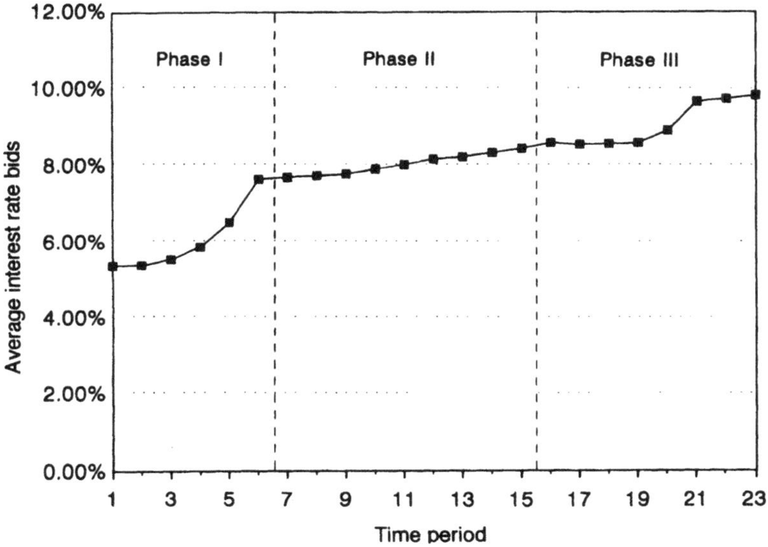

Figure 2.2 Interest rate time path

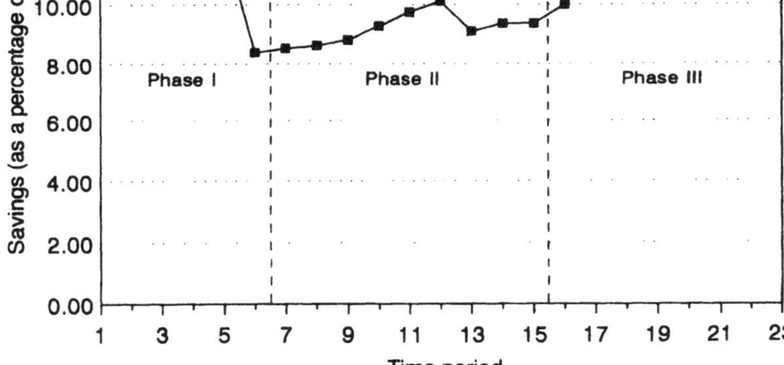

Figure 2.3 Savings time path

Table 2.2 Episodic effects of the regime shift

	Period	B_t^a	G_t^b	R_t^c	S_t^d
Phase 2	15	76	1,900	8.42	9.37
Phase 3	16	190	1,900	8.57	10.01
Percentage change		(150)	(0)	(1.8)	(6.8)

[a] Represents the individual denomination of government debt
[b] Total economy-wide government spending
[c] Average interest rate on government debt in every period
[d] Private savings expressed as percentages of national income

1, where increases in government borrowing were actually lower (100 per cent). (These episodic effects of the regime shift are described in Table 2.2.)

Furthermore, the shift from taxation to bond financing is accompanied by an increase in average household savings in period 16, as predicted by the Ricardian model. Households do indeed increase savings from periods 15 to 16 by 6.80 per cent – $S_{15} = 9.37$ increases to $S_{16} = 10.01$ (see Table 2.2 and Figure 2.3). These increased savings, in turn, exert a dampening effect on interest rates, causing them to rise by only 1.80 per cent in period 16. In the following period, savings increase further to $S_{17} = 11.30$, with the average interest rate consequently dampened to $R_{17} = 8.53$.

However, as phase 3 progresses with total government borrowing held steady at $1,900 for periods 18–23, taxes T_t held at zero, and income Y_t equal to $500 per period, we experience intriguing interest rate effects which seem similar to those experienced earlier in phase 2, but are now significantly more pronounced. Average interest rates begin to drift up, from $R_{17} = 8.53$ to $R_{23} = 9.82$ at the culmination of the experiment, resulting in an interest rate increase of 15.12 per cent (Figure 2.2). This is particularly interesting since average household savings from periods 17 to 23 hold steady at an elevated average level of $11.33 (Figure 2.3).

An examination of the post-experiment survey responses helped resolve this interesting interest rate behaviour. When asked to explain briefly the motivation for the interest rate bidding, consumption and savings decisions throughout the experiment, 73 per cent of the households cited some form of 'anxiety', or apprehension, when the government continued to borrow $1,900 in every period (from

16 to 23) and promised principal plus interest payments in the following semester, with the future tax policy remaining uncertain.

The majority of these respondents – 44 per cent – feared outright debt repudiation, 36 per cent expected huge increase in future taxation, 11 per cent believed that monetisation-induced inflation, along the lines of the present Brazilian, Ukrainian and Russian monetisations, would be inevitable, and the remaining 9 per cent could not specifically articulate their source of apprehension. It was this debt-driven apprehension that led the households to affix implicit and progressively increasing 'risk premiums' to successive issues of government debt which accounted for the upward drift in interest rates in phase 3 (and to a lesser extent in phase 2) in spite of level savings, consumption and government borrowing.

These phase 3 results are consistent with the literature pertaining to the 'sustainability' of bond-financed deficits along the lines of Sargent and Wallace (1981). Here 'sustainability' refers to the ability of the government/treasury to continuously roll over the debt in every period by issuing new debt, without having to resort to either monetisation, or an outright debt repudiation. A sequence of bond-financed deficits is defined as 'non-sustainable' when the real interest on government debt exceeds the rate of growth of the economy and implies an intertemporally increasing debt/income ratio.[21] This, in turn, makes a future monetisation or an outright debt repudiation 'inevitable' as the mounting debt/income ratios cause domestic (and foreign) households to reach some implicit upper limit on the amount of government debt in their portfolios.

In phase 3, the debt/income ratio increases intertemporally due to (i) the exogenously fixed rate of growth of national income and (ii) the burgeoning outstanding debt with the implicit inclusion of the mounting principal and interest payments. This non-sustainability, in turn, implies a real rate of interest that must exceed the growth rate of the economy. It is this interest-rate result that is experimentally confirmed by the interest rate behaviour in phase 3.

In the present experiment, real interest rates on government debt (which are equal to the nominal rates R_t as there is no current monetisation) do indeed increase – drift up – by virtue of the progressively increasing risk premiums imposed by the households. As bond sales mount and as the growth rate of the economy stays exogenously fixed – income is $500 per period per household – the rapidly increasing debt/income ratios are recognised as non-sustainable by households who implicitly add risk premiums to their 'bids' in the bond auctions. Furthermore, these risk premiums are found to increase in the latter stages of phase 3, as the credibility of the government's deficit-financing strategy erodes rapidly.

CONCLUSIONS

An experimentally modelled bond-financed tax cut yields results consistent, in part, with the Barro revival of the Ricardian equivalence theorem. The additional government bond sales are not treated as net wealth and households are indeed found to increase savings immediately following the bond-financed tax cut. The increase in the supply of savings offsets (to some extent) the interest-rate effects arising from the increased demand in government borrowing necessary to maintain the government revenues fixed. This dampening effect on interest rates is particularly significant when compared with the traditional 'crowding out' results obtained in phase 1 when government borrowing was increased in addition to taxation.

However, phases 2 and 3 of this experiment yield evidence of an upward drift in interest rates, even when the demand in government borrowing remains unchanged. This is particularly evident in phase 3 following the unexpected shift in the fiscal regime, with the drift increasing with continuous government borrowing in periods 17–23. Post-experiment survey results attribute this phenomenon to the fact that the majority of the lenders were apprehensive of continually large bond financing. They expected policy makers to eventually have to resort to debt repudiation or deficit monetisation to service the principal and interest payments. The decline in the long-term credibility of fiscal policy stemming from this debt-induced uncertainty increased from periods 17 to 23, and led households to add an increasing implicit 'risk premium' to the government's seemingly insatiable appetite for borrowing.

These results, which are consistent with the theory pertaining to 'non-sustainable' deficit financing, will be discussed again in the historical/empirical Part II of this book where we examine the relationship between confidence and credibility factors and the macroeconomic policies of the North and the South during the American Civil War; the German government during the post-First World War hyperinflation; and the post-1979 European Monetary System.

The present chapter, however, finds that an unexpected switch from taxation to bond financing, with the overall level of government revenues held fixed, does indeed yield household behaviour and interest rate effects consistent with Ricardian equivalence. However, policy makers would be remiss in exploiting this observed Ricardian behaviour by continually relying on a long-term fiscal policy of debt issuance, as the Ricardian results are experimentally found to be confined to the period(s) immediately following the regime shift. Households eventually perceive government debt to be 'riskier' and affix progressively increasing risk premiums to what they correctly perceive to be non-sustainable government bond financing, thereby causing an upward drift in interest rates that begins to negate the earlier Ricardian results.

The logical extension of this experiment (resources allowing in the future) would be to test households over longer periods to determine experimentally the effects on savings and interest rates under two different regimes, namely (i) when bond financing continues unabated, and (ii) the government institutes fiscal reform in an attempt to reverse the trend in phase 3 and decrease the intertemporal debt/income ratio.

APPENDIX: AN EXPERIMENTAL EXAMINATION OF INTEREST-RATE EFFECTS OF FISCAL POLICY

Please read the following directions carefully:

This experiment is designed to determine the effects of fiscal policies – changes in government borrowing and changes in taxes – on interest rates, savings, and consumption. Here, the processes of interest rate determination, bond sales, and government deficit financing attempt to mimic national 'real world' policies. The macroeconomic theories being tested will be discussed in class, in detail, following the conclusion of this experiment. The early results will be presented in the last week of class, if possible.

Please refrain from discussing possible results of the policy experiments, or from guessing the outcome of the experiment with your classmates – your opinion might influence theirs, and hence threaten the integrity of the experiment.

Instructions to participants

1 The classroom is the 'economy' comprised of individual participants, or, 'households', who are producers and consumers. It is a closed economy – there is no trade or capital flow between countries. The experiment director is the fiscal body, or, the government/treasury.
2 Your individual income will be given to you at the beginning of each period. Each time period is a 'round' of the experiment. There will be 20-30 time periods (rounds) in the experiment.
3 You might have a flat lump-sum tax imposed on your income in certain periods.
4 The government will announce the amount it needs to borrow to make up its deficit every period. This amount need not be constant every period. You can 'buy' government (Treasury) bonds by bidding on interest rates in the Treasury auction. Please submit your bids in writing on the note-cards that have been provided.
5 The lowest ten bidders will be sold the government debt in 10 equal denominations. The final rate that the government will offer will be an average of these ten lowest bids.
6 The principal and interest will be credited to you next semester – this is long-term government debt. This is the only means of earning interest in this economy. Your savings will not earn any interest if not lent to the government.
7 This process of announcing the latest lump-sum tax and the required additional government borrowing will be done at the beginning of every period, before the commencement of bidding.
8 Please remember to complete the short post-experiment survey. This is very important. You will get full credit if you have attended all the sessions and followed all the directions carefully. Please remember not to discuss your bids, etc., with other participants.

Please deliberate before lending (buying bonds). Treat the money as real. Assume that your objectives are to meet 'real world' expenses, to provide for a nest-egg of savings to meet any contingencies, and, of course, to invest and earn interest on a portion of your savings.

Please feel free to ask questions, or to suggest procedural changes in any future variations of this experiment. Thank you for your cooperation.

Chapter 3

Monetary credibility and national output

An experimental verification of the Lucas 'islands' explanation of business cycles*

> The aim of monetary policy should surely be not to prevent all fluctuations in the general price level, but to permit those which are necessary to the establishment of appropriate alterations in output and to repress those which tend to carry the alterations in output beyond the appropriate point.
>
> (Dennis H. Robertson, 1926)

> Paradoxically (the) weakness in the short-term evidence linking money to economic activity, and in particular to prices, is *encouraging* from the point of view of monetary business cycle theory.
>
> (Robert E. Lucas, Jr., 1976)

This chapter determines experimentally the changes in expectations resulting from shifts in monetary policy. In particular, we focus on the effects on expectations and national output in two separate cases: (i) when the central bank has lost credibility due to monetary irresponsibility in the past, and (ii) when the central bank attempts to rectify past monetary indiscipline by enacting some form of monetary reform to regain lost credibility.

Recently, the role of monetary stabilisation has generated renewed attention due to the recessions, slow-downs, and periods of sluggish growth experienced by most of the G-7 economies from the early 1990s to the present. Once again, research has been directed towards explaining the aggregate fluctuations in employment and output, and their correlations with inflation.

Mitchell (1951) formalised these aggregate fluctuations, or business cycles, as comovements in the time series of observed macroeconomic variables, and found that cycles of decentralised market economies exhibited similar properties, independent of time periods or administrations. For example, he found output movements across different sectors move together over time (exhibit high 'coherence') and that prices, short-term interest rates and monetary aggregates are procyclical.[1]

This observation of the similarity of business cycles across different regimes has generated substantial research directed towards exploring a unified market-determined cause of business cycles instead of attributing them to political or institutional policies. The unified, or 'single-shock', cause of business cycles was identified with fluctuations in monetary policy in the influential work by Friedman and Schwartz (1963). This, coupled with the Mitchell observation of procyclical prices and money, proved largely instrumental in directing the research focus towards examining possible monetary causes of business cycles.[2]

Lucas (1973) pioneered a large and growing body of research that attempted to explore the monetary causes of business cycles in the context of a rational expectations economy with imperfect information. Particular emphasis was placed on the fact that, since short-term links between fluctuations in money and real economic activity are unclear, individuals making production decisions are forced to indulge continuously in 'signal extractions' to sift out the relative price changes caused by real changes in market demand from the secular inflationary changes caused by changes in the money supply. This hedging behaviour on the part of producers was found to generate an increase in the rate of real output along with an increase in the inflation rate – referred to as the output–inflation tradeoff – and to replicate Mitchell's observation of the procyclicality of prices.

In recent years, however, this procyclical nature of prices documented by Mitchell – explained by Keynes in his *General Theory* as driven by rigid nominal wages and the declining marginal product of labour, and later developed theoretically by the imperfect information models – has been challenged by the real business cycle (RBC) literature.[3] This body of research attributes macroeconomic fluctuations primarily to productivity shocks, and finds price–output comovements to be countercyclical.[4]

This experiment explores whether the Lucas 'islands' approach to explaining business cycles – along with the attendant hypothesis of procyclical prices – can indeed be validated by testing the imperfect information paradigm in an experimental setting with real participants. The experiment simulates the Lucas 'islands' economy by replicating a version of Lucas's (1973) study in an economy where 'producers' have incomplete information and are forced to indulge in signal extractions to make their output decisions. The collective action of these 'producers' then provides us with an 'economy-wide' output response for every time period.

The rest of the chapter is organised as follows. A simplified version of Lucas (1973) adapted for the experiment is presented first, then the experimentation procedure and results are discussed. A brief summary and conclusion follows.

AN ADAPTATION OF THE LUCAS 'ISLANDS' MODEL

The economy is assumed to be comprised of many 'islands' of information (indexed by i), with rational individuals (producers) observing only the price on their specific island in the current time period, p_t(i) along with all past information. Furthermore, producers are scattered over a large number of competitive islands, with demand for the good distributed unevenly over this islands economy, which results in both relative and general price movements.[5]

The observed island-specific price, p_t(i), is assumed to deviate from some general price level p_t by the random amount z, expressed in logs as:

$$p_t\,(\mathrm{i}) = p_t + z \qquad (1)$$

where the general price level p_t is not directly observable by the islanders. This general price level is normally distributed with mean P and variance S_j^2 with the index j = 1–4 denoting four regimes of increasing general price-level variances implemented in the experiment. The deviation z is normally distributed and independent of p_t, with zero mean and variance T^2.

Producers on individual islands therefore independently observe the left-hand-side of (1) but are unable to determine the composition of this observed price. They have imperfect information in that they cannot distinguish the fraction of the observed increase in price that is caused by a general inflationary change, p_t, from the real increase in market demand for their good, denoted by the z component.

In Lucasian terminology, they are unable to distinguish between secular price changes due to inflation on all the islands, and relative price changes due to increases in z. If they attribute an increase in their observed price exclusively to the former, then they do not increase output, whereas an increase attributed to real (relative) price changes is accompanied by an increase in output.

The output supply function for each island is given by:[6]

$$y_t(\mathrm{i}) = k[p_t(\mathrm{i}) - E(p_t / I_t(\mathrm{i}))], \tag{2}$$

where $I_t(\mathrm{i})$ denotes the set of all information available to the producer in market i at time t. The rational agents in this economy are assumed to make their production decisions based on relative price changes, given by the right-hand-side of (2) which denotes the percentage deviation in the observed price $p_t(\mathrm{i})$ from the general price level, p_t.

Since p_t is not directly observable, the producers have to form an expectation of p_t conditional on all available information given by $E(p_t/I_t(\mathrm{i}))$, where $I_t(\mathrm{i})$ consists of two pieces of information: (a) the observed island-specific price $p_t(\mathrm{i})$, and (b) the mean of the general price level (obtained from past time periods) given by P. This signal extraction problem can be solved using the law of recursive projection to give:[7]

$$E(p_t/p_t(\mathrm{i}), P) = (1 - R_j)p_t(\mathrm{i}) + R_j P, \tag{3}$$

where $R_j = [T^2/(S_j^2 + T^2)]$, and is defined as the ratio of the variance in market-specific relative prices (T^2), with respect to the total variance ($T^2 + S_j^2$) where S_j^2 is a measure of the aggregate noise in the economy imparted by fluctuations in monetary policy. Therefore, the higher the variance of the general price level (or the noisier the monetary policy) the smaller the parameter R_j; $dR_j/dS_j^2 < 0$ as j increases from monetary regimes 1 to 4 with 1 being the low-variance or 'well-behaved' monetary policy and regime 4 being the highest variance, or 'noisiest' monetary policy.[8]

Substituting (3) into (2), and aggregating output–supply over all islands, we obtain the economy-wide deviation from trend of aggregate supply:

$$y_t = R_j [p_t(\mathrm{i}) - P], \tag{4}$$

where R_j is the weight that producers attribute to the deviations of the observed price $p_t(\mathrm{i})$ from the historical general price average, P.

In the limiting case when S_j^2 tends to zero (no monetary noise), R_j approaches unity and producers attribute all the increase (deviation) in the observed price to a relative price change and hence respond by increasing (changing) output supply. However, at the other extreme, when S_j^2 approaches infinity (as in a regime with extremely noisy monetary policy), R_j tends to zero. Producers in this case simply attribute any increases (deviations) in the observed price to general inflation, and consequently they refrain from making any output changes.

Diagramatically, this translates to an increase in the slope of the aggregate supply (AS) curve due to the increase in the variance of the general price level. In the presence of any discretionary demand-side stabilisation such as monetary loosening, this results in a progressively deteriorating output–inflation tradeoff as looser monetary policy shifts out aggregate demand over a steeper aggregate supply curve.[9] Theoretically, in the limiting case, as S_j^2 approaches infinity, we would obtain a vertical AS curve at which point discretionary monetary policy would be neutral with respect to real output.

Lucas therefore corroborates Mitchell's description of prices as being procyclical; increases in the rate of growth of prices are accompanied by increases in the rate of output. Furthermore, Lucas finds empirical support for the premise that the output–inflation tradeoff deteriorates as the monetary discipline of the economies decreases. For example, the tradeoff worsens as we move from the 'low' monetary variance – or, low 'noise' – economy of the pre-1970 United States to a relatively higher and 'noisier' monetary variance economy such as that of Argentina (which would have a relatively steeper AS curve).

Our next task is to test this Lucasian islands economy experimentally and verify that producers with imperfect information do indulge in individual signal extractions, and that, on an aggregate scale, this behaviour does indeed generate an output–inflation tradeoff of the type documented by Mitchell. Furthermore, we will attempt to verify that this tradeoff deteriorates as the monetary variance increases, thus precluding any attempts at long-run monetary stabilisation.

EXPERIMENT DESCRIPTION AND RESULTS

The experiment was tested on two samples of 'producers' denoted L1 and L2, comprised of students in the MBA programme at Rutgers. The former sample consisted of thirty-eight MBA students enrolled in the 'Executive MBA' programme while L2 was comprised of sixty-nine students enrolled in the 'Evening MBA' programme. These groups were chosen because of their great similarity – individuals in both groups had full-time day jobs in the same mix of companies in central New Jersey. Both these groups had no prior knowledge of the nature of the imperfect information model being tested here, nor of the results to be expected. Both groups which represented sections of Farrokh Langdana's Aggregate Economic Analysis course, participated in this experiment as part of a novel learning experience designed to relate a theoretical rational expectations model of the economy to actual responses of 'producers'.[10] The experiment was performed at the very beginning of the semester, before the students could begin to develop any sort of macroeconomic framework. The Lucas model, along with the implications of the results of the experiment, was then discussed at the end of the semester, months after the experiment's completion.[11]

Each student was considered a 'producer' on a separate 'island'.[12] This representative producer was then sequentially presented with prices observable only by that producer. There were a total of 120 prices comprised of a randomly generated normal distribution combining a real component z with mean zero and finite variance T^2, and an inflationary component with mean P and variance S_j^2 which increased from $j = 1$ to $j = 4$, with values of 250, 750, 1,250, 1,750. The 120 observed prices were divided into four stacks of thirty cards, with each stack corresponding to a variance regime j. Each card had an 'observed' price $p_t(\mathrm{i})$ on one side and the actual market-clearing output for that particular observation on the other. The island-specificity of prices was accomplished by distributing four stacks of thirty cards to each producer. These cards were distributed singly to each producer by assistants who 'managed' 10–15 producers each. Furthermore, each stack was shuffled to ensure that each producer's currently observed price was not identical to that of the neighbouring producer – Lucas's islands economy, with randomised observed prices on each island, was therefore replicated. The fact that all producers were not simultaneously observing identical prices was repeatedly stressed during every session of the experiment to remove any urge to mimic the neighbouring producer's output decision, or to communicate with classmates before, during, or after the experiment.

After observing each price, the producers made their production decision after (inadvertently) indulging in signal extractions to form an expectation of the real component of the change observed in their island-specific price.[13] Producers could increase output in increments of 2 per cent from 0 per cent (if they chose not to respond with increased output) to a maximum of 14 per cent.[14]

Immediately following each output decision, the producer was allowed to turn over the card to determine the market-clearing output. Only the experiment director had prior knowledge of the value of this exact market-clearing output which was a function of the real component of the observed price.[15] The two faces of the cards were colour coded so that the supervising assistants could immediately spot any premature attempts to flip the card prematurely and 'cheat' by knowing the exact output that would clear the market. Furthermore, once producers coded-in their output decisions, they were not allowed to erase their entries, thereby removing any temptation to 'revise' their past production decisions.

As this procedure was repeated 120 times, producers extracted information over time pertaining to the real and inflationary composition of their observed prices. Since there was no storage technology, or inventory, in this economy, their objective as producers was to minimise over- or underproduction by minimising absolute deviations of actual production from the market-clearing value.[16]

Due to resource constraints, the subject rewards were non-monetary. Producers were given course credit amounting to 5 per cent for (i) participating conscientiously in the complete experiment – all 120 prices – by attempting to target the market-clearing output, (ii) following all the instructions carefully, and (iii) not communicating with other participants. This reward system was particularly useful in motivating students who had missed sessions to come by and complete the missing part of the experiment, prior to the next set of price distributions.

Producers were also unaware that they would encounter four regimes of general price variances after every thirty observations; the cards of all four variances had the same colour coding. This forced them to constantly update their signal extractions as they noticed, or 'caught on' to the fact that the inflationary noise had changed. Sample L1 was fed 120 prices with S_j^2 increasing from regime $j = 1$ to $j = 4$, while L2 was tested with price variances moving in the opposite direction from $j = 4$ to $j = 1$.[17]

The empirical results indicate that prices indeed behave procyclically in this model economy. Increases in prices are accompanied by increases in output. Furthermore, the slope of the aggregate supply curve increases as S_j^2 increases from 250 to 1,750. This is observed in the empirical results presented in Table 3.1 where the R_j values of 0.085, 0.057, 0.036 and 0.034 correspond to the variances S_1^2, S_2^2, S_3^2 and S_4^2.[18] The slope of the aggregate supply curves, which is the

Table 3.1: Regression results for the 'islands' experiment (sample = L1)
Output equation: $[y_t = R_j\, p_t]$

Observations	*Constant*	R_j	R^2	*Degrees of freedom*
1–30 (j = 1; S_1^2 = 250)	5.50	0.085* (0.012)	0.65	28
31–60 (j = 2; S_2^2 = 750) 28	6.06	0.057* (0.006)	0.74	28
61–90 (j = 3; S_3^2 = 1,250)	6.03	0.036* (0.005)	0.67	28
91–120 (j = 4; S_4^2 = 1,750)	6.25	0.034* (0.004)	0.76	28

Note: Standard errors are in parenthesis
* Denotes significance at the 1% level

reciprocal of R_j, therefore increases, with values of 11.76, 17.54, 27.78 and 29.41.

Thus, greater monetary variance or 'noise' produces decreased output–inflation tradeoffs. Accordingly, attempts to exploit the perceived output–inflation tradeoff relentlessly by repeated discretionary monetary stabilisation only succeed in hastening its demise.

This experiment was performed in the reverse direction on sample L2, with producers being started off with the relatively high variance S_4^2, and ending with the low variance S_1^2. In this case, the results are statistically insignificant.[19] Once the producers experience the high-variance economy at the start of their experiment, their expectations of eventually extracting some real component from the sequence of later prices are seriously impaired, presumably due to scepticism regarding any imminent monetary discipline. While, theoretically, the islands model should work in both directions of increasing as well as decreasing monetary noise, the experiment indicates that the islands economy might be unidirectional.

Therefore, this result could allow one to make an even stronger case for monetary discipline and long-term monetary credibility. Not only does greater monetary noise worsen the output–inflation tradeoff, but once individuals assign a low weight to the real content of the price signal that they observe (due to a high monetary-variance economy), any attempts to increase this assigned weight through future monetary reform might be futile. This result may explain the fact that additional conditions – such as international lending tied to monetary discipline – are usually necessary to make the monetary reforms credible.[20] These findings are also consistent with the apparent difficulties experienced by the US and Western European policy makers in attempting to regain their credibility after the inflationary 1970s (see Chapter 6 for some evidence on the European case).

CONCLUSIONS

The Lucas (1973) islands economy, which spawned a huge body of literature explaining procyclical prices as well as the marked differences in the output–inflation tradeoffs of economies with varying degrees of monetary discipline, is experimentally tested in an imperfect information setting. The experiment verifies that producers, hampered by imperfect information, will attempt to signal-extract all possible information, allowing them to form an expectation of relative prices in their market. This experiment finds this hedging behaviour to produce a positive price–output relationship, or procyclical prices.

This output–inflation tradeoff is, however, unexploitable in the long run. Attempts at repeated discretionary monetary stabilisation only increase the monetary noise in this economy, causing producers eventually to assign lower weight to changes in their observed prices when determining their output-influencing relative price changes. This deterioration in the tradeoff is evidenced here by an aggregate supply curve that gets steeper as monetary variance increases.

Furthermore, we find that regimes once-characterised by monetary indiscipline will find it difficult to reverse the low real-demand content assigned by producers to observed changes in prices in the past. The experiment, therefore, corroborates the Lucas 'islands' model only for economies progressing from 'low' to 'high' monetary variances; an economy characterised by a monetary policy reforming in the opposite direction faces continued mistrust on the part of producers, and the loss in monetary credibility is found to persist over the period of the experiment.

An interesting agenda for future research – in addition to testing both groups in both directions of monetary variance – would be to extend the experiment for a prolonged length of time after monetary policy has gone from high variance to monetary reform. These extensions might determine if there is a finite 'critical credibility lag' beyond which the experiment might again conform to the Lucas model in both directions.[21]

APPENDIX: INSTRUCTIONS TO PARTICIPANTS

This experiment is worth 5% of your course grade. You can obtain full credit by participating in all 120 observations, by following all directions carefully, and above all, by not discussing the experiment with your classmates. There are no 'right' or 'wrong' answers. Just consistent ones. Please feel free to ask questions regarding the procedure of the experiment, at any time.

(A) Each student in the Rutgers core macroeconomics class (591) this semester will be a 'producer' on an 'island'.
(B) You, the 'producer' will have to respond to changes in the prices that you 'see' *only* on your island. There are in total 120 prices which you will 'see' sequentially on note-cards which will be presented to you individually, and singly, by the assistants.

Please *do not* move the cards placed on your desk by the assistant – the blue side of the last card should be facing up.

(C) The price that you 'see' on the card placed on your desk by the assistant will *almost NEVER* be the price that your neighbors are 'seeing' on their respective desks (islands) at this time.
(D) You have to decide if the change in price on your card is mainly due to an increase in real demand, or if the change is simply due to inflation. You then make your output decision based on your impression/guess of the nature of the price change that you observe on your card.
(E) You can increase output from 0% to the limit of 14%, in increments of 2%. The output decision is to be entered on the provided op-scan sheet (green and white sheet on which you do your course evaluations). Each circle on this sheet corresponds to a *2% change* in output. *Therefore, circle 1 is 0% (no change) in output, circle 2 is a 2% increase in output, circle 3 is a 4% increase in output . . . circle 8 is the maximum possible 14% increase in output.*
(F) Once you color-in your output decision, you *cannot* erase the entry and revise your production amount. Remember, every entry you make is final!
(G) *After* each output decision is made, I will announce that you can flip over your cards so that the *orange* side is facing up. You will now know the maximum output that would have cleared the market.
(H) Your objective as a producer is to minimize over- or under-

production over the long run by trying to produce as close to the market-clearing output as possible.

Since the prices that you 'see' are generated randomly, there is *no 'formula'* that you can derive. Only the experiment director knows the exact composition of the observed prices.

Therefore, your objective is to minimize over- or under-production over the long run, rather than accomplish the theoretically impossible feat of producing the exact output that would consistently clear the market.

(I) As announced, there is no storage technology; all excess production is lost. There are no inventories here.
(J) Once again, since this economy is driven by the concept of imperfect information, it is *imperative* that you *do not* discuss your past, current, and future output decisions with other participants.

Furthermore, remember that everyone is not 'seeing' identical prices simultaneously, any discussion will jeopardize the results.

Thank you.

Part II

Confidence and credibility factors in historical perspective

Chapter 4

Public confidence and public finance during the American Civil War

Lessons from North and South*

> Thus far, no want of confidence has been exhibited in our currency. It freely circulates everywhere, and the fact that the banking institutions receive and pay out Treasury Notes in their own business is the most certain indication that their credit is unimpaired.
>
> (C. G. Memminger, Confederate Secretary of the Treasury, August 1862)[1]

> Who steals my purse steals trash – if it contains Confederate bills.
>
> (Mrs Mary Boykin Chestnut, August 1864)[2]

INTRODUCTION

By the summer of 1864, public confidence in Confederate currency, like confidence in the success of the Confederate armies, had plummeted from the halcyon heights reached early in the Civil War. While the South's issues of Treasury notes had initially been well received, the rapid inflation that ultimately developed in the Confederacy was sparked by an increasing reluctance of the Southern population to hold, first, the Confederacy's bond issues and, ultimately, the money issues themselves. By 1863, this reaction by the public had put the Confederacy on the road to financial disaster while, in the North, improved public acceptance of the bond issues was critical in keeping inflation under control.

As shown in Figure 4.1, the rate of price increase during the Civil War was much milder in the North than in the South. Between April 1861 and April 1865, wholesale prices in the Eastern Confederacy as measured by Lerner's (1955, p. 24) index rose by more than 9,000 per cent (see Table 4.1). By comparison, Northern prices rose by

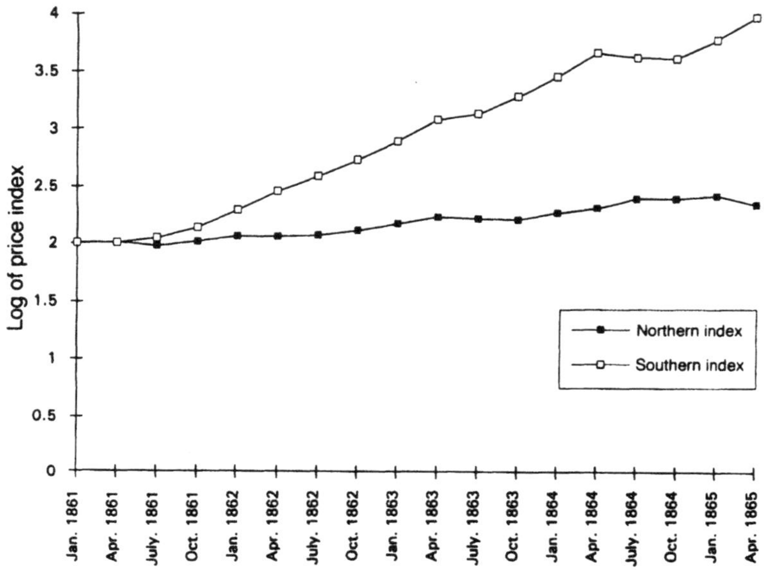

Figure 4.1 Wholesale prices in North and South, 1861–1865

approximately 110 per cent over the April 1861–April 1865 period. In April 1865, the month of General Lee's surrender to General Grant at Appomattox Court House, the Eastern Confederacy price index was more than 43 times higher than the price index for the Northern states.

While large budget deficits and inflation have often been seen to go hand in hand, any explanation of the divergent inflationary trends between North and South must confront the fact that both sides ran extremely big deficits during the Civil War. Even though the North had by far the better inflation record, Northern tax revenues accounted for only 10 per cent of total revenue in the fiscal year ending on 30 June 1862, and 15 per cent in the next fiscal year – before rising above 25 per cent for the fiscal year ending 30 June 1864 (Mitchell, 1903, p. 129). Over the course of the war, the ratio of the deficit to total expenditures ranged from 80 to 95 per cent in the South and from 69 to 89 per cent in the North (see pp. 69–75).

The wartime deficits required massive issues of debt in both North and South. A critical distinction, however, is that the composition of the debt was markedly different. The Confederacy's interest-bearing debt remained smaller than the non-interest-bear-

Table 4.1 Indices of wholesale commodity prices, 1861–1865

	April 1861	*April 1862*	*April 1863*	*April 1864*	*April 1865*
Eastern Confederacy	101	281	1,178	4,470	9,211
Northern states	101	113	166	199	212
Ratio: Confederacy/North	1.00	2.49	7.10	22.46	43.45

Sources: Lerner 1955, p. 24; Mitchell 1903, p. 256; and authors' calculations

Notes: Each index is constructed such that January–April 1861 = 100. In the case of the index for the Northern states, the original series (Mitchell, 1903, p. 256) had 1860 as the base year and was recalibrated by the authors. Both indices are based on arithmetic means. Complete quarterly series are given in Appendix Table A4.1.

ing portion right up until the Confederate Currency Reform Act of 17 February 1864, which imposed a one-third tax on Confederate Treasury notes not exchanged for bonds by 1 April 1864. On the other hand, the North's reliance on non-interest-bearing debt as a means of funding expenditures was always smaller than the revenue collected from interest-bearing debt. Indeed, after June 1863, receipts from non-interest-bearing debt accounted for less than 5 per cent of expenditures.

It is easy to criticise the Confederate policy makers' seemingly excessive reliance on non-interest-bearing Treasury notes. Such criticism misses the point, however, that in both the North and the South unbacked paper currency issues were utilised only because tax or bond financing was considered infeasible. The shortfall of tax revenue was inevitable for both sides given the rapid escalation of the war and the lack of an established system for collecting direct taxes. The North, though, not only funded a larger share of her deficits through interest-bearing debt but also successfully shifted away from short-term debt issues in favour of bonds during the critical middle stages of the war. While the Confederate government was itself well aware of the importance of absorbing excess issues of money and short-term debt through encouraging their conversion into bonds, its efforts were stymied by public unwillingness to hold Confederate bonds. A series of increasingly desperate measures by the Confederate government culminated in the outright repudiation that was imposed in 1864.

This denouement stands in sharp contrast to the situation at the beginning of the war when, in spite of the North's material advantages and stronger initial financial position, confidence factors had seemed to favour the South. The North experienced considerable difficulty in finding subscribers for its bonds in 1861 and 1862. It was only later in the war that public confidence was sufficient to provide a ready market for US government bonds without requiring hefty discounts from par. The South's own problems in disposing of its bond issues began, meanwhile, with the effects of the Union blockade in stopping the cotton sales that were to be used to purchase the Confederacy's $50 million loan. These difficulties were then exacerbated by the Confederate Treasury's suspension of specie payments on the bonds in August 1862 and subsequent adverse military developments that made it doubtful that specie payments would ever be resumed.

The pivotal blow may well have been the bloody repulse of the Confederate invasion of the North at Sharpsburg, Maryland, on 16–17 September 1862, followed by Lincoln's Emancipation Proclamation that – at least in theory – freed the slaves being held in the Southern states. These events ended any immediate hopes for a quick Southern victory. At the same time, the South's prospects of redeeming her debt issues with future surpluses began to look increasingly bleak. As discussed below, the peaking out of Confederate real money balances in October 1862 certainly appears to indicate a loss in public confidence at that time. From that point on, the government's revenue from money creation – and its command over real resources – went into decline. The fact that the Confederacy's expenditures trended downward in real terms while those of the North continued to increase can only have added to the daunting odds faced by the South throughout its struggle for nationhood.

TRENDS IN MONEY SUPPLY AND MONEY DEMAND DURING THE CIVIL WAR

By mid-1863, the nominal money stock in the Eastern Confederacy probably exceeded that in the Northern states. Given the wide variety of monies circulating in both sections of the country at the time, aggregate figures are subject to a good deal of uncertainty. However, Table 4.2 provides data from Godfrey (1978) on the sum of Confederate Treasury notes plus state and private bank issues in seven states for which continuous data are available through the close of 1864. The totals for July of each year are then compared with data from Mitchell (1903) on the money stock in the Northern

Table 4.2 Nominal and real money stocks, 1861–1865 ($ millions)

	1861	*1862*	*1863*	*1864*	*1865*
Eastern Confederacy:					
Nominal money stock	50	290	683	717	—
Real money stock	45	76	52	18	—
Northern states:					
Nominal money stock	202	333	630	827	957
Real money stock	213	287	394	346	506
Ratios (Confederacy/North):					
Nominal money stock	0.25	0.87	1.08	0.87	—
Real money stock	0.21	0.26	0.13	0.05	—

Sources: Godfrey 1978, pp. 118–119; Lerner 1955, p. 24; Mitchell 1903, pp. 179, 256; and authors' calculations.

Notes: The Confederate money stock figures are as of July in each year, and comprise Confederate Treasury notes plus state and private bank issues in seven states (Godfrey, 1978, pp. 118–119). These figures are deflated by the July wholesale price index to obtain the real money stock in January–April 1861 dollars. Full quarterly series are provided in Table 4.3. The Northern money stock figures are as of the end of the fiscal year on 30 June, and comprise legal tender Treasury notes plus state and national bank issues (Mitchell, 1903, p. 179). These figures are again deflated by the July wholesale price index to obtain the real money stock in January–April 1861 dollars

states at the end of each fiscal year (i.e. as of 30 June). By totalling the legal tender Treasury notes plus state and local bank issues, an attempt has been made to obtain a series as comparable as possible to that available for the Confederacy. This practice excludes other categories such as specie money, postage and fractional currency and notes that were not legal tender, estimates of which are, in any event, in Mitchell's (1903, p. 181) words 'mere guesses'.

The data as presented are consistent with a rapid expansion in the money stock in both North and South through 1863. The Confederate money stock is estimated to have grown approximately 1,266 per cent between July 1861 and July 1863, while the North's money stock grew by approximately 211 per cent over this same period. After this point, the rates of increase decline. In the South, this is explained by the implementation of the Confederate Currency Reform Act of 17 February 1864 that initially reduced the estimated money stock from $963 million in January 1864 to $683 million in April 1864 (full quarterly data on the Confederate money stock are shown in Table 4.3 and are graphed in Figure 4.2).[3] In the North, the reduced rate of money supply growth occurred as the issue of

Table 4.3 Quarterly series on Confederate nominal and real money stock totals, 1861–1865 ($ millions)

	1861	*1862*	*1863*	*1864*	*1865*
Nominal money stock (Confederate, state and local issues in seven states)					
January	47	134	548	963	860
April	49	208	608	683	—
July	50	290	683	717	—
October	73	411	814	769	—
Real money stock (in January–April 1861 dollars)					
January	47	69	72	34	15
April	49	74	52	15	—
July	45	76	52	18	—
October	54	78	43	19	—

Sources: Godfrey 1978, pp. 118–119; Lerner 1955, p. 24; and authors' calculations

Notes: The money supply data cover Alabama, Florida, Georgia, Mississippi, North Carolina, South Carolina and Virginia and are drawn from the seemingly definitive work of Godfrey (1978, pp. 118–119). The real money stock is computed by dividing the nominal figures by Lerner's (1955, p. 24) wholesale price index that is constructed from 28 commodities in Richmond, Virginia; 23 in Fayetteville, North Carolina; 34 in Augusta, Georgia; and 25 in Wilmington, North Carolina. The nominal and real money stock series differ significantly from Lerner's (1955, p. 29) own calculations as explained by Godfrey (1978). Lerner's real money stock index, in fact, ends in January 1864 and peaks in October 1861 – whereas Godfrey's data suggest that the real money stock actually rose until October 1862 and did not fall below the January 1861 level until after July 1863

'greenback' Treasury notes was stopped and the North was able to use increased issues of bonds and other interest-bearing debt to take their place (see pp. 79–82).

Whatever parallels one may be able to draw regarding the behaviour of the nominal money stock in the North and South, the respective real money stocks – obtained by using wholesale price indices to deflate the nominal series – reveal a strikingly different pattern. Between July 1861 and July 1863, the 1,266 per cent increase in the Confederacy's nominal money stock was accompanied by only a 16 per cent increase in the real money stock. Moreover, the real money stock actually began to decline after the autumn of 1862. The North's real money stock increased by approximately 85 per cent between 30 June 1861 and 30 June 1863, and the North was clearly better able to keep the growth of the money supply

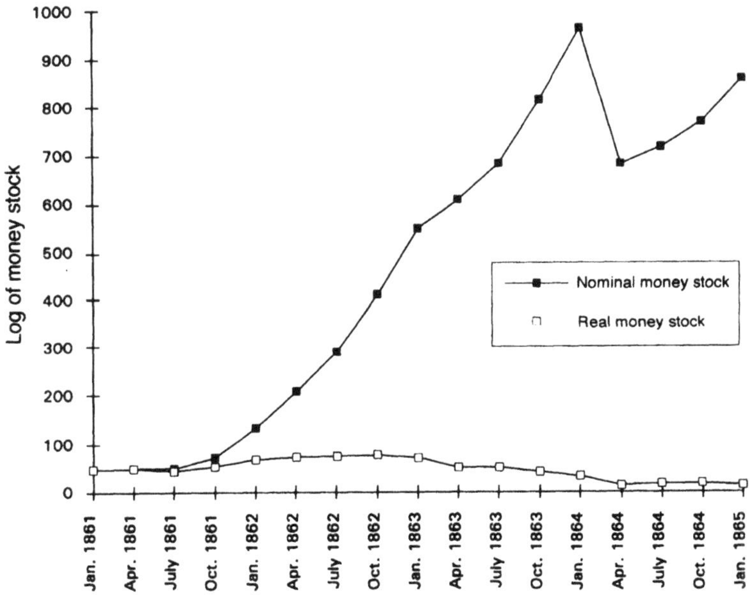

Figure 4.2 Confederate nominal and real money stocks

ahead of the growth in prices. This is consistent with the fact that the much lower rate of inflation in the North gave individuals less incentive to economise on cash balances as a means of avoiding the inflation tax. In the Confederacy, however, the rapid inflation eventually produced a declining real money supply as the public literally proved themselves able to spend money faster than the Confederacy could print it.

Confederate real money balances fell below the January 1861 level by October 1863, and, when the data series ended in January 1865, real balances stood at less than one-third of the January 1861 level. Not surprisingly, there was widespread resort to barter and increasing circulation of greenbacks in the South in the latter stages of the war. Indeed, in April 1865, greenbacks were even 'used to pay off Confederate soldiers at the rate of $1 in "greenbacks" for $15 in Confederate notes' (Schwab, 1901, pp. 162–163). Private bank notes also began to command an increasing premium over Treasury notes. As early as January 1864, Richmond bank notes were said to be worth 3 Confederate dollars (Pecquet, 1987, p. 222).

Nevertheless, if inflation was rising throughout this 1861–1863 period in both North and South, this still leaves the question of why real money balances increased at all. This issue is especially pertinent to the Confederate situation, where real money balances continued to increase through October 1862 even though wholesale prices rose by 421 per cent between January 1861 and October 1862.[4] Even in the North, the rising real money balances through the fiscal year ending 30 June 1863 were accompanied by a 60 per cent rise in prices relative to the January 1861 level.

One reason for the public's apparent willingness to hold the depreciating currency may have been the fact that the paper currency was, to some extent, replacing the specie money that had been in use before the war. Mitchell (1903, p. 178), for example, refers to the director of the mint's estimate that there was from $275 to $300 million of specie in the country in 1861. Adding $275 million to the 1861 Northern money stock given in Table 4.2 would reverse the conclusion that the real money stock grew between 1861 and 1862. It would not, however, alter the finding that the real money stock grew between 1862 and 1863. Mitchell (1903, p. 179) estimates that the specie in circulation remained steady from 1862 on at about $26 million, with the vast majority of this circulation being confined to the Pacific coast states (where the specie continued to be produced during the war).[5]

The role of the new money in displacing specie money also does not seem to explain the rising real money balances in the Confederacy as it is doubtful that the banks in the Confederate states held more than about $25 million in specie when war broke out (Schwab, 1901, p. 142). Newcomb (1865, p. 55) was perhaps not so far from the truth in claiming that the Confederate states 'had scarcely any financial resources worthy the name to start with, and what they had were exhausted in the beginning'. Indeed, with little specie and almost no tax revenue, the Confederate government's ability to succeed in having the public acquiesce in holding these notes seems almost a source of wonder. Were individuals irrational not only in raising their real cash balances during the early part of the war but also in being willing to accept Confederate Treasury notes at all if they were not backed by any tangible resources?

An explanation may perhaps be found in terms of whether the rise in prices – like the resort to large deficits funded in large part by printing money – was seen, at first, as a temporary rather than a permanent phenomenon. This general point has been made by Keynes (1924, p. 50), who observes that the

> public is so much accustomed to thinking of money as the ultimate standard, that, when prices begin to rise, believing that the rise must be temporary, they tend to hoard their money and to postpone purchases, with the result that they hold in monetary form a *larger* aggregate of real value than before [emphasis in original].[6]

Particularly given a situation where individuals in both North and South were anticipating a short war of only a few months (see, for example, Lerner, 1954, p. 508), even a large deficit financed mostly by note issue need not raise inflationary expectations if the war-induced deficits are believed to be of short duration and if the public believes that the government has the capability of extracting future surpluses so that the notes issued will eventually be redeemable at par in specie. A similar argument applies to the public's willingness to hold the government's bond issues, and Toma (1991) points to the acceptance of very low rates of interest on these bonds during the Second World War as being rational provided that bond holders believed that the duration of the war would be sufficiently short, and the postwar budgetary surpluses sufficiently large, to enable redemption without inflation.

If this argument is correct, then the subsequent decline in real money balances, and apparent loss of confidence in the currency in both North and South, would reflect not only the state of the existing finances and existing inflation rates but also expectations about the duration of the war and the final outcome of the conflict. The peaking out of Confederate real money balances in October 1862 comes after the Battle of Sharpsburg (or Antietam, as it was known in the North) that was fought on 16–17 September 1862. This battle ended General Lee's invasion of the North and frustrated Southern hopes for a victory on Northern soil that had been expected to spur intervention by the European powers. This battle produced more than 25,000 casualties (Livermore, 1900, pp. 92–93) and was soon followed by Lincoln's Emancipation Proclamation, altogether surely dispelling any prospect of a quick end to hostilities.[7] The consequences of a long drawn out war of attrition were, of course, particularly devastating to the South given its more limited initial pool of resources.

Interestingly, the Northern reaction to the events of September 1862 also appeared to be negative. Guinnane *et al.* (1993) find evidence of a significant structural 'break' in the gold price of greenbacks on 23 September 1862. While pointing out that the unprecedented casualties in the 16–17 September battle may have led to heightened estimates of the war's future costs, Guinnane *et al.* (p. 13) argue that the 'more likely cause of the structural break is that the Emancipation Proclamation destroyed any hope for a peaceful settlement to the war'. There could be no reconciliation with the South in the face of a proclamation that dispossessed the slave-owners and planters who had played a leading role in the secession movement. Indeed, the Confederate government, to the very end, rejected plans to enlist blacks as a means of compensating for the denudation of its armies. While Guinnane *et al.* (1993) isolate six other structural breaks in the gold premium during the Civil War, the September 1862 break is the first in their 1862-1865 sample (the others lie between 8 January 1863 and 8 March 1865).

There is, unfortunately, no way to separate effectively the response of real money balances to military events from effects associated with the swathe of rising deficits, rising rates of note issue and rising inflation. However, in an earlier empirical study (Burdekin and Langdana, 1993), we did find some evidence that the Confederate inflation rate was better explained on the basis of a dummy variable representing the military situation than by the state of Confederate fiscal policy. It is possible that the same is true with respect to real money balances. Certainly, deteriorating finances and rising inflation were a fact of life throughout the Confederacy's existence. If these trends alone explain the decline in real money balances, then why did people wait until nearly two years into the war to recognise them? It may be that awareness of the permanency of the unfortunate financial situation was the key to initiating the trend towards declining real money balances, and that this awareness was, to at least some extent, a reflection of military (and political) events.[8]

Confederate real money balances certainly appear to have declined substantially during 1863. The quarterly inflation rate – as calculated from the Lerner price index given in Appendix Table A4.1 – reached 54.6 per cent in April 1863 and real money balances fell to $52 million at this time, down sharply from the $78 million level reached in October 1862. In the midst of General Lee's advance into Pennsylvania following the rout of General Hooker's forces at the Battle of Chancellorsville, July 1863 saw the quarterly inflation rate temporarily decline to 12.6 per cent while real money balances held steady at the reduced level of $52 million. With word of Lee's retreat from Gettysburg on 4 July and the surrender of Vicksburg by General Pemberton on the same day, the rise in inflation and decline in real money balances resumed in earnest, however. The quarterly inflation rate peaked at 59.6 per cent in April 1864 just prior to the operation of the Confederate Currency Reform Act. At that time, real money balances reached their nadir of $15 million, which was less than one-third of the level attained in early 1861 and less than one-fifth of the maximum reached in October 1862.

In the North, real money balances declined between 30 June 1863 and 30 June 1864 before rising to a new peak on 30 June 1865. The temporary decline between mid-1863 and mid-1864 coincided with a decline in the gold value of the currency towards its lowest value for the war in July 1864, when the average value in gold of $100 in greenbacks stood at only $38.70 (see Mitchell, 1903, pp. 210–211). Between July 1863 and July 1864 wholesale prices in the North rose 49 per cent, up from the 38 per cent rate of increase over the July 1862–July 1863 period (see the data in Appendix Table A4.1). At the same time, the rate of growth of the nominal money stock as given in Table 4.2 declined from 89 per cent between 30 June 1862 and 30 June 1863 to 31 per cent between 30 June 1863 and 30 June 1864.

The decline in Northern real money balances may reflect a higher velocity of circulation as individuals sought to dispose of the depreciating currency. Another factor was the incentive to exchange this currency for US government bonds, however, as higher gold prices made the North's specie-paying bonds more attractive in relation both to the greenback and to other short-term debt instruments whose interest was paid in greenbacks. The Confederate government, on the other hand, was unable to live up to its initial promises of making bond interest payments in specie (see pp. 75–79) and so higher gold prices did not encourage a similar exchange into bonds in the South. In fact, the deteriorating military situation led to increased pessimism that these bonds would ever be redeemed, making it ever more difficult for the Confederate Treasury to find new subscribers for its loan offerings.

THE SETTING FOR FISCAL POLICY

The Confederacy, like the North, began the war with no system for collecting direct taxes. Moreover, the Union blockade and the partially self-imposed cotton embargo severely limited revenue

Table 4.4 Confederate and Federal spending and revenue flows, 1861–1865 ($ millions)

	1861	*1862*	*1863*	*1864*	*1865*
Confederate states:					
Nominal expenditures	70.7	258.1	773.1	998.0	—
Nominal deficit	68.9	245.9	727.1	799.6	—
Real expenditures	56.0	108.5	89.2	28.3	
Real deficit	54.3	104.1	84.0	22.2	—
Receipts from interest debt/expenditures	0.28	0.31	0.43	0.37	—
Receipts from non-interest debt/ expenditures	0.43	0.60	0.66	0.54	—
Northern states:					
Nominal expenditures	66.6	469.6	718.7	865.0	1,296.8
Nominal deficit	25.1	417.6	606.0	600.4	963.1
Real expenditures	65.9	434.8	502.6	462.6	571.3
Real deficit	24.8	386.7	423.8	321.1	424.3
Receipts from interest debt/expenditures	0.35	0.58	0.48	0.76	0.67
Receipts from non-interest debt/ expenditures	—	0.34	0.35	0.05	0.002

Sources: Memminger 1861a, b, 1862a, b, 1863a, b, 1864a; Trenholm 1864; Lerner 1955, p. 24; Studenski and Krooss 1952, p. 152; Mitchell 1903, pp. 129, 256; and authors' calculations

Notes: The Confederate spending and revenue figures each cover two Treasury Reports, and span the periods 17 February 1861–16 November 1861; 17 November 1861–1 August 1862; 2 August 1862–30 September 1863; and 1 October 1863–1 October 1864. Full details from the individual Treasury Reports are provided in Appendix Tables A4.2–A4.4. Deflation of the nominal figures by the average value of the wholesale price index over the period in question yields the real expenditure and deficit series in January–April 1861 dollars. The Northern spending and revenue figures each cover the fiscal year ending on 30 June and are deflated by the average value of the wholesale price index to yield the real expenditure and deficit series in January–April 1861 dollars

from import and export duties. The Confederate budget deficit accounted for more than 97 per cent of expenditures in the period from 17 February to 16 November 1861 (see the data provided in Table 4.4). A 'War Tax' was passed on 15 August 1861 at the rate of 50 cents per $100 of the taxable items assessed by the Treasury, but had a very low yield. In 1862, its first year of operation, less than 5 per cent of revenues were realised from this tax. The Tithe Act, or the 'Tax-in-Kind', on 24 April 1863 supplemented a combined property tax and graded income tax with a tax-in-kind that was primarily aimed at supplying provisions for the army.[9] While these tax initiatives did somewhat reduce the Confederacy's reliance on deficit financing after October 1863, the receipts from non-interest-bearing notes still accounted for more than half of total expenditures (see Table 4.4). The ratio of the deficit to total expenditures was 95 per cent in the 17 November 1861–1 August 1862 period; 94 per cent in the 2 August 1862–30 September 1863 period; and 80 per cent in the 1 October 1863–1 October 1864 period.[10]

While the South's reliance on deficit financing changed little during the war, its command over real resources appears to have declined after 1862. That is, while nominal expenditures and nominal expenditures continued to rise rapidly, real expenditures and the real deficit – as calculated by dividing the nominal values by the average value of the Lerner price index for the period in question – fell after 1862. While the exact point of transition cannot be determined on the basis of the data available, real expenditures for 2 August 1862–30 September 1863 are only 82 per cent of real expenditures for the 17 November 1861–1 August 1862 period (even though the latter period is approximately four months shorter). There is a similar drop in the real deficit. The decline in the Confederacy's command over real resources, in fact, roughly coincides with the decline in real money balances that appeared to set in during the last months of 1862. Thereafter, Confederate real expenditures, real deficits and real money balances trended downward throughout the remainder of the war.

Whatever the Confederacy's financial problems, the North's finances were, in many respects little better. Figure 4.3 illustrates the heavy reliance on deficit financing by both North and South. The deficit reached 89 per cent of expenditures in the fiscal year ending 30 June 1862 and was still at 84 per cent during the 1862–1863 fiscal year. In the 1863–1864 and 1864–1865 fiscal years the deficit's share of total expenditures declined to the somewhat lower totals of 69 per cent and 74 per cent, respectively. As with the Confederacy, new tax laws were passed early in the war but collection difficulties and exemptions severely limited the revenue received by the Treasury. Excise taxes and the new income tax had become important revenue sources by 1864, however, and tax revenues funded approximately 25 per cent of total expenditures in 1864 and 1865 as compared to only 10 per cent in 1862.

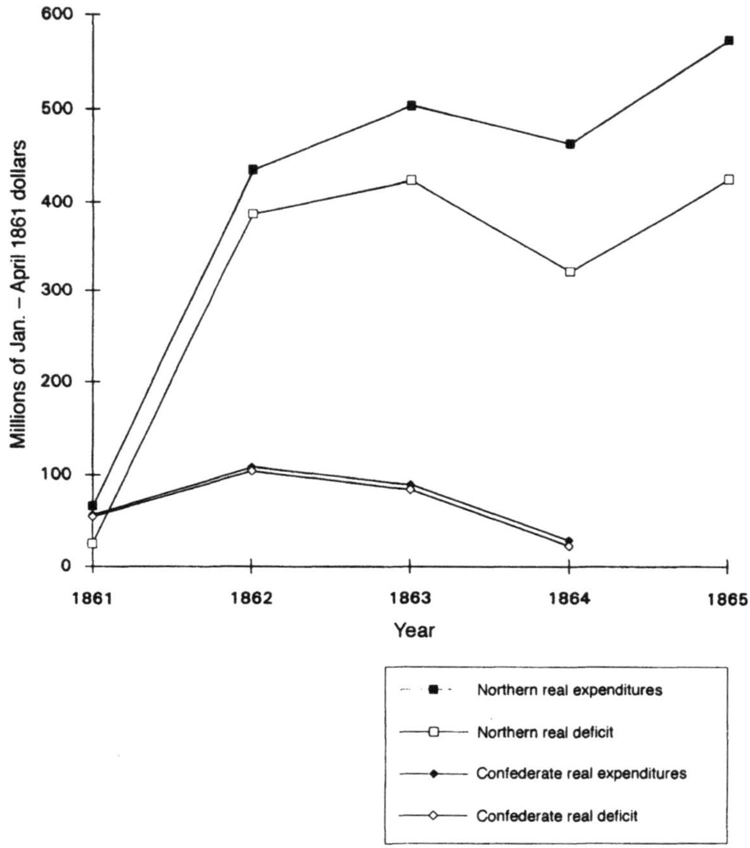

Figure 4.3 **Confederate vs. Northern expenditures and budget deficits in constant dollars**

Manufacturers' sales taxes, in particular, were raised until they amounted to an estimated 8–20 per cent of the cost of production in 1865 (see Studenski and Krooss, 1952, pp. 151–153).

Nevertheless, the North's deficit/expenditure ratios in the fiscal years prior to 30 June 1863 ranged between 84 and 89 per cent while the South's ranged between 94 and 95 per cent over roughly the same period.[11] Both sides reduced their reliance on deficit financing by approximately 15 percentage points in the 1863–1864 reporting periods. In total, approximately 20 per cent of the North's war-time revenues came from taxes as compared to a little over 8 per cent for the South (see Ball, 1991, p. 255). While there is no denying that the North's fiscal policy was more effective than that of the South, the dependence upon debt finance by both sides was extreme by historical standards. Even the North's deficit/expenditure ratios were, for example, well above those incurred by the United States during the mass mobilisation effort undertaken for the Second World War. At that time, the US deficit/expenditure ratio peaked at 69 per cent in 1943 before declining to just over 50 per cent in 1944 and 1945 (*Economic Report of the President*, 1994, table B–79).

Table 4.4 shows that the North's real expenditures, as well as the real deficit, appeared to increase until the fiscal year ending on 30 June 1863. There was then a temporary decline in each category over the next fiscal year before real expenditures and the real deficit rose to new highs in the 1864–1865 fiscal year. Confederate real expenditures fell drastically in relation to Northern real expenditures. While 1864 real expenditures by the North exceeded the 1862 levels, 1864 real expenditures by the South stood at only 26 per cent of the 1862 totals. The rising disparity in real spending (and revenue) levels after 1862 surely made the South's task increasingly impossible the longer the war progressed.

The South's declining real expenditure levels after 1862 are hardly surprising given that non-interest-bearing notes were accounting for more than half of expenditures and that real money balances declined sharply during 1863. Nominal issues of non-interest-bearing notes totalled \$506.1 million between 2 August 1862 and 30 September 1863 as compared to \$155.8 million between 17 November 1861 and 1 August 1862 (Table 4.5). Real receipts from these note issues declined, however, from an estimated \$66.7 million in the 1861–1862 period to \$54.2 million in the 1862-1863 period (see Appendix Table A4.2). In short, by 1863 the South's revenues from the inflation 'tax' were declining and – in the absence of sufficient conventional tax revenues to take their place – total revenues and real expenditures fell as well.

The decline in the South's real revenue gains from money creation was the inevitable result of collapsing 'confidence' in the Confederate currency and a shift away from the favourable situation to which Secretary Memminger had alluded in August 1862 – when real money balances were, in fact, near their peak levels. While the decline in real money balances appears to have been temporarily held in check by military successes in the spring and early summer of 1863, the trend

Table 4.5 Distribution of Confederate and Federal debt receipts, 1861–1865 ($ millions)

	1861		*1862*		*1863*		*1864*		*1865*	
Confederate states:										
Total debt receipts	50.2		235.7		841.3		908.2		—	
Bonds	18.0	(36%)	19.6	(8%)	189.8	(23%)	303.8	(33%)	—	
Other interest debt	2.0	(4%)	60.4	(26%)	145.4	(17%)	61.1	(7%)	—	
Non-interest debt	30.2	(60%)	155.8	(66%)	506.1	(60%)	543.3	(60%)	—	
Northern states:										
Total debt receipts	23.0		432.5		596.1		697.7		875.0	
Bonds	23.3	(101%)	59.6	(14%)	172.5	(29%)	468.2	(67%)	344.2	(39%)
Other interest debt	−0.3	(−1%)	214.4	(49%)	170.4	(29%)	185.9	(27%)	528.1	(60%)
Non-interest debt	0.0	(0%)	158.5	(37%)	253.2	(42%)	43.6	(6%)	2.7	(1%)

Sources: Memminger 1861a,b, 1862a,b, 1863a,b, 1864a; Trenholm 1864; Mitchell 1903, p. 129; and authors' calculations

Notes: The Confederate debt figures span the periods 17 February 1861–16 November 1861; 17 November 1861–1 August 1862; 2 August 1862–30 September 1863; and 1 October 1863–1 October 1864. Besides bonds, other interest debt comprises call certificates and interest-bearing Treasury notes, and the non-interest debt is non-interest-bearing Treasury notes outstanding. The Northern debt figures each cover the fiscal year ending on 30 June. Besides bonds, other interest debt comprises interest-bearing notes, temporary loans and certificates of indebtedness. The non-interest debt in this case is greenbacks plus old demand notes of 1861 and fractional currency toward rising inflation and declining real money balances soon resumed. Once it became clear that no quick victory would be forthcoming, a financial policy based upon little more than the printing press quickly began to prove disastrous for the Southern economy.

Given that the North also obtained less than 10 per cent of its revenue from taxes during the 1861–1862 and 1862–1863 fiscal years, resort to debt finance could have had similar effects in that section of the country as well. However, as discussed below, the North ultimately proved more successful in financing its deficits with interest-bearing debt that was less prone to circulate as currency, hence making the yawning gap between receipts and expenditures less inflationary than in the South. As seen in Figure 4.4, the North's receipts from interest-bearing debt always exceeded those from the non-interest-bearing portion, whereas the reverse was true for the Confederacy.

PROBLEMS WITH BOND FINANCING

Ironically, at the beginning of the war it was the North's credit that seemed to be in question. Upon passage of the Act of 17 December 1860 that authorised the issue of $10 million in 1-year US Treasury notes, $5 million of these notes were offered the following day. Mitchell (1903, p. 7) states that, in the midst of South Carolina's secession and low public confidence in the Buchanan administration, the

> response showed how low the national credit had sunk; $1,831,000 was offered at 12 per cent. or less; $465,000 more at rates between 15 and 36 per cent. All offers at 12 per cent. or under were accepted.

To put these numbers in perspective, 'New York State 7's were [then] selling at a premium, evidencing the weakness of Federal credit' (Studenski and Krooss, 1952, p. 138*n*). Of $25 million in 6 per cent bonds authorised by the Federal Congress in February 1861, only $8 million could be sold at 90 or above (i.e. at less than a 10 per cent discount below par). Things were little better in May 1861 when Salmon P. Chase, Lincoln's appointee as Secretary of the Treasury, sold $7.3 million in 6 per cent bonds at an average price of only 85.34 (Studenski and Krooss, 1952, p. 140).

Both governments sought to gain specie by new loans authorised in the first year of the war. On 28 February 1861, the Confederate

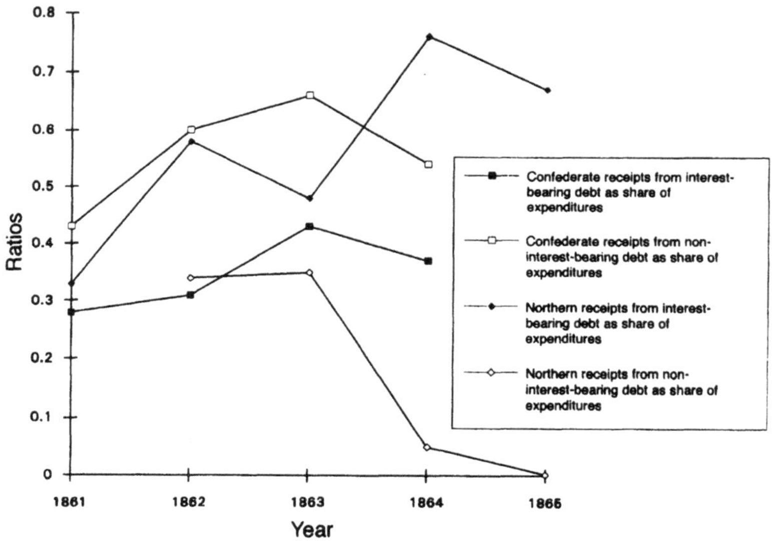

Figure 4.4 Confederate vs. Northern reliance on debt and note issues

Provisional Congress authorised a $15 million loan paying 8 per cent interest. Then $5 million worth of bonds were offered on 17 April 1861 with payment to be made in specie on the terms of 6 per cent down and the remainder due on or before 1 May. Although most Southern banks had suspended specie payments before the loan was even offered, the banks aided the Confederacy by exchanging for specie, at par, all of their notes that were to be used for purchasing the bond issue – as well as making large subscriptions on their own account (Todd, 1954, p. 30). Consequently, the full $15 million was taken up by 15 October 1861. A second $50 million loan was authorised on 16 May 1861, again bearing 8 per cent interest, and payable either in specie, produce or foreign bills of exchange. The early success of this second loan was such that President Davis, in an address to the Provisional Congress, stated:

> In the single article of cotton, the subscriptions to the loan proposed by the Government cannot fall short of fifty millions of dollars, and will probably exceed that amount; and scarcely an article required for the consumption of the Army is provided otherwise than by subscription to the produce loan.[12]

The North, meanwhile, secured a $50 million bank loan in 3-year, 7.3 per cent notes during August 1861, with $5 million in specie being delivered immediately to the government. The banks were only able to sell $45 million of these notes to the public, however, and the entire amount of a second $50 million issue in October was retained by the banks. Drains on the banks' specie reserves were exacerbated by the issue of $33 million in demand notes by Secretary Chase that were, in short order, presented to the banks for exchange into specie (Studenski and Krooss, 1952, p. 142). Following the very large budget deficit presented in Chase's Treasury Report of 10 December 1861, and receipt on 16 December of warlike news from England over the *Trent* affair,[13] banks in New York City alone were subject to losses of specie that reached $7.4 million in a single week (Mitchell, 1903, pp. 37–40). There was a general suspension of specie payments by the banks on 30 December 1861.

Amid fears that attempts to close the growing budget deficit by a large new bond issue would yield only '75 to 60 cents on the dollar' (see Mitchell, 1903, pp. 48–49), the Federal Congress soon authorised the first issues of non-interest-bearing 'greenbacks' under the Legal Tender Act of 25 February 1862. The greenbacks, while non-interest bearing, were convertible at par into 6 per cent bonds (until this privilege was revoked on 1 July 1863). Apparently, few took advantage of this conversion right, however, and Chase's attempts to sell these bonds at par were largely unsuccessful (Studenski and Krooss, 1952, p. 145). With sales of demand notes and certificates of deposit insufficient to meet the Treasury's growing revenue needs, the initial $150 million issue of greenbacks was followed by further $150 million issues in July 1862 and January–March 1863. Through the end of the 1862–1863 fiscal year, Federal finance remained plagued with weak demand for US bond issues, budget deficits in excess of 84 per cent of total expenditures, and heavy reliance on greenbacks and short-term debt instruments. While receipts from interest-bearing debt always exceeded receipts from the non-interest-bearing portion, Table 4.5 shows that long-term loans accounted for just 14 per cent of total debt receipts in the 1861–1862 fiscal year and the figure rose only to 29 per cent in the 1862–1863 fiscal year.

In the early stages of the war, therefore, Northern finances were, to say the least, not on a firm basis. Nor had the North matched the apparent initial enthusiasm for the first Confederate bond issues. Meanwhile, the gold value of $100 in greenbacks followed a steady decline down to a temporary low of $58.1 in gold on 28 February 1863 (Mitchell, 1903, p. 196). The North benefited, however, from the fact that by this time the Confederacy's finances were even more unsound and, by 1863, the inflationary spiral in the Confederate states was accompanied by an accelerating flight from the currency. Confederate bond issues received a perhaps fatal setback when, in the face of the growing Federal blockade of Southern ports, the cotton sales that were to fund the lion's share of the $50 million loan of 16 May 1861 were not to be had. A second $50 million loan, authorised on 19 August 1861 and payable in Confederate Treasury notes as well as specie and foreign bills of exchange, did not secure the hoped for number of new subscriptions (see Todd, 1954, pp. 34–39).

Between 17 February 1861 and 16 November 1861, the Confederate government took in $18 million from bond issues and $30.2 million from non-interest-bearing notes. Between 17 November 1861 and 1 August 1862, bond sales realised only an additional $19.6 million. The share of total debt receipts accounted for by long-term loans declined from 36 per cent in the 17 February 1861–16 November 1861 period to just 8 per cent in the 17 November 1861–1 August 1862 period (see Table 4.5). The Confederacy's growing revenue shortfall was largely made up by $155.8 million in issues of non-interest-bearing notes between 17 November 1861 and 1 August 1862. The revenue from bond sales was also supplemented with $60.4 million in short-term interest-bearing debt – comprising interest-bearing notes and call certificates – between 17 November 1861 and 1 August 1862.

Issues of 3.65 per cent and 7.3 per cent interest-bearing Treasury notes were authorised under the Acts of 9 March 1861 and 17 April 1862, respectively. While it was hoped that the latter 7.30 per cent issue would be 'withdrawn from circulation and held as an investment, the notes circulated freely, adding to the redundancy of the currency' (Todd, 1954, p. 108). Over $120 million of these notes were put into circulation during 1862 (Godfrey, 1978, p. 43). Call certificates, meanwhile, were issued by the Confederate Treasury under the Act of 24 December 1861 in return for individuals depositing $500 in Treasury notes. These call certificates, while initially yielding 6 per cent while bonds had an 8 per cent coupon rate, were freely exchangeable for Treasury notes for the full amount of principal and interest due. Given their high degree of 'moneyness', call certificates are included alongside Treasury notes and state and bank money issues in Godfrey's (1978) aggregate money supply measure employed in Tables 4.2 and 4.3.

NORTHERN RESURGENCE AND CONFEDERATE FINANCIAL COLLAPSE

By the summer of 1862, not only was the South relying primarily on non-interest-bearing notes – whose value was backed only by the promise to redeem these notes out of the future resources the South would have available in the event of victory – but also a majority even of the interest-bearing debt was circulating as currency. While bonds did account for a larger portion of the interest-bearing debt after August 1862, this was only achieved through a series of funding acts designed to induce the exchange of Treasury notes and call certificates for Confederate bonds. Inducements soon gave way to confiscatory measures as the public increasingly ignored the deadlines imposed on the privilege of exchanging Treasury notes for Confederate bonds under the Funding Acts of 13 October 1862 and 23 March 1863 (see Todd, 1954, pp. 64ff). Thus, as a last resort, compulsory measures were adopted under the Currency Reform Act of 17 February 1864. Holders of Treasury notes were given the option of exchanging the notes for 4 per cent bonds by 1 April 1864 or else exchanging them for new notes at a rate of three old notes for two new notes.

The growing unwillingness on the part of the public to purchase Confederate bonds, while perhaps initially reflecting the effects of the Union blockade, was fuelled by the Treasury's default on paying bond interest payments in specie.[14] From August 1862, payments were made only in Treasury notes.[15] Ball (1991, p. 131) emphasises the importance of the Confederate Treasury's inability to augment its specie supply in 1861–1862:

> Had the government levied specie taxes and borrowed the banks' coin and foreign exchange early in the war, the treasury would have been in a much stronger position. . . . Specie-paying bonds, with inflation-proof interest, would have encouraged funding and allowed bond sales at a premium in treasury notes, thus checking the rise in the public debt.

Certainly, following the Confederacy's suspension of specie payments, the price in gold of the 8 per cent bonds of 28 February 1861 plunged from $79 in August 1862 to $41 the following month

– eventually declining to just $2 by March 1865 (see Ball, 1991, p. 127).[16] As shown in Table 4.6, the real value of the Confederacy's interest-bearing debt barely increased between 1 August 1862 and 30 September 1863 – despite more than quadrupling in nominal terms. By 1 October 1864 the real value of the interest-bearing debt outstanding had sunk below the 1862 level while the real value of the non-interest-bearing portion even declined to less than the 16 November 1861 figure.

The North's ability to continue making bond payments in specie throughout the war probably helped limit the decline in the gold price of Northern bonds, and, in the face of rising inflation, encouraged voluntary exchanges of legal tender notes for bonds in the North of the type that Secretary Memminger tried so vainly to induce in the South. As late as May 1864, Memminger was still searching for a way to repair the damage caused by the suspension of specie payments. In

Table 4.6 Confederate and Federal debt levels, 1861–1865 ($ millions)

	1861	*1862*	*1863*	*1864*	*1865*
Confederate states:					
Nominal values					
Interest debt	20.1	98.6	442.4	819.9	—
Non-interest debt	30.2	181.8	552.0	577.6	—
Real values					
Interest debt	12.5	25.9	27.4	19.2	—
Non-interest debt	18.7	47.8	34.1	13.5	—
Northern states:					
Nominal values					
Interest debt	90.4	365.4	707.8	1,360.0	2,217.7
Non-interest debt	0.2	158.8	412.0	455.8	462.9
Real values					
Interest debt	95.2	315.0	442.4	569.0	1,173.4
Non-interest debt	0.2	136.9	257.5	190.7	244.9

Sources: Memminger 1861a,b, 1862a,b, 1863a,b, 1864a; Trenholm 1864; Lerner 1955, p. 24; Studenski and Krooss 1952, p. 152; Mitchell 1903, p. 256; and authors' calculations

Notes: The Confederate debt figures are calculated as of 16 November 1861; 1 August 1862; 30 September 1863; and 1 October 1864. These figures are deflated by the value of the wholesale price index for the month in question to obtain the real debt series in January–April 1861 dollars. The Northern debt figures are as of the end of each fiscal year, as given by Studenski and Krooss (1952, p. 152). These numbers are deflated by the July wholesale price index to obtain the real debt series in January–April 1861 dollars.

a letter to Senator Hunter, Memminger (1864b) urged consideration of a plan for purchasing needed war materials through the use of 'specie certificates'. These certificates would have committed the government to repaying the full specie value of the loan. However, even had they been adopted by the Confederate Congress, their potential for spurring renewed interest in the Confederacy's bond issues would have depended upon a faith in the government's promises that was seemingly altogether lacking by that time.

In the North, for the 1862–1863 fiscal year, 35 per cent of expenditures were financed by issues of non-interest-bearing notes and 48 per cent by interest-bearing debt. About half of the interest-bearing debt was comprised of bonds and the other half was short-term debt instruments. In the following 1863–1864 fiscal year, receipts from non-interest-bearing notes dropped to less than 5 per cent of expenditures, and 67 per cent of total debt receipts were now due to bond sales. Paradoxically, the accelerating depreciation of the greenback may actually have aided Northern bond sales – but only insofar as the bonds were gold backed. Whereas the value of the payments on the Southern bonds depreciated along with the Treasury notes in which interest was paid, in the North 'when gold was at a high premium the true interest earned by a gold-bearing security doubled and sometimes trebled the nominal rate written in the bond' (Dewey, 1934, p. 310). The gold yield on 20-year 6 per cent US bonds due in 1881 is calculated by Roll (1972, pp. 488–491) as averaging 9.76 per cent during the 1863–1864 fiscal year before rising to a peak of 16.9 per cent on 6 August 1864 just prior to the fall of Atlanta.[17]

Northern bond sales also benefited from the energetic campaign launched by Jay Cooke, who sold $362 million worth by January 1864. As described by Studenski and Krooss (1952, p. 153):

> Cooke hired some 2,500 subagents to comb the country, selling bonds in every whistle stop to anyone who could raise $50. He advertised in all the foreign-language newspapers, distributed throwaways, and rang doorbells.

Other factors helping Northern bonds were increased confidence in military victory following Southern defeats at Gettysburg and Vicksburg in July 1863, rising tax revenues, and the new uniform currency laid out in the National Banking Act that was passed in February 1863.

Developments in the North appear to be consistent with Calomiris's (1991, p. 91) emphasis on the role that reduced fiscal uncertainty and greater confidence in debt redemption may have had in reducing the reliance on short-term debt. The rise in Northern bond sales amidst strengthening tax revenues and more favourable military prospects in 1863 was, in fact, followed by a return to more short-term debt issues in 1864 – at a time when there may well have been reduced confidence on both the fiscal and military fronts. The gold premium – and the gold yield on US bonds – reached new highs in the summer of 1864 accompanied by the apparent stalling of Northern military offensives in both the Western and Eastern theatres and soaring real deficit and expenditure levels. These difficulties were, of course, only temporary in nature, however. In early September 1864, news of the fall of Atlanta marked the beginning of the end for the Confederacy and the gold premium began to fall again.

The South's financial situation in the last months of the war is largely unknown, as data from the Treasury Reports end on 1 October 1864. However, the wholesale price index (with January–April 1861=100) more than doubled between October 1864 and April 1865, rising from 4,001 to 9,211 (see Appendix Table A4.1). George A. Trenholm, Memminger's successor as Secretary of the Treasury, attempted in vain to stem the rise in the gold premium by buying and selling gold at the end of 1864 (Morgan, 1985, p. 119). Right at the death, the Confederate Congress, on 18 March 1865, made a final attempt to gain specie by authorising the Secretary to borrow $3 million in coin by offering new 6 per cent specie-paying bonds. In the event of inability to collect this loan, a 25 per cent tax was to be imposed on all coin, bullion and foreign exchange effective from 1 April 1865. Schwab (1901, p. 82) states that the government was actually able to borrow approximately $300,000 in specie from the banks in Virginia before Richmond was evacuated on 2 April 1865 – a testimony to the relentless efforts of the Confederate financiers.

CONCLUSIONS

In essence, the South's financial position became untenable by the close of 1862. While the North also ran huge budget deficits, its greater tax capacity, ability to maintain specie payments on its bonds, and, by 1863 its improving military situation, combined to mitigate the consequences of these deficits. The South faced increasing difficulties in selling its bonds, particularly after the suspension of specie payments in the summer of 1862, and was forced to rely on non-interest-bearing notes as its chief revenue source throughout the war. Once the permanency of this policy became clear when General Lee's retreat from Maryland in September 1862 was followed by the Emancipation Proclamation, the loss of public confidence was reflected in a decline in real money balances that accelerated further with the military reverses of the following summer.

The critical effect of this decline in real money balances seems inescapable. In the face of falling revenue from money creation – and with no means of making up the shortfall – expenditures by the Confederacy declined in real terms for the duration of the war. This meant that the Confederacy's command over real resources fell while that of the North continued to increase – and would appear to underscore the arguments of, for example, Ramsdell (1944), Eaton (1954) and Ball (1991) that the weaknesses of Confederate finance dealt a fatal blow to the Southern war effort. The Civil War experience also provides a vivid illustration of the role of confidence factors in the consequences of deficit financing. The North was able to restore confidence in its bond issues and curtail its money issues. The Confederacy had no hope of doing so. In light of its always weak financial base, the early support for its bond and money issues could only be sustained so long as there was confidence in its ability to secure a quick military victory.

APPENDIX

Table A4.1 Quarterly wholesale price series, 1861–1865

	1861	*1862*	*1863*	*1864*	*1865*
Eastern Confederacy:					
January	101	193	762	2,801	5,824
April	101	281	1,178	4,470	9,211
July	111	380	1,326	4,094	—
October	136	526	1,879	4,001	—
Northern states:					
January	100	114	146	181	253
April	101	113	166	199	212
July	95	116	160	239	189
October	103	127	158	240	204

Sources: Lerner 1955, p. 24; Mitchell 1903, p. 256; and authors' calculations. See notes to Table 4.1.

Table A4.2 Nominal and real values of Confederate revenue and spending flows

	17 Feb 1861– 1 May 1861	*2 May 1861– 30 June 1861*	*1 July 1861– 16 Nov 1861*	*17 Nov 1861– 18 Feb 1862*	*18 Feb 1862– 1 Aug 1862*
Revenue: Nominal values					
Taxes	732,455.05	65,505.38	152,964.06	321,262.64	10,706,435.18
Taxes + est. value of tax-in-kind	732,455.05	65,505.38	152,964.06	321,262.64	10,706,435.18
All non-debt financial revenue[a]	1,121,722.51	310,635.62	345,129.39	516,061.29	11,658,531.18
Bonds	0	7,450,749.65	10.592,277.00	13,109,633.37	6,460,686.59
Total interest earning debt	0	8,567,149.65	11,496,977.00	13,109,633.37	66,845,786.59
Non-interest bearing notes	0	0	30,178,355.00	63,590,795.00	92,189,420.00
Revenue: Real values					
Taxes	730,045.90	60,096.68	116,588.46	174,362.36	3,741,284.96
Taxes + est. value of tax-in-kind	730,045.90	60,096.68	116,588.46	174,362.36	3,741,284.96
All non-debt financial revenue[a]	1,118,033.00	284,986.81	263,055.94	280,087.54	4,073,987.90
Bonds	0	6,835,550.14	8,073,381.86	7,115,133.44	2,257,639.37
Total interest bearing debt	0	7,859,770.32	8,762,939.79	7,115,133.44	23,358,768.07
Non-interest bearing notes	0	0	23,001,794.97	34,513,321.57	32,214,914.21
Average value of price index	100.33	109.00	131.20	184.25	286.17

	17 Feb 1861– 1 May 1861	*2 May 1861– 30 Sept 1861*	*1 Oct 1861– 16 Nov 1861*	*17 Nov 1861– 18 Feb 1862*	*18 Feb 1862– 1 Aug 1862*
Spending: Nominal values					
Debt service	-	-	-	-	5,534,149.93
Government purchases	993,308.32	41,983,609.29	27,689,798.15	94,823,861.15	157,724,103.86
Total spending	993,308.32	41,983,609.29	27,689,798.15	94,823,861.15	163,258,253.79
Spending: Real values					
Debt service	-	-	-	-	1,933,868.30
Government purchases	990,041.18	36,380,943.93	18,646,328.72	51,464,782.17	55,115,527.10
Total spending	990,041.18	36,380,943.93	18,646,328.72	51,464,782.17	57,049,395.40
Average value of price index	100.33	115.40	148.50	184.25	286.17

Sources: Memminger 1861a,b, 1862a,b, 1863a,b, 1864a; Trenholm 1864; Todd 1954, pp. 148, 156; Lerner 1955, p. 24

[a] Excludes tax-in-kind

	2 Aug 1862– 31 Dec 1862	*1 Jan 1863– 30 Sept 1863*	*1 Oct 1863– 1 Apr 1864*	*1 Apr 1864– 1 Oct 1864*	*Cumulative sum*
	6,626,643.82	5,071,889.43	60,457,177.78	57,737,327.98	141,871,661.32
	6,626,643.82	11,071,889.43	94,457,177.78	79,737,327.98	203,871,661.32
	14,385,929.82	31,583,661.72	112,530,728.83	85,889,989.89	258,342,390.25
	34,937,599.41	154,840,601.40	273,016,123.90	30,751,450.00	531,159,121.32
	148,035,295.41	187,157,901.40	313,171,623.90	51,724,610.00	800,108,977.32
	123,365,465.00	382,781,330.00	265,690,928.50	277,576,950.50	1,235,373,244.00
	1,205,721.22	420,750.05	2,204,454.98	1,347,271.68	10,000,576.29
	1,205,721.22	918,493.61	3,444,199.74	1,860,630.68	12,251,423.61
	2,617,527.26	2,620,094.05	4,103,217.09	2,004,199.97	17,365,189.56
	6,356,914.01	12,845,152.09	9,955,009.08	717,569.71	54,156,349.70
	26,935,097.42	15,526,106.77	11,419,202.33	1,206,967.92	102,183,986.06
	22,446,409.21	31,754,490.48	9,687,909.88	6,477,119.37	160,095,959.69
	549.60	1,205.44	2,742.50	4,285.50	-

	2 Aug 1862– 31 Dec 1862	*1 Jan 1863– 30 Sept 1863*	*1 Oct 1863– 1 Apr 1864*	*1 Apr 1864– 1 Oct 1864*	*Cumulative sum*
	36,193,172.07	91,256,739.00	128,046,836.59	342,560,327.11	603,591,224.70
	217,520,309.14	428,111,820.00	255,063,722.45	272,378,505.59	1,496,289,037.95
	253,713,481.21	519,368,559.00	383,110,559.04	614,938,832.70	2,099,880,262.65
	6,585,366.10	7,570,409.06	4,668,982.18	7,993,473.97	28,752,099.61
	39,577,931.06	35,514,983.74	9,300,409.21	6,355,816.26	253,346,763.37
	46,163,297.16	43,085,392.80	13,969,391.39	14,349,290.23	282,098,862.98
	549.60	1,205.44	2,742.50	4,285.50	-

Table A4.3 Confederate revenue and spending rates (measured in $/month)

	17 Feb 1861– 1 May 1861	*2 May 1861– 30 June 1861*	*1 July 1861– 16 Nov 1861*	*17 Nov 1861– 18 Feb 1862*
Revenue:				
Nominal values				
Taxes	301,599.14	32,752.69	33,742.07	107.087.55
Taxes + est. value of tax-in-kind	301,599.14	32,752.69	33,742.07	107,087.55
All non-debt financial revenue[a]	461,885.74	155,317.81	76,131.48	172,020.43
Bonds	0	3,725,374.83	2,336,531.69	4,369,877.79
Total interest earning debt	0	4,283,574.83	2,536,097.87	4,369,877.79
Non-interest bearing notes	0	0	6,656,990.07	21,196,931.67
Revenue:				
Real values				
Taxes	300,607.14	30,048.34	25,718.04	58,120.79
Taxes + est. value of tax-in-kind	300,607.14	30,048.34	25,718.04	58,120.79
All non-debt financial revenue[a]	460,366.53	142,493.41	58,027.05	93,362.51
Bonds	0	3,417,775.07	1,780,893.06	2,371,711.15
Total interest earning debt	0	3,429,885.16	1,933,001.42	2,371,711.15
Non-interest bearing notes	0	0	5,073,925.36	11,504,440.52
	17 Feb 1861– 1 May 1861	*2 May 1861– 30 Sept 1861*	*1 Oct 1861– 16 Nov 1861*	*17 Nov 1861– 18 Feb 1862*
Spending:				
Nominal values				
Debt service	-	-	-	-
Government purchases	409,009.31	8,396,721.86	18,058,564.01	31,607,953.72
Total spending	409,009.31	8,396,721.86	18,058,564.01	31,607.953.72
Spending:				
Real values				
Debt service	-	-	-	-
Government purchases	387,075.78	7,276,188.79	12,160,649.17	17,154,927.39
Total spending	387,075.78	7,276,188.79	12,160,649.17	17,154,927.39

Sources: As in Table A4.2

[a] Excludes tax-in-kind

18 Feb 1862–1 Aug 1862	*2 Aug 1862–31 Dec 1862*	*1 Jan 1863–30 Sept 1863*	*1 Oct 1863–1 April 1864*	*1 Apr 1864–1 Oct 1864*
1,985,299.24	1,325,328.76	563,543.27	10,076,196.30	9,622,888.00
1,985,299.24	1,325,328.76	1,230,209.94	15,742,862.96	13,289,554.66
2,161,846.84	2,877,185.96	3,509,295.75	18,755,121.47	14,314,998.32
1,198,008.11	6,987,519.88	17,204,511.27	45,502,687.32	5,125,241.67
12,395,245.20	29,607,059.08	20,795,322.38	52,195,270.65	8,620,768.33
17,094,726.89	24,673,093.00	42,531,258.89	44,281,821.42	46,262,825.08
693,748.20	241,144.24	46,750.01	367,409.16	224,545.28
693,748.20	241,144.24	102,054.85	574,033.29	310,105.11
755,441.46	523,505.45	291,121.56	683,869.52	334,033.33
418,635.12	1,271,382.80	1,427,239.12	1,659,168.18	119,594.95
4,331,427.19	5,387,019.48	1,725,122.97	1,903,200.39	201,161.32
5,973,626.48	4,489,281.84	3,528,276.72	1,614,651.65	1,079,519.90

18 Feb 1862–1 Aug 1862	*2 Aug 1862–31 Dec 1862*	*1 Jan 1863–30 Sept 1863*	*1 Oct 1863–1 April 1864*	*1 Apr 1864–1 Oct 1864*
1,026,199.99	7,238,634.41	10,139,637.67	21,341,139.43	57,093,387.85
29,246,853.70	43,504,061.83	47,567,980.00	42,510,620.41	45,396,417.60
30,273,053.69	50,742,696.24	57,707,617.67	63,851,759.84	102,489,805.45
358,598.10	1,317,073.22	841,156.56	778,163.70	1,332,245.66
10,220,097.74	7,915,586.21	3,946,109.31	1,550,068.20	1,059,302.71
10,578,695.84	9,232,659.43	4,787,265.87	2,328,231.90	2,391,548.37

Table A4.4 Aggregated Confederate revenue and spending totals

	1 May 1861	*30 June 1861*	*16 Nov 1861*	*18 Feb 1862*
Revenue: Nominal values				
Taxes	732,455.05	797,960.43	950,924.49	1,272,187.13
Taxes + est. tax-in-kind	732,455.05	797,960.43	950,924.49	1,272,187.13
All non-debt financial revenue[a]	1,121,722.51	1,432,358.13	1,777,487.52	2,293,548.81
Stock & bonds outstanding	0	7,450,749.65	18,043,026.65	31,152,660.02
Total interest earning debt outstanding	0	8,567,149.65	20,064,126.65	33,173,760.02
Non-interest bearing notes outstanding	0	0	30,178,355.00	93,769,150.00
Revenue: Real values				
Taxes	725,203.02	732,073.79	590,636.33	602,932.29
Taxes + est. tax-in-kind	725,203.02	732,073.79	590,636.33	602,932.29
All non-debt financial revenue[a]	1,110,616.35	1,314,090.03	1,104,029.52	1,086,989,96
Stock & bonds outstanding	0	6,835,550.14	11,206,848.85	14,764,293.85
Total interest earning debt outstanding	0	7,942,339.13	12,462,190.47	15,722,161.15
Non-interest bearing notes outstanding	0	0	18,744,319.88	44,440,355.45
Price index	101	109	161	211

	1 May 1861	*30 Sept 1861*	*16 Nov 1861*	*18 Feb 1862*
Spending: Nominal values				
Debt service	-	-	-	-
Government purchases	993,308.32	42,976,917.61	70,666,715.76	165,490,576.91
Total spending	993,308.32	42,976,917.61	70,666,715.76	165,490,576.91
Spending: Real values				
Debt service	-	-	-	-
Government purchases	983,473.58	33,575,716.88	43,892,370.04	78,431,553.03
Total spending	983,473.58	33,575,716.88	43,892,370.04	78,431,553.03
Price index	101	128	161	211

Sources: As in Table A4.2

[a] Excludes tax-in-kind

1 Aug 1862	31 Dec 1862	30 Sept 1863	1 Apr 1864	1 Oct 1864
11,978,622,31	18,605,266.13	23,677,155.56	84,134,333.34	141,871,661.32
11,978,622.31	18,605,266.13	29,677,155.56	124,134,333.34	203,871,661.32
13,952,079.99	28,338,009.81	59,921,671.53	172,452,400.36	258,342,390.25
41,577,250.00	88,986,400.00	292,915,620.00	589,196,000.00	645,350,850.00
98,602,750.00	266,947,370.00	442,365,270.00	804,065,170.00	819,856,140.00
181,802,935.00	289,157,692.00	551,997.869.00	505,257,603.00	577,598,018.00
3,152,269.03	2,712,137.92	1,464,264.41	2,038,137.92	3,315,533.10
3,152,269.03	2,712,137.92	1,835,321.93	3,007,130.17	4,764,469.77
3,671,600.00	4,130,905.22	3,705,731.08	4,177,625.98	6,037,447.77
10,941,381.58	12,971,778.43	18,114,756.96	14,273,158.91	15,081,814.68
25,948,092.11	38,913,610.79	27,357,159.55	19,478,322.92	19,159,993.92
47,842,877.63	42,151,267.06	34,137,159.49	12,239,767.51	13,498,434.63
380	686	1,617	4,128	4,279

1 Aug 1862	31 Dec 1862	30 Sept 1863	1 Apr 1864	1 Oct 1864
5,534,149.93	41,727,322.00	132,984,061.00	261,030,897.59	603,591,224.70
323,214,680.77	540,734,989.91	968,846,809.91	1,223,910,532.36	1,496,289,037.95
328,748,830.70	582,462,311.91	1,101,830,871.91	1,484,941,430.95	2,099,880,262.45
1,456,355.25	6,082,700.00	8,224,122.51	6,323,422.91	14,105,894.48
85,056,494.94	78,824,342.55	59,916,314.77	29,648,995.47	34,968,194.38
86,512,850.19	84,907,042.55	68,140,437.28	35,972,418.38	49,074,088.86
380	686	1,617	4,128	4,279

Chapter 5

Deficit finance, expectations and real money balances

The operation of the inflation tax in Germany after the First World War

> In actual fact the Reich is, through the currency depreciation, much more lightly burdened with debt than formerly. On March 31, 1914, the total funded and floating debt of the Reich amounted to 4,918 million gold marks; . . . reckoning in gold marks at a dollar rate of 3,000, the debt of the Reich on October 10, 1922, amounted to 875,842,000 marks, or something over one-sixth of the pre-war debt. It must, of course, be borne in mind that the capital of everyone in Germany, and therewith the ability to take up a new loan, has correspondingly fallen as the currency has depreciated.
>
> (*Manchester Guardian Commercial*, 26 October 1922)

> The Reichsbank to-day issues 20 thousand milliards of new money daily. The note-issue at present amounts to 63 thousand milliards: in a few days . . . we shall be able to issue in one day two-thirds of the total circulation.
>
> (Reichsbank President Havenstein, 7 August 1923[1])

INTRODUCTION

In Chapter 1 we discussed how deficits become 'non-sustainable' when they necessitate large amounts of monetisation. Such non-sustainability is typically accompanied by rampant inflation, deteriorating real debt and real wealth levels, and plummeting confidence in the government's monetary and fiscal policies. All these features were evident in the Confederate experience of 1861–1865 that was discussed in Chapter 4. The present chapter explores the interaction between deficit finance, confidence and inflation in the still more extreme setting of post-First World War Germany.

The years between Germany's military defeat in 1918 and the November 1923 currency stabilisation saw the German government continue the wartime practice of running substantial budget deficits that were financed, in large part, by selling debt direct to the Reichsbank (the German central bank). As the Reichsbank issued credits in exchange for this debt, the deficit was monetised and the stage was set for an inflationary spiral that decimated the real value of the ballooning public debt. The rate of decline in the real value of the government's outstanding debt peaked in 1922, when the real debt fell by 89 per cent. This was not due to any lack of zeal in issuing new debt, however. Between January and December 1922, there was a better than five-fold increase in the government's Treasury bill issues.

Despite increasing difficulties in marketing the government's rapidly depreciating debt to the German public, the Reichsbank continued to purchase this debt until, in December 1922, the Reichsbank was holding fully 79.2 per cent of the outstanding Treasury bills (Holtfrerich, 1986, p. 68). D'Abernon (1927, p. 11) summarises the relationship between the Reichsbank and the government as follows:

> Throughout the inflation period no real budgeting was done: the Government lived on borrowing, open credits being available at the Reichsbank against Treasury bills. It was an era of unrestricted and unlimited floating debt.

In addition to its monetisation of government debt, the Reichsbank issued further credits in exchange for private commercial bills.[2] This latter practice intensified after June 1922 in response to a 'credit famine' that may have reflected not only shrinking real money balances and increased difficulties in financing working capital but 'also a growing reluctance [on the part of the credit banks] to give their capital away in mark-denominated loans' (Balderston, 1991, p. 561). The Reichsbank note issues, meanwhile, were themselves being spent at such at a rate that, in 1922, real notes in circulation declined by nearly 75 per cent while wholesale prices rose by 4,126 per cent (see Table 5.1).

While Germany's financial disarray accelerated markedly during 1922, the government's prolonged reliance on the printing press is reflected in the fact that deficit finance accounted for an average of approximately half of total government expenditures in the April 1919–December 1922 period as did the estimated ratio of inflation

Table 5.1 German inflation, real money balances and real debt, 1919–1923

Date	Real monetary base	Real notes in circulation	Real debt outstanding	Yearly wholesale price inflation
		(in millions of 1913 marks)		(%)
December 1919	5,870	4,446	17,300	228
December 1920	5,817	4,778	16,000	79
December 1921	3,981	3,256	8,700	142
December 1922	1,124	868	950	4,126
October 1923	812	352	210	481,068,520

Sources: Young 1925, pp. 526–530; Webb 1989, p. 49; and authors' calculations

Notes: The real monetary base is calculated by adding non-government deposits at the Reichsbank to the quantity of notes in circulation. Real debt comprises both Treasury bills and government bonds. Finally, the wholesale price inflation rate is based upon the rise in the wholesale price index relative to the value for December of the year before. While the October 1923 figure is calculated over 10 months, the 12-month inflation rate relative to October 1922 is a still more astronomical 1,253,498,133%

tax revenue to total spending (see Table 5.2). As in the case of the Confederacy discussed in the previous chapter, the operation of the inflation tax was initially facilitated by relative stability in the level of real money balances, or inflation tax base. Real money balances ended 1920 at approximately the same levels as those of December 1919 despite 79 per cent inflation for the year. In 1921, real money balances declined by just over 30 per cent while inflation accelerated to 142 per cent. Meanwhile, as shown in the empirical work below for the June 1920–May 1923 period, there is evidence that month-to-month fluctuations in the government's real budget deficit continued to be positively correlated with month-to-month movements in real money balances.[3] That is, the rising rates of money growth required to finance larger real deficits appear to have temporarily outstripped the additions to inflation produced by the spending of the extra cash balances.

The implication that the public may have been slow to grasp the true nature of the German government's financial policies is supported by the fact that the one-month forward mark/£ exchange rate remained at a premium relative to the spot rate between April 1920 and May 1922 (see Appendix Table A5.1). This implies that market participants continued to expect that the mark would

Table 5.2 Deficit finance in Germany, 1919–1923

Period	*Total real spending*	*Real deficit*	*Deficit/ spending ratio*	*Jessen's estimate of inflation tax revenue/ spending*
	(in millions of 1913 marks)		*(%)*	*(%)*
April–December 1919	8,645	6,151	71	62
January–December 1920	7,097	3,927	55	53
January–December 1921	10,393	4,157	40	43
January–December 1922	6,238	2,207	35	43
January–October 1923	7,324	5,471	75	–

Sources: Webb 1986, pp. 48–50, 67–69; Holtfrerich 1986, p. 150; and authors' calculations

Notes: Jessen's estimate is based on a calculation of the gold mark value of the yield from the printing of money taken as a percentage of aggregate Reich expenditures. This estimate, originally published in A. Jessen, *Finanzen, Defizit und Notenpresse 1914–22* (Berlin, 1923, p. 50), is as given by Holtfrerich (1986, p. 150). The remainder of the figures are obtained by aggregating the monthly revenue and spending series compiled by Webb (1986)

strengthen against the pound sterling over the month ahead even though rampant inflation in Germany resulted in near-continuous depreciation of the mark from May 1921 until the stabilisation achieved after the currency reform announced on 15 October 1923.[4] The trends in the spot mark/£ exchange rate over this period are shown in Figure 5.1 based on the monthly data presented in Appendix Table A5.2. The persistent forward premium through May 1922 does not necessarily imply that individuals behaved irrationally at this time, however. After all, the decline in the external value of the mark after 1918 was punctuated by temporary recoveries in early 1920 and again in early 1921. The permanent nature of the renewed decline that set in after May 1921 may be clear *ex post* but may not have been obvious to market participants at the time.

Webb (1989, p. 54) suggests that expectations of price stability

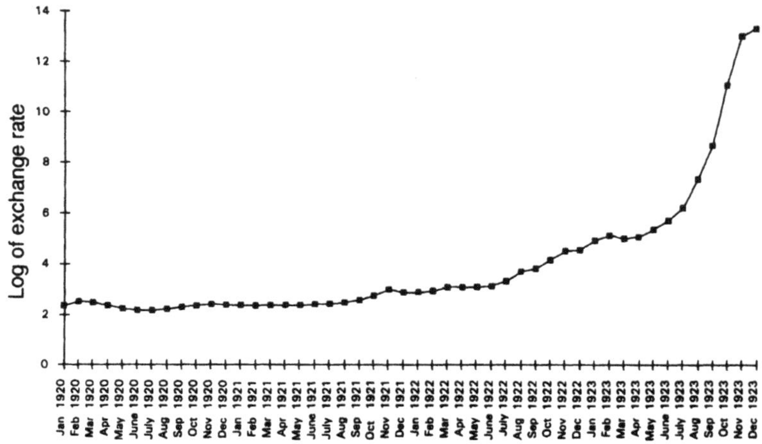

Figure 5.1 The mark/pound exchange rate, 1920–1923

were justified in the July 1920–June 1921 period by genuine prospects for budgetary balance (or surplus). The new income taxes and emergency levy imposed by Minister of Finance Matthias Erzberger were accompanied by growth in the real tax base given by the 11 per cent increase in net national output between 1920 and 1922. New reparation demands by the Allies under the London Ultimatum of May 1921 drove expenditures higher, however, fuelling a renewed worsening of the government's budget deficit.[5] As expected, and actual inflation rates rose, the real revenue yield from the new taxes – that were themselves denominated in nominal terms – was adversely affected. Nevertheless, even after that time, hopes for a compromise on reparations may have encouraged a belief that the mark would again recover. Webb (1989, p. 56) believes that recovery of the mark could have ensued had France been willing to reschedule reparations at the May 1922 Genoa Conference. In spite of the higher inflation, the German government did, in fact, achieve a temporary – but substantial – reduction in the real budget deficit that reduced the pressure on the monetary base in the first half of 1922 (see Appendix Table A5.1).

It is now a matter of historical record that reparation payments were not, in fact, rescheduled at the Genoa Conference and the German government was placed in escalating crisis. Holtfrerich (1986, p. 70) points to a shift in expectations in mid-1922, reflecting 'an upsurge of pessimism about the mark's future domestic and international purchasing power that precipitated a "flight from the mark", not simply as a "store of value" but even as a "unit of account"'. This pessimism proved, of course, to be well-justified. French invasion of the Ruhr in January 1923 was met with a policy of 'passive resistance', whereby the government compensated Ruhr workers for non-production in the French occupied territory. While these events were accompanied both by sharply declining real money balances and increasingly higher forward exchange rate discounts after the summer of 1922, the delay in these market reactions suggests that belief in the government's ability to restore budgetary order remained long after the sequence of large budgetary deficits began. As was true in the case of the Confederacy, these policies did not provoke widespread flight from the currency until it became clear that they were no longer likely to be reversed. What military defeats did to the Confederacy, defeats at the negotiations table may have done to Germany.

The operation of the inflation tax in Germany is analysed in more detail in the next section. Then the behaviour of real money balances or inflation tax base is examined in empirical work undertaken over the June 1920–May 1923 period. The real government budget deficit is employed along with the change in the forward exchange market discount in explaining movements in the real money stock during the German hyperinflation. Additional analysis and concluding comments are provided in the final sections.

REAL MONEY BALANCES AND THE INFLATION TAX

The German government's reliance on inflation finance after the First World War marked an extension of the policies followed during the war itself.[6] The percentage of wartime expenditures financed by deficits in Germany was not in itself much higher than that of Great Britain. For Germany (Reich and states combined), the deficit/expenditure ratio between 1914/1915 and 1918/1919 averaged 83 per cent as compared to a ratio of 74 per cent for Great Britain over the same time period (Balderston, 1989, pp. 225–227). However, while Great Britain was able to finance these deficits primarily with debt issued to the public – a large portion being placed abroad – up until 1917 only one-quarter of Germany's Treasury bill issues were held by the market. The remaining three quarters of the German debt 'was held by the *Reichsbank*, where it entered the secondary reserve against the note issue and explained more than half of the wartime increase of that issue' (Balderston, 1989, p. 238). In fact, between 31 December 1913 and 31 December 1918, there was a six-fold increase in the German monetary base.

While deficit/spending ratios in Germany were somewhat lower after the Armistice of 11 November 1918, the average ratio remained around 50 per cent for 1919–1922 and rose to 75 per cent for the first 10 months of 1923. Over this period, the government continued to rely on the inflation tax to supply its revenue needs. Inflation tax revenue (or 'seignorage') is given by the product of the real money stock and the rate of monetary growth, or – if we restrict our attention to the case where output is held constant – by the real money stock times the inflation rate. Despite declines in real money balances in the face of higher inflation, inflation tax revenue continues to rise up until the point where the rate of price increase no longer outweighs the rate of decline in real money balances. The revenue-maximising inflation rate is attained when the elasticity of demand for real money balances with respect to inflation reaches unity (for further analysis, see Friedman, 1971; Banaian 1995).

As real money balances decline in the face of rising inflation, seignorage revenues can only be maintained at their previous levels if the government is able to raise the inflation 'tax rate' – through still faster rates of money supply growth – to compensate for the falling 'tax base' (i.e. as represented by the real money stock). That is, higher inflation rates must be met by still faster rates of money growth in the future in order to compensate for attempts by individuals to avoid the inflation tax by unloading their pre-existing real money balances. Accordingly, Sargent and Wallace (1973) associate their well-referenced finding of feedback from inflation to subsequent rates of money creation with the government's resort to revenue from money creation as a means of financing its real expenditures.[7]

The German government's continued ability to extract seignorage in the postwar period is supported by Cukierman's (1988, p. 20) calculation that inflation tax revenues, as a percentage of November 1920 real money balances, actually rose from 42.77 per cent in 1921 to 50.27 per cent in 1922, and to an annualised 71.06 per cent in the first 10 months of 1923. While the positive correlation between money growth and seignorage could not endure in the long run, Cukierman attributes the apparent short-term success of this strategy to lags in the adjustment of inflationary expectations. In this respect, Cukierman (1988, p. 35) argues that 'the policymaker always possesses the ability to increase current seignorage because inflationary expectations, being based on information up to the previous period, are temporarily given.' It is certainly a matter of record that the forward exchange rate tends to underestimate the actual future rate of currency depreciation over the 1920–1923 period. The existence of adjustment lags may also explain the fact that actual real money balances consistently adapted more sluggishly than those predicted under perfect foresight (Cukierman, p. 39).

As noted earlier, the underestimation of the rate of currency depreciation may have been quite rational to the extent that it was believed that the postwar policies of deficit finance were temporary rather than permanent. Tax reforms and the potential for reduced reparations payments may well provide a valid explanation for the forward exchange premium that persisted until June 1922. Frenkel (1977, p. 656*n*) further emphasises that 'in the absence of a previous experience with an environment of hyperinflation, while agents learn the new structure, mistakes would occur and expectations would initially under-predict the actual course of events'.[8] Another factor in this under-prediction may have been the apparent increased demand for inflation tax revenue by the German government over the 1921–1923 period. Jacobs (1977) contrasts the German experience with that of the post-Second World War hyperinflations in Austria, Hungary, Poland and Russia – as well as the post-Second World War hyperinflations in China, Greece and the second Hungarian hyperinflation – where government behaviour is instead more consistent with attempts to simply maintain a given level of real revenue. Cukierman (1988, p. 37) points out that the passive resistance policy of early 1923, in particular, may have helped produce a situation where

> in the presence of larger short-run instability in [the] government's desire for seignorage, it takes longer for the public to detect changes in governmental objectives. As a consequence the negative effect of a current monetary acceleration on the policy-maker's ability to collect seignorage in the future occurs later, making it more profitable for him to obtain more current seignorage by picking a higher rate of monetary expansion.

Certainly, if the magnitude of the money supply and inflation increases were underestimated, this suggests the presence of a lag between the accumulation of extra nominal cash balances and the spending of these balances. As a result, deficit-induced increases in the nominal money stock may also have a positive impact on the real money stock in the short run.

Did lags in the adjustment of money demand therefore permit the German government (via the Reichsbank) to achieve some temporary control over real monetary aggregates? Despite the well-accepted link between the real value of the government's financing requirements (i.e. the real budget deficit) and nominal money growth, it is conventionally assumed that real money balances can be treated as entirely demand-determined – that is, following Cagan (1956), dependent only upon the expected inflation rate. Cukierman's recent analysis, and evidence of a sustained positive relationship between money growth and seignorage, seems to offer a potentially important qualification to this view. In the next section, the hypothesised linkage between real government financing requirements and real money supply growth is quantified using monthly data.

EMPIRICAL RESULTS

Two different definitions of real money balances are employed in the empirical work. In addition to utilising a series on total notes in circulation, a measure of the monetary base is obtained by adding non-government deposits at the Reichsbank to total currency.[9] Both money supply measures are then divided by the level of the wholesale price index to put the series on a real basis. Figure 5.2 plots these two measures of real money balances against the government's monthly real budget deficit, all expressed in millions of 1913 marks. The data on these series – and data sources – are given in Appendix Table A5.1. Table A5.1 also provides data on the forward exchange discount, which (following Frenkel, 1977) is used in the analysis as a proxy for inflationary expectations. While application of the forward exchange discount in this context has been criticised, Keil (1993, p. 1295*n*) points out that the assumptions required to equate the forward exchange discount with inflationary expectations are reasonable under conditions of hyperinflation – where deviations in real interest rates across countries, deviations from purchasing power parity, and movements in the foreign expected inflation rate are likely dominated by the changes in domestic inflationary expectations.

The real deficit (RDEF) and the series on real money balance are converted to billions of 1913 marks. The series on real notes in

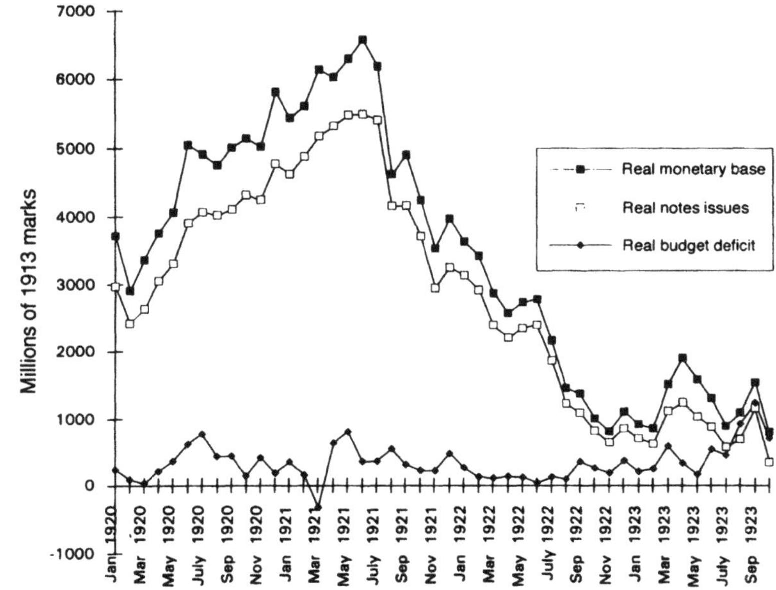

Figure 5.2 Real money balances and the real budget deficit in Germany, 1920–1923

circulation and the real monetary base are then transformed by taking first differences of the logarithms to yield the variables analysed below (denoted as RDNOTES and RDMB, respectively). While it is well-accepted that the German government financed larger budget deficits by faster rates of nominal money issue, regression of the real deficit on the rates of real money growth focuses on the question of the government's apparent ability to extract rising seignorage rates over the hyperinflation period. In particular, we consider whether the government was able to manipulate real money balances by not only printing money at a faster rate when the real deficit increased but printing it at a rate faster than the public expected. While impossible to do over the longer run, this strategy may well have been facilitated by the very belief in the short-lived and reversible nature of the policies of inflation finance that seems to underlie the behaviour of the forward exchange discount over much of the hyperinflation period.

The effect on real money balances arising from the real budget deficit is assessed in conjunction with the negative demand-side effects arising from inflationary expectations (as proxied by the forward exchange discount). After all, in order for larger deficits to induce rising real money balances the positive effect on nominal money growth must outweigh the price increases that result from faster turnover of these cash balances as individuals seek to avoid the inflation tax. The forward exchange discount is expected to have a negative effect on real money balances because higher inflation expectations encourage the public to turn over the given money stock at a faster rate, thereby driving prices up and real money balances down. In the empirical analysis below, the forward discount on the mark/£ exchange rate is multiplied by 100 and then put in first difference form to obtain the variable denoted as FDISC below.

The earliest date for which all the source data are available is April 1920, which after allowance for differencing and for a lagged dependent variable forms the basis for the 1920:6–1923:5 estimation period.[10] The correlations between RDMB, RDNOTES, RDEF and FDISC over the sample estimation period are given in Table 5.3. There is a very high positive correlation between RDMB and RDNOTES of 0.977. Both real monetary aggregates reveal a positive correlation with the real deficit (0.287 for RDMB and 0.330 for RDNOTES) as well as the expected negative correlation with FDISC (−0.590 for RDMB and −0.659 for RDNOTES). There is a negative correlation between RDEF and FDISC that is consistent with the inflationary consequences of these deficits not being foreseen at the time. This negative correlation may also reflect the 'wrong way' bets on the mark through much of this period. In

Table 5.3 Correlation matrix for the regression variables, June 1920–May 1923

Variable	*RDMB*	*RDNOTES*	*RDEF*	*FDISC*
RDMB	1.000			
RDNOTES	0.977	1.000		
RDEF	0.287	0.330	1.000	
FDISC	−0.590	−0.659	−0.239	1.000

Sources: See Appendix Table A5.1 for details on the raw data

Notes: RDMB is the logarithmic growth rate of the real monetary base; RDNOTES is the logarithmic growth rate of total currency in circulation; RDEF is the real budget deficit; and FDISC is the first difference of the forward exchange discount

any event, the apparent failure of inflationary expectations accurately to track the movements in the real deficit may well have been critical to the government's scope for extracting higher rates of seignorage.

In order to assess the stationarity of the data (with seasonal means removed by prior regression on a set of seasonal dummies), unit root tests are applied by regressing the first difference of each of RDMB, RDNOTES, RDEF and FDISC on the lagged value of the original variable.[11] (Under the null hypothesis of a unit root the coefficient on the lagged term will not be significantly different from zero.) Additional allowance is made for a set of lagged first difference terms on the right-hand side – and results are given with the maximum lag length set at 9 and 3 (corresponding to Schwert's, 1987, p. 88, ℓ_{12} and ℓ_4 criteria) as well as at 1 (as would correspond to a simple AR(1) process). Finally, results are also reported for the non-augmented form of the Dickey–Fuller test with no lagged difference terms included. All empirical estimates are obtained using the heteroscedasticity-consistent covariance matrix available in the Time Series Processor (TSP) software package.

The results of the unit root tests as given in Table 5.4 show that (according to the critical values given in Fuller, 1976, p. 373) the null hypothesis of a unit root can be rejected at the 5 per cent level or

Table 5.4 Testing for unit roots in the German monetary and fiscal data, March 1921–May 1923 ($N = 27$)

	t-tests against the presence of a unit root under different decision rules for inclusion of lagged first difference terms			
	Non-augmented Dickey–Fuller (0 lags)	*AR (1) process (1 lag)*	*Schwert's ℓ_4 criterion (3 lags)*	*Schwert's ℓ_{12} criterion (9 lags)*
RDMB	$t=-4.96$*	$t=-5.87$*	$t=-1.76$***	$t=-2.31$**
RDNOTES	$t=-7.15$*	$t=-5.73$*	$t=-1.82$***	$t=-2.09$**
RDEF	$t=-3.37$*	$t=-3.86$*	$t=-2.81$**	$t=-2.11$**
FDISC	$t=-7.42$*	$t=-6.14$*	$t=-2.15$**	$t=-2.66$**

Notes: The results above correspond to regressions of the form $\Delta X = \beta X(-1) + \Sigma(L)\gamma\Delta X$, where ΔX denotes the first difference of the variable in question, $X(-1)$ denotes the lagged value, and (L) is the lag operator. The lag order is set successively at 0, 1, 3 and 9 in accordance with the criteria listed above. Critical values for the t-statistic on β are taken from the first grid of table 8.5.2 in Fuller (1976, p. 373)

*, ** and *** denote significance at the 1%, 5% and 10% levels, respectively

higher in all cases except those of RDMB and RDNOTES under the l_4 criterion – where the unit root is still at least rejected at the 10 per cent level. (Allowance for the 9-lag maximum under the l_{12} criterion accounts for the reduced March 1921–May 1923 sample period pertaining to the regressions in Table 5.4.) With the results of the univariate analysis in any event seeming to affirm the stationarity of the selected data series, these series are now employed in addressing the relationship between the real deficit and real money growth.

The results of regressing RDMB and RDNOTES on RDEF with and without additional allowance for the expectations variable (FDISC) are given in columns (1)–(4) of Table 5.5. Note that a lagged dependent variable, a constant and eleven seasonal dummies are also entered on the right-side of each regression equation. It should be added that the exogeneity of each of RDEF and FDISC was confirmed using the exogeneity test suggested by Hausman (1978, p. 1260).[12] Also, the effects of adding lagged values of RDEF and FDISC – as well as a second lag of the dependent variable – were examined, but these extra terms were always insignificantly different from zero.

Columns (1) and (2) of Table 5.5 show RDEF to be positive and significant at the 1 per cent level in the regressions that exclude FDISC. When FDISC is added to the regressions of columns (3) and (4), FDISC is significant at the 1 per cent level with the expected negative sign. While the significance of RDEF is reduced in these latter two regressions, it still remains significant at the 5 per cent level in the regression for RDNOTES (column 4) and is at least significant at the 10 per cent level in the regression for RDMB (column 3). Thus, there is some evidence that both inflationary expectations and real government financing needs exerted their expected impact on real money stock growth over the June 1920–May 1923 period.

Another question, however, concerns whether changes in the deficit – as well as changes in the forward exchange discount – might affect inflationary expectations (and credibility), and hence exert an additional negative impact on real money growth. This possibility was tested by adding the first difference of the real deficit (FRDEF) to the regressions with FDISC to yield the results reported in columns (5) and (6) of Table 5.5. Here, FRDEF is significant at the 5 per cent level with the expected negative sign in the regression for RDMB (column 5), while, at the same time, RDEF remains positive and is now easily significant at the 5 per cent

Table 5.5 Estimation results for Germany, June 1920–May 1923 (estimation procedure OLS)

Right-hand-side variables	*Dependent variable in the regressions*					
	RDMB (1)	*RDNOTES (2)*	*RDMB (3)*	*RDNOTES (4)*	*RDMB (5)*	*RDNOTES (6)*
Constant term	0.126***	0.081	0.171*	0.134*	0.127**	0.107**
	(0.068)	(0.066)	(0.047)	(0.037)	(0.052)	(0.046)
Lagged dependent variable	0.252**	0.204**	0.426*	0.394*	0.327**	0.333*
	(0.120)	(0.090)	(0.133)	(0.076)	(0.126)	(0.085)
RDEF	0.302*	0.345*	0.127***	0.143**	0.243**	0.210**
	(0.108)	(0.114)	(0.075)	(0.067)	(0.090)	(0.091)
FDISC	–	–	−0.027*	−0.032*	−0.027*	−0.032*
			(0.005)	(0.005)	(0.005)	(0.005)
FRDEF	–	–	–	–	−0.148**	−0.085
					(0.069)	(0.066)
Summary statistics						
$\bar{R}^2$	0.414	0.345	0.657	0.708	0.673	0.704
SE	0.141	0.145	0.108	0.097	0.105	0.098
ρ	−0.093	−0.033	−0.292	−0.014	−0.164	0.038
	(0.213)	(0.211)	(0.218)	(0.222)	(0.232)	(0.228)

Notes: Eleven seasonal dummies were included in the regressions alongside the variables listed above
coefficient standard errors are in parentheses
*, **, and *** denote significance at the 1%, 5% and 10% levels, respectively
SE denotes the standard error of the regression
ρ denotes the estimated value (with standard error) of the autoregressive parameter, rho, obtained when allowance is made for an AR(1) process.

Table 5.6 Specification tests applied to the model

	(1)	*(2)*	*(3)*	*(4)*	*(5)*	*(6)*
RESET test	$F^{6}_{16}=0.66$	$F^{6}_{16}=0.44$	$F^{9}_{12}=1.14$	$F^{9}_{12}=0.68$	$F^{12}_{8}=1.10$	$F^{12}_{8}=0.66$
Differencing test	$F^{2}_{20}=0.85$	$F^{2}_{20}=0.42$	$F^{3}_{18}=3.86^{**}$	$F^{3}_{18}=2.01$	$F^{4}_{16}=2.25$	$F^{4}_{16}=1.38$
Constant variance (VR test)	$F^{4}_{4}=1.86$	$F^{4}_{4}=2.16$	$F^{3}_{3}=3.15$	$F^{3}_{3}=2.38$	$F^{2}_{2}=3.12$	$F^{2}_{2}=1.59$
Parameter stability (AOC test)	$F^{14}_{8}=0.73$	$F^{14}_{8}=0.80$	$F^{15}_{6}=0.51$	$F^{15}_{6}=0.73$	$F^{16}_{4}=0.28$	$F^{16}_{4}=0.65$
Farley–Hinich test	$F^{2}_{20}=0.47$	$F^{2}_{20}=0.86$	$F^{3}_{18}=0.37$	$F^{3}_{18}=1.12$	$F^{4}_{16}=1.10$	$F^{4}_{16}=1.52$

Notes: The RESET test is performed adding second and third and fourth powers of the right-side variables to the regressions

The differencing test is performed adding the sum of the lead and lag values of the right-side variables to the regressions (except in the case of a lagged dependent variable – where just the second lag of that variable is entered)

The VR (variance ratio) and AOC (analysis of covariance) tests are applied for the subsamples of June 1920–November 1921 and December 1921–May 1923

The Farley-Hinich test adds time-interactive counterparts of each right-side variable

*, ** and *** denote significance at the 1%, 5% and 10% levels, respectively

level. FRDEF is, however, not significant in the regression for RDNOTES – and the results are little affected by its inclusion. The gains from allowing for the possible dual role for the deficit as an argument in the formation of inflationary expectations – as well as a measure of demands for inflationary finance stemming from the government – therefore appear concentrated on monetary base growth alone.

Meanwhile, the results in Table 5.5 all appear to be free of first-order serial correlation in that the estimated values of ρ are always insignificantly different from zero. When a battery of specification tests is applied to each of the equations – as shown in Table 5.6 – the RESET test (using powers of the right-side variables as suggested by Thursby and Schmidt, 1977), the augmented differencing test (Davidson *et al.*, 1985), the variance ratio (VR) and analysis of covariance (AOC) tests for structural change (see Phillips and McCabe, 1983) and the Farley–Hinich test for parameter drift (Farley and Hinich, 1970) yield only one significant test statistic out of a total of thirty. Consequently, the null hypothesis of no specification error appears to be well-accepted on the basis of these additional tests – although, in the case of the VR and AOC tests, a qualification arises from the fact that there are barely sufficient observations to permit the required re-estimation over the split sample.

DISCUSSION AND FURTHER ANALYSIS

The empirical results presented in this chapter provide support for the premise that both inflationary expectations and real government financing needs were significant determinants of growth in the real money stock during the June 1920–May 1923 period of the German hyperinflation. The present finding that deficit financing requirements significantly influenced the growth in the real money stock itself stands in marked contrast to the conventional view that real money balances could be treated as being entirely demand-determined at this time. These results are, however, obtained in a context where the measure of inflationary expectations, the change in the forward exchange discount, is known to lag the actual inflation rate for much of the sample. If the forecasts embodied in the forward exchange discount were formed rationally as discussed earlier, then – whether right or wrong – they should at least incorporate all available information.

Webb (1989, p. 133) reports the results of regressing the forward exchange rate on a set of news variables gathered from the front page and the financial page of Berlin's *Vossische Zeitung*. These news variables encompass the number of columns devoted to domestic revolts; changes in government spending programmes; changes in tax rates; adjustment of railroad and postal rates and government salaries; changes in Allied reparation demands; German agreements to pay reparations; sanctions imposed by the Allies; losses of territory; and agreements on major international loans. Webb totals the number of columns devoted to these announcements in such a way that a 'plus' sign always indicates 'good' fiscal news and a 'minus' sign 'bad' news, and the resulting variable – TOTNEWS – is entered in a forward exchange discount regression equation. Webb finds that TOTNEWS exerts the expected negative effect on the forward exchange discount (good news implying prospects for smaller deficits, and hence lower rates of inflation and money growth, in the future) and is significant in the regression at the 1 per cent level.

Webb's (1989) results suggest that, even if the forward exchange discount did not accurately reflect the actual course of future fiscal policies and future inflation rates, it did, however, respond to news of these developments that was available to market participants during the hyperinflation period. At the same time, if the forward exchange discount accurately incorporated news announcements, these same news variables should be insignificant if added to the regressions performed in the last section for the growth in real money balances. That is, their influence should already be incorporated in the forward exchange discount. When Webb's news variables (as presented in Keil, 1993, p. 1299) are added individually to the specifications laid out in Table 5.5 above, they are jointly insignificant based upon the application of a standard *F*-test.[13] Also, if the aggregate measure, TOTNEWS, is entered in place of the individual news items, the coefficient on TOTNEWS is statistically insignificant and smaller than its standard error in each case.

CONCLUSIONS

By the summer of 1923, rising deficits combined with rising rates of debt monetisation by the Reichsbank had caused the inflation and exchange rate processes in Germany to explode (see also the analysis provided in Burdekin and Langdana, 1992, chapter 2). Up until this point, however, the German government was able to sustain high levels of deficit finance and, apparently, rising rates of seignorage revenue. This chapter has suggested that, at least through May 1923, the government retained some ability to manipulate real money balances in support of its revenue. While higher actual and expected inflation did indeed lead to a trend toward declining real money balances in the post-First World War period, the government was apparently able to take advantage of persistent hopes for a resolution to the government's financial problems. Rather like the US debt service policy during the Second World War that was discussed in Chapter 1, the policies apparently succeeded because the government retained some of the credibility it had built up by producing low inflation rates in the past.

In the next chapter, we turn to the more recent experience under the pegged exchange rates established under the European Monetary System during the post-1979 period. In this case, member countries hoped to restore lost reputations for delivering price stability. We have seen that, during the historical cases examined in this chapter and in the preceding chapter on the American Civil War, reputations may prevail even after the fundamentals have seriously deteriorated provided that the deterioration is seen as being temporary. The analysis in the next chapter suggests that, once public confidence had been lost, the attempt to use exchange rate pegging as a disinflation device was not sufficient to restore credibility as an inflation-fighter – and that there is little evidence of any immediate gains from the adoption of the pegged exchange rate system.[14]

APPENDIX

Table A5.1 Monthly data on German real monetary aggregates, the real deficit, wholesale prices and the forward exchange discount, 1920–1923

Date	*Real monetary base*	*Real notes in circulation*	*Real budget deficit*	*Wholesale price index*	*Forward exchange discount*
	(in millions of 1913 marks)			*(1913=100)*	*(mark/£)*
Jan 1920	3,723	2,972	232	1,260	–
Feb 1920	2,909	2,428	82	1,690	–
Mar 1920	3,366	2,642	33	1,710	–
Apr 1920	3,758	3,053	207	1,570	−0.006
May 1920	4,068	3,312	359	1,510	−0.008
June 1920	5,048	3,911	622	1,380	−0.005
July 1920	4,916	4,071	775	1,370	−0.008
Aug 1920	4,756	4,028	434	1,450	−0.004
Sept 1920	5,011	4,116	439	1,500	−0.006
Oct 1920	5,144	4,326	142	1,470	−0.007
Nov 1920	5,027	4,257	417	1,510	−0.006
Dec 1920	5,817	4,778	184	1,440	−0.009
Jan 1921	5,444	4,626	355	1,440	−0.012
Feb 1921	5,615	4,886	157	1,380	−0.011
Mar 1921	6,138	5,180	−315	1,340	−0.009
Apr 1921	6,023	5,326	642	1,330	−0.007
May 1921	6,289	5,484	815	1,310	−0.008
June 1921	6,574	5,498	360	1,370	−0.006
July 1921	6,182	5,412	361	1,430	−0.005
Aug 1921	4,629	4,170	556	1,920	−0.006
Sept 1921	4,915	4,173	312	2,070	−0.004
Oct 1921	4,252	3,721	224	2,460	−0.004
Nov 1921	3,541	2,952	217	3,420	−0.003
Dec 1921	3,981	3,256	475	3,490	−0.004
Jan 1922	3,638	3,144	265	3,670	−0.003
Feb 1922	3,433	2,927	127	4,100	−0.002
Mar 1922	2,878	2,406	107	5,430	−0.000
Apr 1922	2,586	2,208	136	6,360	−0.000
May 1922	2,746	2,352	119	6,460	−0.000
June 1922	2,792	2,407	42	7,030	0.001
July 1922	2,171	1,868	130	10,160	0.003
Aug 1922	1,461	1,240	96	19,200	0.023
Sept 1922	1,383	1,104	358	28,700	0.041
Oct 1922	1,018	829	261	56,600	0.120
Nov 1922	821	655	190	115,100	0.107
Dec 1922	1,124	868	375	147,480	0.066
Jan 1923	930	713	209	278,500	0.148
Feb 1923	867	629	252	558,500	0.209
Mar 1923	1,518	1,129	593	488,800	0.046
Apr 1923	1,908	1,256	337	521,200	0.102
May 1923	1,588	1,048	172	817,000	0.122
June 1923	1,320	892	546	1,938,500	0.181
July 1923	905	583	458	7,478,700	0.462
Aug 1923	1,110	703	938	94,404,100	0.356
Sept 1923	1,545	1,178	1,251	2,394,889,300	–
Oct 1923	812	352	716	709,480,000,000	–

Sources: Young 1925, pp. 526–530; Webb 1985, pp. 482–483; 1986, pp. 48–50, 67-69; and authors' calculations.

Table A5.2 Monthly data on the mark/£ spot exchange rate, 1920–1923

	1920	*1921*	*1922*	*1923*
January	233	243	811	83,190
February	335	237	907	130,750
March	305	244	1,245	99,526
April	235	249	1,285	113,584
May	179	247	1,294	219,821
June	154	261	1,410	507,567
July	152	278	2,200	1,594,760
August	171	307	5,074	21,040,000
September	203	390	6,502	449,375,000
October	236	582	14,145	112,503,000,000
November	265	1,041	32,146	9,604,000,000,000
December	254	794	34,858	18,349,000,000,000

Source: D'Abernon 1927, pp. 9–11
Notes: Figures given are the average number of marks per pound sterling in the spot exchange market each month

Chapter 6

Does exchange rate pegging foster monetary credibility?

The European Monetary System and the 1980s disinflation*

> At the centre of our policy to get inflation down has been entry into the European Exchange Rate Mechanism on October 5. Belonging to this anti-inflationary club sends an important message to the financial markets and to our competitors. . . . Despite this, we still hear siren voices telling us we should devalue the currency by realigning our ERM rates. We will not heed those voices. Consequently, there is no question of a cut in interest rates that is not fully justified by our position in the ERM.
>
> (Norman Lamont, UK Chancellor of the Exchequer, 30 December 1990)[1]

INTRODUCTION

The prominence of Germany during the European Monetary System (EMS) era lent support to the view that the EMS simply functioned as a Deutsche mark zone during the 1980s (Mastropasqua *et al.*, 1988; Giavazzi and Giovannini, 1989; Herz and Röger, 1992). Other countries were seen as matching Germany's anti-inflationary policies – and hence 'importing' its legendary monetary credibility – by preventing their currencies from depreciating outside the range permitted by the EMS exchange rate 'bands'. It was, however, the very unwillingness of other countries to match the Bundesbank's anti-inflationary policies, at a time when they were beset with domestic recessions, that underlay the recent near-collapse of the EMS. The United Kingdom – along with Italy – withdrew from the Exchange Rate Mechanism (ERM) of the EMS in September 1992, following which the UK government embarked on the very sequence of interest rate cuts that Ex-Chancellor of the Exchequer Lamont seemed definitively to rule out in his remarks of less than two years before. Other EMS countries held on for less than a year before agreeing to the drastic widening of exchange rate bands in August 1993 that allowed them greater monetary discretion.[2]

Despite the recent breakdown of the EMS, advocacy of pegged exchange rates by such agencies as the International Monetary Fund has never been stronger. Edwards (1993, p. 2) points to the growing support for the view that 'exchange rate policy in the developing countries should move towards greater rigidity – and even complete fixity – as a way to introduce financial discipline and provide a nominal anchor'. Edwards (1993) finds, however, that, among the Latin American countries, there is little evidence that an exchange rate peg aids in the disinflation process unless it is accompanied by restrictive domestic macroeconomic policy measures of the type adopted by, say, Mexico. This is consistent with the fact that, while even hyperinflations have been abruptly ended with the adoption of a new pegged exchange rate, this was only possible because of the drastic fiscal tightening undertaken in such cases as post-First World War Germany (see Chapter 5).[3]

The disinflation undertaken in most Western European countries over the 1980s coincided with the initial period of operation of the EMS, whose ERM began in March 1979. It has been argued that the EMS arrangements assisted the disinflation process in the member countries by making inflationary policies more 'costly'. In particular, with the exchange rate held constant, inflationary policies imply a loss of competitiveness as exports become relatively more expensive abroad and imports become cheaper at home. If market participants recognise the domestic authorities' new-found incentive to avoid this problem by following policies more consistent with price stability, timely reductions in wage claims and inflationary expectations could mitigate the adverse effects of disinflationary policies on domestic unemployment – with the policy maker enjoying credibility gains via the exchange rate commitment (Giavazzi and Pagano, 1988).

One problem in applying this line of argument to the EMS is that flexibility to vary exchange rates did not disappear after 1979, and there were more than ten EMS realignments between 1979 and 1987. It is true that the subsequent 'hardening' of the exchange rate arrangements after 1987 appears to have been associated with a narrowing of interest rate differentials (see, for example, Giovannini, 1990; Weber, 1991; Fratianni and von Hagen, 1992). Analysis of forward exchange rate premia also provides some support for a gradual build-up of credibility during the 1980s (Westbrook, 1993; Burdekin *et al.*, 1994). The actual role played by the exchange rate arrangements in all this remains unclear, however. The disinflation was accompanied by domestic policy tightening as well as reduced exchange rate devaluation, and the hardening of the EMS in the 1980s would have been impossible in the absence of such key domestic policy commitments as the 1983 French austerity programme (see also Woolley, 1992, on this point).

There certainly seems to be room for scepticism in considering whether or not the EMS could have suddenly restored policy makers' credibility as inflation fighters. After all, the spiralling inflation of the 1970s – like the inflations experienced during the American Civil War and in post-First World War Germany – did not develop overnight. At first, continued expansionary policies appeared to let policy makers achieve lower unemployment as money wages (and inflationary expectations) lagged behind the actual rate of price movements. It was not until after many years of such policies that the inflation–unemployment tradeoff seemed to disintegrate as individuals adjusted their behaviour, and adopted new institutions such as wage indexation, so as to offset the expansionary effects of inflationary policy (see Friedman, 1977).

One has to wonder whether credibility lost over a period of many years could be regained by the simple expedient of announcing one's membership in a new system of pegged exchange rates. If it is true that the EMS exchange rate arrangements added to policy makers' credibility during the 1980s, however, then one would expect that the unemployment costs of disinflation among EMS members would at least have been lower than for non-members. Interestingly, De Grauwe (1989) suggests that the inflation–unemployment tradeoffs in the EMS countries actually worsened in relative terms during the 1980s. In comparing the EMS record with that of other non-EMS European countries, De Grauwe (1989, p. 164), states that in

> both groups of countries we observe similar reductions in inflation during the eighties. The unemployment trends, however, appear to have been different. In the EMS countries we do not observe a decline in the unemployment rate, whereas in the non-EMS European countries we observe such a decline from 1986 on.[4]

While De Grauwe's analysis is essentially descriptive in nature, this issue is empirically tested below as we consider whether EMS membership led to a shift in Phillips curve tradeoffs in 1979. By comparing the experience of EMS member countries with four European non-EMS countries we are also able to examine whether any such shift in 1979 was EMS-specific. We also allow for a second shift in 1983 so as to investigate whether any shifts in the inflation, output and wage processes were delayed until after the second oil shock, rather than applying to the whole period of operation of the EMS (cf, Collins, 1988).

METHOD OF ANALYSIS

In addressing the question of whether EMS arrangements have really made a difference to the participating countries, we estimate inflation, output growth and wage growth equations for four EMS founder members (Belgium, France, Italy and the Netherlands) as well as for four European non-participants (Austria, Finland, Sweden and the United Kingdom) using quarterly data for the second quarter of 1971–fourth quarter of 1989.[5] The sample period predates the 'shocks' associated with the temporary entry of sterling into the ERM in October 1990 and the September 1992 and July/August 1993 EMS crises, and also sets the founding date of the EMS almost exactly at the mid-point of the sample period.

The price, real output and wage variables are specified in log first difference form so that regressions are performed in terms of the growth rates of these series. In view of the empirical evidence of a continued influence of US monetary policy on the EMS member countries (see, for example, Burdekin, 1989; Lastrapes and Koray, 1990; Sheehan, 1992; Katsimbris and Miller, 1993), lagged values of both German and US monetary base growth are included alongside lagged values of domestic money growth and the inflation, output and wage variables. Allowance is also made for interaction between German/US money growth and domestic money growth in the following three-equation model from Burdekin (1994):[6]

$$\begin{aligned}\mathrm{DP} = a_0 &+ a_1(L)\mathrm{DMB} + a_2(L)\mathrm{USMB} + a_3(L)\mathrm{GEMB} \\ &+ a_4(L)\mathrm{USMBI} + a_5(L)\mathrm{GEMBI} + a_6(L)\mathrm{DP} \\ &+ a_7(L)\mathrm{DY} + a_8(L)\mathrm{DW} + u_t, \qquad (1)\end{aligned}$$

$$\begin{aligned}\mathrm{DY} = b_0 &+ b_1(L)\mathrm{DMB} + b_2(L)\mathrm{USMB} + b_3(L)\mathrm{GEMB} \\ &+ b_4(L)\mathrm{USMBI} + b_5(L)\mathrm{GEMBI} + b_6(L)\mathrm{DP} \\ &+ b_7(L)\mathrm{DY} + b_8(L)\mathrm{DW} + v_t, \qquad (2)\end{aligned}$$

Table 6.1 Total lag lengths for the right-hand-side variables

	Right-hand-side variables								*Overall degrees of*
Equation	*DMB*	*USMB*	*GEMB*	*USMBI*	*GEMBI*	*DP*	*DY*	*DW*	*freedom*
Belgium									
Inflation rate	4	3	4	3	4	4	—	—	45
Output growth	1	4	—	4	—	3	4	4	47
Wage growth	4	3	—	3	—	4	2	4	47
France									
Inflation rate	4	4	—	4	—	4	1	4	48
Output growth	4	4	4	4	4	2	—	—	47
Wage growth	4	2	4	2	4	3	4	1	45
Italy									
Inflation rate	—	4	2	4	2	1	4	4	47
Output growth	—	—	4	—	4	4	4	—	52
Wage growth	4	2	2	2	2	1	4	4	47
Netherlands									
Inflation rate	—	2	4	2	4	2	3	1	38
Output growth	1	3	1	3	1	—	3	—	44
Wage growth	4	1	2	1	2	4	2	2	38

Austria									
Inflation rate	3	4	4	4	4	1	4	4	34
Output growth	—	4	4	4	4	3	4	3	36
Wage growth	1	2	2	2	2	4	4	4	41
Finland									
Inflation rate	—	—	4	—	4	4	4	—	45
Output growth	1	2	4	2	4	4	4	—	40
Wage growth	4	—	4	—	4	4	3	1	41
Sweden									
Inflation rate[a]	4	—	4	—	4	4	1	—	49
Output growth	4	—	1	—	1	2	4	4	50
Wage growth	4	4	4	4	4	1	4	3	38
United Kingdom									
Inflation rate	—	4	2	4	2	1	3	1	51
Output growth	—	—	2	—	2	1	1	2	60
Wage growth	1	1	—	1	—	4	4	3	54

[a]Denotes regression performed on rho-transformed variables to correct for negative first order serial correlation

Table 6.2 Mean and standard deviation of each right-hand-side variable

Country	*Right-hand-side variables*							
	DMB	*USMB*	*GEMB*	*USMBI*	*GEMBI*	*DP*	*DY*	*DW*
Belgium								
Mean	0.012	0.017	0.016	0.001	0.001	0.015	0.007	0.021
SD	(0.046)	(0.024)	(0.052)	(0.001)	(0.002)	(0.009)	(0.065)	(0.025)
France								
Mean	0.019	0.017	0.017	0.001	0.001	0.020	0.007	0.028
SD	(0.062)	(0.024)	(0.052)	(0.002)	(0.003)	(0.010)	(0.006)	(0.016)
Italy								
Mean	0.037	0.017	0.016	0.001	0.001	0.029	0.008	0.036
SD	(0.048)	(0.024)	(0.052)	(0.002)	(0.004)	(0.015)	(0.014)	(0.022)
Netherlands								
Mean	0.019	0.017	0.012	0.001	0.001	0.010	0.004	0.012
SD	(0.039)	(0.024)	(0.051)	(0.001)	(0.002)	(0.009)	(0.054)	(0.014)

Austria								
Mean	0.017	0.017	0.016	0.001	0.002	0.013	0.007	0.019
SD	(0.060)	(0.024)	(0.050)	(0.001)	(0.003)	(0.008)	(0.093)	(0.019)
Finland								
Mean	0.045	0.018	0.016	0.001	0.002	0.023	0.010	0.028
SD	(0.088)	(0.024)	(0.050)	(0.003)	(0.005)	(0.012)	(0.066)	(0.030)
Sweden								
Mean	0.026	0.017	0.015	0.001	0.002	0.020	0.006	0.026
SD	(0.089)	(0.024)	(0.051)	(0.004)	(0.004)	(0.010)	(0.119)	(0.033)
United Kingdom								
Mean	0.020	0.017	0.016	0.001	0.002	0.024	0.006	0.030
SD	(0.065)	(0.024)	(0.052)	(0.002)	(0.004)	(0.017)	(0.014)	(0.016)

Note: SD denotes the variable's standard deviation over the sample period.

$$\begin{aligned}\mathrm{DW} = c_0 &+ c_1(L)\mathrm{DMB} + c_2(L)\mathrm{USMB} + c_3(L)\mathrm{GEMB} \\ &+ c_4(L)\mathrm{USMBI} + c_5(L)\mathrm{GEMBI} + c_6(L)\mathrm{DP} \\ &+ c_7(L)\mathrm{DY} + c_8(L)\mathrm{DW} + w_t, \end{aligned} \tag{3}$$

where DMB is the rate of domestic monetary base growth, USMB is the rate of US monetary base growth, GEMB is the rate of German monetary base growth, USMBI is the interaction between domestic and US monetary base growth, i.e. DMB*USMB, GEMBI is the interaction between domestic and German monetary base growth, i.e., DMB*GEMB, DP is the domestic inflation rate (CPI measure), DY is domestic real output growth, DW is the rate of domestic wage growth, (L) is the lag operator, and u, v and w are error terms.

The maximum lag length was initially set at four lags, which leaves us with an estimation period beginning in the second quarter of 1971 (full documentation of the data is provided in the Appendix). Final lag values were determined using the Akaike (1974) Information Criterion. Two dummy variables (D1979 and D1983) were then added to each equation. D1979 is set equal to one from the second quarter of 1979 until the end of the sample, and covers the period following the establishment of the EMS in March 1979. D1983 is set equal to one from the second quarter of 1983 until the end of the sample, reflecting the onset of the 'disinflationary period' in early 1983 as well as the 'policy shifts' that Weber (1991) attributes to the period between the major realignments of June 1982 and March 1983 (see also von Hagen and Fratianni, 1990). At the same time, inclusion of the post-1983 dummy together with the post-1979 dummy allows the results to pick up any temporary effects that might be specific to the 1979–1982 period alone.

Table 6.1 lays out the number of lags attached to each variable following the application of the lag length reduction technique and also reports the overall degrees of freedom for the estimating equations. Summary statistics on the data are given in Table 6.2, which lists the mean and standard deviation for each variable over the sample period. Full analysis of the individual equations, together with tests for shifts in the effects of German money on the EMS and non-EMS countries, are provided in Burdekin (1994).[7] The individual results are also provided in Appendix Tables A6.1–A6.6.[8] In this chapter, however, we restrict our attention to the following two key issues that are raised by this empirical work. First, we examine the overall support for shifts in the inflation, output and wage processes in 1979 and 1983 based on system-wide tests that are undertaken in the next section. Second, we present the results of tests for shifts in the Phillips curve slopes in EMS and non-EMS countries in 1979 and, again, in 1983.

ASSESSING WHETHER EMS MEMBERSHIP MADE A DIFFERENCE

An initial comparison of the experience of the EMS and non-EMS countries is given by the results presented in Tables 6.3 and 6.4. Here, the relevance of US and German money, as well as the evidence of shifts in the inflation, output and wage processes in 1979 and 1983, is addressed using a series of system-wide likelihood-ratio tests. These tests assess the effects of excluding the variable in question from the entire three-equation system that is estimated for each country. In the case of the US and German variables, the column denoted 'number of terms' sums together the total lags of these variables that enter the three equations for the country in question. The 'restricted log likelihood' is the log likelihood computed with these terms excluded. The 'value of the likelihood ratio' is obtained by taking the difference between the restricted and unrestricted log likelihoods and multiplying by −2 (see Maddala, 1977, pp. 43–44).

The results in Table 6.3 confirm the importance of German and US money for France, Italy and the Netherlands, even though German money does not appear to play a significant role in the Belgian case. The interactions of German and US money growth with domestic money growth are, however, significant at the 1 per cent level for all four EMS countries. While these results are consistent with the important role ascribed to German monetary policy by many observers of the EMS, it is important to note that the significant role played by German money does not appear to be a figment of the EMS period alone. The post-1979 dummy is significant for Italy but insignificant for the other three countries, which is evidence against any significant shift in the inflation, output and wage processes following the establishment of the EMS. Rather, any shift appears to have been postponed to 1983. The post-1983 dummy is significant at the 1 per cent level for France and the Netherlands and is significant at the 10 per cent level for Belgium.

Table 6.5 reports the results of applying the same set of likelihood-ratio tests to the four non-EMS countries. Austria, Finland, Sweden and the United Kingdom all evidence significant effects of

Table 6.3 Significance of US and German variables and EMS shift dummies: four EMS countries

Country	*Variable*	*Number of terms*	*Restricted log likelihood*	*Value of the likelihood ratio*	*χ^2 Critical values (5%/1%)*
Belgium	USMB & USMBI*	20	721.73	43.38	31.41/37.57
	GEMB & GEMBI	8	737.13	12.58	15.51/20.09
	USMBI & GEMBI*	14	728.19	30.46	23.69/29.14
	Post-1979 dummy	3	741.08	4.68	7.82/11.34
	Post-1983 dummy***	3	740.27	6.30	7.82/11.34
	Both EMS dummies***	6	738.04	10.76	12.59/16.81
France	USMB & USMBI*	20	870.13	63.46	31.41/37.57
	GEMB & GEMBI*	16	880.91	41.90	26.30/32.00
	USMBI & GEMBI*	18	875.93	51.86	28.87/34.81
	Post-1979 dummy	3	899.18	5.36	7.82/11.34
	Post-1983 dummy*	3	895.79	12.14	7.82/11.34
	Both EMS dummies*	6	889.58	24.56	12.59/16.81

Italy	USMB & USMBI*	12	724.07	26.64	21.03/26.22
	GEMB & GEMBI**	16	721.85	31.08	26.30/32.00
	USMBI & GEMBI*	14	719.75	35.28	23.69/29.14
	Post-1979 dummy*	3	729.95	14.88	7.82/11.34
	Post-1983 dummy	3	736.60	1.58	7.82/11.34
	Both EMS dummies*	6	727.06	20.66	12.59/16.81
Netherlands	USMB & USMBI*	12	657.94	36.64	21.03/26.22
	GEMB & GEMBI*	14	649.57	53.38	23.69/29.14
	USMBI & GEMBI*	13	650.26	52.00	22.36/27.69
	Post-1979 dummy	3	674.71	3.10	7.82/11.34
	Post-1983 dummy*	3	666.56	19.40	7.82/11.34
	Both EMS dummies*	6	665.52	21.48	12.59/16.81

Unrestricted log likelihoods:
Belgium = 743.42
France = 901.86
Italy = 737.39
Netherlands = 676.26
*, **, and *** denote significance at the 1%, 5% and 10% levels, respectively

Table 6.4 Significance of US and German variables and EMS shift dummies: four non-EMS countries

Country	*Variable*	*Number of terms*	*Restricted log likelihood*	*Value of the likelihood ratio*	χ^2 *Critical values (5%/1%)*
Austria	USMB & USMBI*	20	705.58	49.58	31.41/37.57
	GEMB & GEMBI*	20	706.37	48.00	31.41/37.57
	USMBI & GEMBI*	20	704.59	51.56	31.41/37.57
	Post-1979 dummy*	3	722.60	15.54	7.82/11.34
	Post-1983 dummy	3	728.37	4.00	7.82/11.34
	Both EMS dummies*	6	720.55	19.64	12.59/16.81
Finland	USMB & USMBI*	4	632.59	13.62	9.49/13.28
	GEMB & GEMBI*	24	616.02	46.76	36.42/42.98
	USMBI & GEMBI*	14	623.41	31.98	23.69/29.14
	Post-1979 dummy	3	637.36	4.08	7.82/11.34
	Post-1983 dummy	3	637.56	3.68	7.82/11.34
	Both EMS dummies	6	635.42	7.96	12.59/16.81

Sweden	USMB & USMBI*	8	692.99	26.72	15.51/20.09
	GEMB & GEMBI*	18	671.81	69.08	28.87/34.81
	USMBI & GEMBI*	13	682.64	47.42	22.36/27.69
	Post-1979 dummy*	3	695.91	20.88	7.82/11.34
	Post-1983 dummy*	3	699.99	12.72	7.82/11.34
	Both EMS dummies*	6	690.89	30.92	12.59/16.81
United Kingdom	USMB & USMBI*	10	709.22	36.76	18.31/23.21
	GEMB & GEMBI*	8	715.80	23.60	15.51/20.09
	USMBI & GEMBI*	9	715.86	23.48	16.92/21.67
	Post-1979 dummy	3	724.90	5.40	7.82/11.34
	Post-1983 dummy	3	726.77	1.66	7.82/11.34
	Both EMS dummies***	6	722.23	10.74	12.59/16.81

Unrestricted log likelihoods:
Austria = 730.37
Finland = 639.40
Sweden = 706.35
United Kingdom = 727.60
*, ** and ** denote significance at the 1%, 5% and 10% levels, respectively.

Table 6.5 Tests for shifting Phillips curve slopes in the EMS countries

Multiplicative dummies	*Belgium*	*France*	*Italy*	*Netherlands*
Inflation equation:				
DY*D1979	—	−0.313	−0.575	0.060
		(0.199)	(0.442)	(0.050)
DY*D1983	—	0.022	−0.032	0.030
		(0.196)	(0.566)	(0.071)
Net effect	—	−0.291**	−0.606	0.090
		(0.140)	(0.388)	(0.086)
Output equation:				
DP*D1979	−0.262	0.112	−0.343	—
	(0.420)	(0.137)	(0.211)	
DP*D1983	0.551	0.442*	0.117	—
	(0.606)	(0.164)	(0.225)	
Net effect	0.290	0.554*	−0.226	
	(0.696)	(0.201)	(0.277)	
Wage equation:				
DY*D1979	−0.551*	2.658*	−0.705**	0.157*
	(0.160)	(0.684)	(0.343)	(0.056)
DY*D1983	−0.002	−3.900*	0.005	−0.084
	(0.236)	(0.823)	(0.933)	(0.097)
Net effect	−0.553**	−1.242***	−0.699	0.073
	(0.224)	(0.648)	(0.860)	(0.117)

Notes: The above results were obtained by adding the multiplicative dummy variables to the specifications laid out in Tables A6.1–A6.6. The 1979 and 1983 multiplicative dummies were entered together in the equations

both German and US money over the sample period. Of these four countries, Austria has followed a unilateral exchange rate peg with the Deutsche mark (DM) during the EMS period. Policy making in the other countries also may, at times, have been significantly influenced by the exchange rate with the DM, such as during the 1987 British policy of 'shadowing' the DM (see Belongia and Chrystal, 1990, on this episode). In any event, whatever role the influence of German monetary policy may have played in creating a 'DM-zone' during the 1980s disinflation, the present test results suggest these effects to have been as prevalent among the non-EMS European countries as among the member countries.

Of the set of non-EMS countries, both Austria and Sweden yield some evidence of a shift in the inflation, output and wage processes after 1979 (as compared to only one instance among the EMS members). The significant 1979 shift for Austria coincides with the September 1979 revaluation that established Austria's hard currency policy *vis-à-vis* the DM (Hochreiter and Winckler, 1994). Given that the September revaluation so closely follows the March 1979 commencement of operations for the ERM, there is, however, no way to distinguish between these two events in the econometric testing. There is less evidence of a 1983 shift, and the post-1983 dummy is significant only for Sweden. Otherwise, Finland yields no evidence of a shift in either 1979 or 1983, while for the United Kingdom the two dummies taken together are marginally significant even though neither the 1979 or 1983 dummies are significant individually.

TESTING FOR SHIFTS IN THE PHILLIPS CURVE

This section focuses on the more specific issue of whether there was any shift in the price–output or wage–output tradeoffs in the EMS members and non-members either in 1979 or in 1983. In particular, we examine the stability of the slope coefficients on DY in the inflation and wage equations, and the coefficients on DP in the output equation, over the potential 1979 and 1983 breakpoints. If EMS membership conferred credibility gains on the participating countries, we would expect to see more favourable Phillips-curve type tradeoffs in these countries after 1979. We can also see whether De Grauwe's observation that Phillips curve tradeoffs instead became more favourable outside the set of EMS countries is supported in the results for Austria, Finland, Sweden and the United Kingdom.

Multiplication of each of the elements in the lag distribution for DY (or DP in the case of the output equation) by the D1979 and D1983 dummy variables yields two sets of multiplicative dummy variables (one for 1979 and one for 1983) that are added to the set of right-hand-side variables appearing in the regression for each country. Tables 6.5 and 6.6 report the coefficient sums for the multiplicative dummies for the EMS members and non-members together with the net effects of the 1979 and 1983 dummies in each equation.[9]

The 1979 multiplicative dummies, while not significant in any of the inflation and output equations estimated for the eight countries,

Table 6.6 Tests for shifting Phillips curve slopes in the non-EMS countries

Multiplicative dummies	*Austria*	*Finland*	*Sweden*	*United Kingdom*
Inflation equation:				
DY*D1979	−0.032	0.019	0.030	0.418
	(0.079)	(0.228)	(0.022)	(0.264)
DY*D1983	0.366*	−0.164	−0.034***	−0.703**
	(0.058)	(0.129)	(0.019)	(0.326)
Net effect	0.334*	−0.145	−0.004	−0.284
	(0.077)	(0.238)	(0.021)	(0.359)
Output equation:				
DP*D1979	−0.645	−0.612	−0.369	−0.327
	(0.474)	(0.533)	(0.265)	(0.228)
DP*D1983	0.103	0.640	0.413	0.197
	(0.554)	(0.756)	(0.513)	(0.235)
Net effect	−0.542	0.028	0.044	−0.130
	(0.573)	(0.814)	(0.545)	(0.225)
Wage equation:				
DY*D1979	0.170	0.653*	−0.874*	0.944**
	(0.168)	(0.250)	(0.322)	(0.369)
DY*D1983	−0.216***	−0.356***	0.355	−0.016
	(0.115)	(0.189)	(0.268)	(0.364)
Net effect	-0.046	0.297	−0.519	0.928***
	(0.212)	(0.218)	(0.371)	(0.505)

See notes to Table 6.5.

are significant in the wage equations for every country besides Austria.[10] Even here, however, the suggested positive impact on the tradeoff between output growth and wage inflation for France and the Netherlands (among the EMS countries), and for Finland and the United Kingdom (among the non-EMS members), implies that the tradeoff actually worsened after 1979. That is, a given expansion in output is now associated with a larger increase in wage inflation. Only for Belgium, Italy and Sweden is there evidence of the negative sign that would be consistent with an improvement in the tradeoff.

In any event, as with the system-wide results reported in the section above, similarity in the findings for the EMS and non-EMS countries (coupled in this case with ambiguity in the direction of the effect) seems to offer little support for the hypothesis that EMS membership fostered any immediate credibility gains. The 1983 multiplicative dummies are themselves largely insignificant for the EMS countries. The results for France stand out, however, in evidencing a pronounced improvement in the Phillips curve tradeoff based upon the results for both the output equation and the wage equation.

Table 6.5 reveals a significant positive coefficient on DP*D1983 in the French output equation and a significant negative coefficient on DY*D1983 in the wage equation. Taken together, these results suggest that, after 1983, a given increase in the inflation rate was associated with a larger increase in output; while a given increase in output produced a smaller wage increase in the post-1983 period than had been the case before.[11] These findings offer support for the premise that France may have enjoyed a flattening of its Phillips curve tradeoff after 1983. It is unclear, however, whether this result should be attributed to a delayed EMS effect or simply to the generalised emphasis on austerity and shift in public attitudes towards inflation at that time (Collins and Giavazzi, 1992).[12]

CONCLUSIONS

This chapter has focused on the effects of EMS membership on the inflation, output and wage processes of eight European countries, with the results for four EMS participants being compared to the findings for four non-participants. While the empirical work does indicate widespread influences of German (and US) money on participants and non-participants alike, there is not much support for any shift in the relationships at the date when the EMS was founded. It appears, therefore, just as credibility may not be quickly lost, it may also not be easily regained without more drastic changes than those involved in an announced commitment to a pegged exchange rate system.

Only in the wage equations is there any consistent evidence of a shift in Phillips curve relationships after 1979. However, even here these findings apply to both EMS and non-EMS members alike, and are as often consistent with a worsening of the Phillips curve tradeoff as with an improvement. As suggested by Burdekin *et al.* (1994), whatever credibility gains the EMS countries may have attained after 1979 likely resulted from the observed commitment to tighter domestic policies. This may explain the fact that the domestic policy tightening in France in 1983, and willingness to tolerate temporarily higher unemployment as a result, does appear to have been followed by an improvement in the Phillips curve tradeoff.

We should certainly acknowledge that, even if the EMS did not offer any 'quick fix' to the so-called 'credibility problem' faced by many of the member countries at the end of the 1970s, this does not preclude at least some of the member countries' policy makers gaining credibility over this period. Even in France's case, however, this credibility does not appear to have been earned until several years after the establishment of the EMS. Other countries too, whether or not they participate in exchange rate arrangements like the EMS, may have to survive a similar 'proving' process. The post-1990 New Zealand experience with inflation targeting, for example, appears to have become credible only after mid-1992 (Svensson, 1993) – when continuation of the policy despite very high real interest rates and rising unemployment offered proof to market participants of the authorities' commitment to the new policy.

APPENDIX: DESCRIPTION OF THE INTERNATIONAL DATA

The output data for Belgium are courtesy of the Banque Nationale de Belgique (Brussels, Belgium) and the monetary base and output data for the Netherlands are courtesy of De Nederlandse Bank (Amsterdam, Netherlands). All other data are taken from the *International Financial Statistics* tape (International Monetary Fund, Washington, DC).

The exact definitions of the data series follow below, with the *International Financial Statistics* line numbers where appropriate:

$$\text{DMB} = \log(\text{MBASE}) - \log(\text{MBASE}(-1)) \quad (1)$$

where MBASE is the domestic monetary base (line 14);

$$\text{DP} = \log(\text{CPI}) - \log(\text{CPI}(-1)) \quad (2)$$

where CPI is the consumer price index (line 64);

$$\text{DY} = \log(\text{OUTPUT}) - \log(\text{OUTPUT}(-1)) \quad (3)$$

where OUTPUT is real gross national product (measured in 1980 prices) for Belgium and the Netherlands, and is real gross domestic product (in 1985 prices) in all other cases (line 99b.p for Austria, Finland and Sweden; line 99b.r for France, Italy and the United Kingdom);

$$DW = \log(WAGE) - \log(WAGE(-1)) \tag{4}$$

where WAGE is average monthly earnings for Austria (line 65..b) and the United Kingdom (line 65..c); hourly earnings for Belgium (line 65), Finland (line 65ey), the Netherlands (line 65) and Sweden (line 65); average labour costs for France (line 65); and the contractual wage per person excluding family allowances for Italy (line 65ey);

$$USMB = \log(USMBASE) - \log(USMBASE(-1)) \tag{5}$$

where USMBASE is the US monetary base (line 14);

$$GEMB = \log(GEMBASE) - \log(GEMBASE(-1)) \tag{6}$$

where GEMBASE is the German monetary base (line 14).

Table A6.1 Inflation equations for the EMS countries, second quarter of 1971–fourth quarter of 1989 (dependent variable DP)

Explanatory variables	*Belgium*	*France*	*Italy*	*Netherlands*
DMB	0.195***	−0.005	—	—
	(0.102)	(0.021)		
USMB	−0.009	0.044	0.128	−0.163*
	(0.105)	(0.093)	(0.161)	(0.052)
GEMB	−0.029	—	0.089**	−0.146*
	(0.043)		(0.044)	(0.034)
USMBI	0.199	1.483***	3.565**	1.557**
	(1.209)	(0.846)	(1.694)	(0.651)
GEMBI	−1.129**	—	−0.536***	1.187*
	(0.560)		(0.324)	(0.408)
DP	0.747*	0.737*	0.576*	0.501*
	(0.116)	(0.157)	(0.141)	(0.117)
DY	—	0.074	0.262**	0.204*
		(0.092)	(0.128)	(0.041)
DW	—	0.081	0.237**	0.095**
		(0.122)	(0.114)	(0.043)
D1979	0.002	0.002	0.004	0.001
	(0.002)	(0.001)	(0.003)	(0.001)
D1983	−0.004**	−0.005*	−0.004	−0.004*
	(0.002)	(0.002)	(0.004)	(0.002)
Summary statistics				
R^2	0.784	0.854	0.806	0.896
σ	0.004	0.004	0.007	0.003

Notes: The coefficients reported are for the sums of the lags, with standard errors in parentheses

A constant and three seasonal dummies were also included in all regressions

Owing to data limitations, sample periods for Belgium and Italy are curtailed at the second quarter of 1989 and third quarter of 1989, respectively. The Netherlands estimation period is restricted to the second quarter of 1974-third quarter of 1989

*, ** and *** denote significance at the 1%, 5% and 10% levels, respectively

Table A6.2 Inflation equations for the non-EMS countries, second quarter of 1971–third quarter of 1989 (dependent variable DP)

Explanatory variables	*Austria*	*Finland*	*Sweden*[a]	*United Kingdom*
DMB	−0.045 (0.035)	—	0.004 (0.020)	—
USMB	−0.233** (0.104)	—	—	−0.228 (0.148)
GEMB	−0.111* (0.033)	0.043 (0.065)	−0.071** (0.031)	−0.073 (0.044)
USMBI	−0.328 (0.954)	—	—	2.952*** (1.783)
GEMBI	−0.066 (0.318)	0.010 (0.448)	0.711** (0.313)	−0.174 (0.388)
DP	0.228** (0.113)	0.935* (0.121)	0.458* (0.115)	0.602* (0.100)
DY	0.443* (0.119)	0.490* (0.148)	0.036 (0.062)	0.273 (0.170)
DW	0.252* (0.085)	—	—	0.208** (0.102)
D1979	−0.00001 (0.002)	−0.002 (0.002)	0.001 (0.001)	−0.005*** (0.003)
D1983	−0.003*** (0.002)	−0.0002 (0.002)	−0.005* (0.001)	−0.0004 (0.003)
Summary statistics				
R^2	0.796	0.756	0.807	0.811
σ	0.004	0.006	0.006	0.007

Notes: Sample periods for Austria, Finland and Sweden are curtailed at the first quarter of 1988, fourth quarter of 1987 and second quarter of 1989, respectively

[a] The Swedish regression was performed on rho-transformed variables to correct for negative first-order serial correlation over sample beginning in the third quarter of 1971

Table A6.3 Output equations for the EMS countries, second quarter of 1971–fourth quarter of 1989 (dependent variable DY)

Explanatory variables	*Belgium*	*France*	*Italy*	*Netherlands*
DMB	0.262**	−0.050**	—	0.215***
	(0.107)	(0.021)		(0.123)
USMB	−0.540	−0.198**	—	0.389
	(0.358)	(0.080)		(0.388)
GEMB	—	0.073***	0.078	−0.199*
		(0.040)	(0.139)	(0.067)
USMBI	−10.373**	1.614*	—	−2.679
	(4.308)	(0.609)		(4.205)
GEMBI	—	0.088	0.907	4.335**
		(0.263)	(0.964)	(1.756)
DP	−1.154*	−0.341*	−0.119	—
	(0.398)	(0.103)	(0.180)	
DY	−0.344	—	−0.215	−1.351*
	(0.274)		(0.357)	(0.293)
DW	0.535***	—	—	—
	(0.286)			
D1979	0.0001	−0.002	−0.003	0.0001
	(0.007)	(0.001)	(0.003)	(0.009)
D1983	0.008	−0.005**	0.003	0.007
	(0.005)	(0.002)	(0.004)	(0.007)
Summary statistics				
R^2	0.954	0.690	0.382	0.886
σ	0.014	0.004	0.011	0.018

See notes to Table A6.1

Table A6.4 Output equations for the non-EMS countries, second quarter of 1971–third quarter of 1989 (dependent variable DY)

Explanatory variables	*Austria*	*Finland*	*Sweden*	*United Kingdom*
DMB	—	0.140**	−0.065	—
		(0.055)	(0.055)	
USMB	−0.221	0.143	—	—
	(0.269)	(0.306)		
GEMB	0.189**	0.249	0.109*	0.157**
	(0.084)	(0.195)	(0.037)	(0.074)
USMBI	5.468*	3.180**	—	—
	(1.864)	(1.568)		
GEMBI	0.228	−2.105***	0.905*	0.185
	(0.767)	(1.128)	(0.306)	(0.864)
DP	−0.516	−0.958**	−0.428	−0.217**
	(0.390)	(0.462)	(0.284)	(0.103)
DY	−0.469	−1.423*	−0.742**	−0.303*
	(0.331)	(0.439)	(0.343)	(0.111)
DW	0.109	—	0.353**	−0.014
	(0.192)		(0.149)	(0.127)
D1979	−0.009*	−0.001	0.005	−0.003
	(0.003)	(0.007)	(0.004)	(0.004)
D1983	0.003	−0.013**	0.002	0.004
	(0.003)	(0.006)	(0.004)	(0.004)
Summary statistics				
R^2	0.992	0.943	0.990	0.298
σ	0.008	0.016	0.012	0.012

See notes to Tables A6.1 and A6.2

Table A6.5 Wage equations for the EMS countries, second quarter of 1971–fourth quarter of 1989 (dependent variable DW)

Explanatory variables	*Belgium*	*France*	*Italy*	*Netherlands*
DMB	0.032 (0.242)	−0.065 (0.047)	−0.069 (0.120)	−0.306* (0.075)
USMB	0.261 (0.218)	−0.053 (0.116)	−0.217 (0.169)	−0.022 (0.038)
GEMB	—	0.128** (0.064)	0.084 (0.068)	0.060 (0.049)
USMBI	5.429*** (2.945)	0.996 (0.914)	1.206 (1.763)	−2.169* (0.729)
GEMBI	—	0.780 (0.590)	0.259 (0.599)	0.467 (0.512)
DP	0.470*** (0.256)	1.610* (0.259)	1.160* (0.189)	0.938* (0.253)
DY	0.212*** (0.123)	0.336 (0.457)	0.085 (0.191)	−0.032 (0.054)
DW	0.219 (0.178)	−0.255** (0.125)	−0.155 (0.148)	0.134 (0.118)
D1979	−0.010** (0.004)	−0.005 (0.003)	−0.012* (0.004)	−0.004*** (0.002)
D1983	−0.001 (0.004)	−0.004 (0.004)	−0.002 (0.005)	0.006** (0.003)
Summary statistics				
R^2	0.845	0.817	0.810	0.870
σ	0.010	0.007	0.009	0.005

See notes to Table A6.1

Table A6.6 Wage equations for the non-EMS countries, second quarter of 1971–third quarter of 1989 (dependent variable DW)

Explanatory variables	*Austria*	*Finland*	*Sweden*	*United Kingdom*
DMB	−0.096***	0.110***	0.297*	0.038
	(0.054)	(0.066)	(0.084)	(0.029)
USMB	0.327	—	−0.361	0.149**
	(0.210)		(0.301)	(0.076)
GEMB	0.021	0.310**	−0.226	—
	(0.072)	(0.141)	(0.157)	
USMBI	2.579	—	−3.186***	−0.192
	(1.690)		(1.701)	(0.891)
GEMBI	−1.981*	−1.858***	0.185	—
	(0.669)	(0.965)	(0.999)	
DP	1.661*	1.091*	0.604*	0.143
	(0.463)	(0.365)	(0.233)	(0.177)
DY	0.974*	0.739*	0.434	−0.823**
	(0.327)	(0.212)	(0.376)	(0.322)
DW	−1.042*	−0.419*	−0.345***	0.105
	(0.246)	(0.099)	(0.207)	(0.178)
D1979	−0.017*	−0.010***	−0.024*	−0.006
	(0.004)	(0.006)	(0.005)	(0.004)
D1983	−0.001	0.002	0.013*	−0.003
	(0.004)	(0.006)	(0.005)	(0.004)
Summary statistics				
R^2	0.682	0.813	0.861	0.615
σ	0.011	0.013	0.012	0.010

See notes to Tables A6.1 and A6.2

Part III

Consumer confidence and macroeconomic stabilisation in the 1990s

Chapter 7

Consumer confidence in today's macroeconomy

Definition, measurement and potential importance

In order to lower interest rates and invigorate the recently sluggish economies of North America, Western Europe and Japan, there has been pressure for looser monetary policy. In the United States, the discount rate dropped significantly from 7 per cent in the fourth quarter of 1990 to 3.0 per cent before being raised again during 1994. In the European Union (EU), the pressure of rising unemployment and stagnating economic growth was instrumental in the turmoil in the European exchange rate markets in 1992 and 1993. Italy and the United Kingdom withdrew from the EU's Exchange Rate Mechanism (ERM) in September 1992. Other slowing economies such as France also eventually proved unwilling and/or unable to match the tight monetary policies pursued by the German Bundesbank and consequently disengaged from the formerly rigid ERM exchange rate bands in August 1993.

The attendant monetary loosening was evident in, for example, the falling UK interest rates which, in early 1994, were close to their lowest level since July 1988. However, even though nominal interest rates have fallen sharply, the economies indulging in monetary loosening have yet to experience a significant rebound in the level of private capital investment necessary for any sustained economic recovery.

One explanation offered by some analysts for the apparent weak effects of attempted monetary stimulation with respect to economic growth is the sharp and prolonged decline in investor and consumer confidence in the industrialised economies since 1989. This 'crisis in confidence' of the early 1990s has been attributed to a combination of factors that in the United States include the tax increases of 1989 and 1993, together with the worldwide effects of the Iraqi invasion of Kuwait in 1990 and the temporary surge in world oil prices.

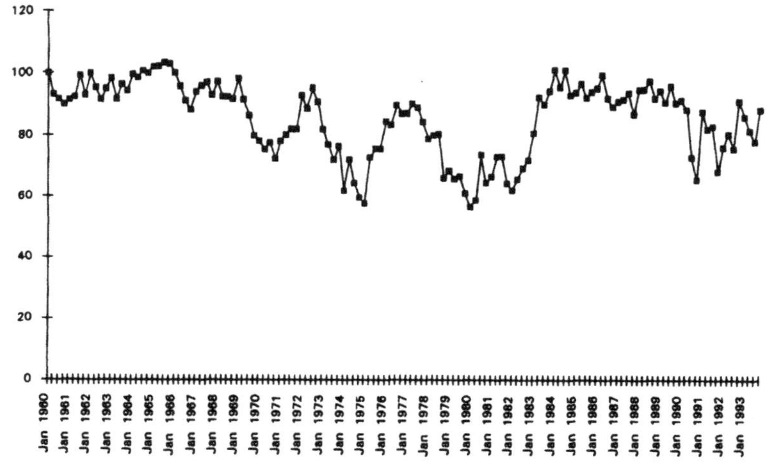

Figure 7.1 University of Michigan index of consumer sentiment

Continuing negative influences have been the unprecedented level of private and corporate debt relative to GDP, collapsing real estate prices, and the European and Japanese recessions.[1]

In the United States, the University of Michigan's survey of consumer sentiment from August to October 1990 recorded the largest decline in any 3-month period since its inception in 1947. The 91-month-old American economic expansion ended in mid-1990 when the decline in consumer confidence (seen in Figure 7.1) was followed by a sharp drop in economic activity.[2] Similarly in the United Kingdom, the consumer confidence index plunged from a high of around 110 in mid-1988 to a low of 63 by the first quarter of 1990. Sentiment received a boost following the conclusion of the Gulf War, however, and by April 1992, both economies were experiencing an apparent reversal of the declining trend in consumer confidence.[3]

However, the outlook for an increase in consumer and investor confidence in the industrialised countries is tempered by the seemingly excessive public and private debt built up during the 1980s and the early 1990s.[4] The US budget deficit, which had been reduced from 6.3 per cent of GDP in 1983 to 2.9 per cent in 1989 following the Gramm–Rudman–Hollings spending cuts, rose again to exceed 4.9 per cent of GDP in 1992.[5] With the deficit still at 4 per cent of GDP in 1993, a number of prominent economists lent their support to a proposed Balanced Budget Amendment to the US Constitution that was narrowly defeated in the Senate in March 1994.

One reason for the defeat of this amendment may be the rapid real growth in the latter part of 1993 that, in combination with the tax hikes imposed by the Clinton administration, produced a slight decline in the deficit/GDP ratio relative to the 1992 level. However, fears of inflation exacerbated by an economy (controversially) thought to be near 'overheating' led the Federal Reserve to raise both the federal funds rate and the discount rate in 1994. This reversal of the downward trend in interest rates (long-term as well as short-term) threatens to hurt consumer confidence and raise the cost of the administration's deficit financing.

Currently, Europe remains heavily influenced by the fiscal and monetary requirements of the German unification, which may have served to dampen any incipient rise in consumer confidence. German government budget deficits (including those of the German privatisation agency, Treuhandanstalt) which approached an unprecedented peace-time level of 7 per cent of GDP by the end of 1993, resulted in continuing tight monetary growth by the Bundesbank until the first moves towards ease were made in early 1994. The EU's Exchange Rate Mechanism (ERM) had previously limited the ability of other participating European countries to lower their interest rates, resulting in the recent currency crises in Europe.[6]

Given the rather questionable prognosis for global economic recovery in the near future, stemming, in part, from stubborn problems with budget deficits and consumer confidence, a pertinent and timely policy issue for the 1990s might be the design and implementation of fiscal and monetary stabilisation polices that explicitly incorporate investor and consumer confidence as suggested, for example, in Chapters 8 and 9 of this volume.

In this section, we divide overall consumer and investor confidence into two components, namely (i) the exogenous component of confidence which is a function of uncontrollable external factors such as the 1990 Iraqi invasion of Kuwait, and the oil shocks of 1973 and 1979 and (ii) the endogenous component of confidence which is a function of past, current and expected fiscal and monetary policies and their results on output, inflation, employment and interest rates.

An example of the endogenous component of consumer and investor confidence is the effect of proposed tax increases on overall business and consumer sentiment.[7] For example, the US tax hike of 1988–1989 that was designed to shrink the burgeoning budget deficits, came at a time when the US economy was on the brink of recession, and when consumer and producer confidence levels were 'flattening out' following the debt-heavy growth of the 1980s. The tax increases served only to pummel the confidence indexes further and to exacerbate the 'crisis in confidence'. This, in turn, played a role in the ensuing decline in economic activity in 1990–1991, which resulted in, ironically, even larger US budget deficits due to the induced increases in welfare payments coupled with a shrinking tax base!

It is this endogenous (policy-influenced and market-determined) component of the overall level of confidence in the economy that we explicitly incorporate into our analyses of macroeconomic stabilisation policies and business cycle effects presented in the following two chapters. Among the general policy issues that we address are:

1 Does the inclusion of endogenous confidence terms that include the interactions between past, current and expected future macroeconomic policies and economic activity, allow policy makers to develop an optimal monetary/fiscal policy mix that stabilises output and employment? Can a consumer confidence index be used as an effective policy instrument?
2 What role does consumer confidence play in determining economic performance? How does low consumer confidence along with expectations of higher inflation compromise the efficacy of traditional stabilisation policies?

Before proceeding with the theoretical modelling, definitions of the relevant confidence indexes and a brief review of the specification and role of consumer confidence in the recent macroeconomic literature and in policy making, are in order.

CONSUMER CONFIDENCE INDEXES: DEFINITIONS AND MEASUREMENT

In the United States, two major measures of consumer confidence, derived from large-scale surveys of US households, are available. These are the University of Michigan's Index of Consumer Sentiment and the Conference Board's Consumer Confidence Index.

The University of Michigan index, developed by Katona and Mueller (1953), is designed to measure 'those factors which are capable of giving rise to independent variation in the rate of consumer spending and saving, namely, changes in people's perceptions, attitudes, motivations, and expectations'.[8]

This index of consumer sentiment is comprised of information obtained from a monthly telephone survey of about 500 households. Participants are asked to provide qualitative responses to questions pertaining to current family financial situations, expected financial outlook one year into the future, expected business conditions 12 months hence, long-term (5-year) expectations of business conditions, and current buying plans for large household durable goods (appliances).

The Michigan Index of Consumer Sentiment is comprised of the average of responses to all five questions, while the Index of Consumer Expectations averages only the responses to the three questions pertaining to expected economic conditions. In addition, the Michigan survey also collects (and includes) information pertaining to consumer perceptions about real estate conditions, inflation, interest rates, employment opportunities, the auto market, and so on.

The Conference Board's Consumer Confidence Index is similar in construction to the Michigan index. Here, information is obtained from mailed surveys to about 5,000 households every month, with an average response of about 3,500 surveys. This index combines qualitative survey responses to five questions relating to current and expected future conditions. These five questions focus on the current general business conditions, expected business conditions 6 months hence, current job opportunities in their area, potential job openings 6 months into the future, and expected family income 6 months into the future.

The Conference Board explicitly inquires about the respondent's job and income prospects instead of the more general 'financial condition' questions in the Michigan survey. Furthermore, the Conference Board survey focuses on nearer-term expectations relative to the Michigan index; participants are asked about business conditions and household employment over the next 6 months as opposed to 5 years.

Because of these differences, the two consumer confidence indexes are not always identical or perfectly correlated. Between January 1978 and March 1991, for example, while both indexes rose and fell at the same time, the Conference Board index displayed greater fluctuation and the respective peaks and troughs of time paths of the two indexes often did not coincide.[9]

THEORIES OF THE MAJOR ROLE OF CONSUMER CONFIDENCE: A REVIEW

At least five roles have been ascribed to consumer confidence by policy makers and analysts:

1 Consumer sentiment is a causal factor – consumer confidence independently influences macroeconomic activity.
2 Sentiment is an instrument that accurately forecasts economic fluctuations.
3 Consumer confidence is a catalyst, magnifying the effects of macroeconomic shocks.
4 The confidence index is an indicator of consumers' forecasts of future economic conditions.
5 The index captures current and exclusive respondent-specific economic information.[10]

The first role – that of confidence as a causal variable – can be traced back to Pigou (1927, p. 30) where an 'initiating impulse' of industrial fluctuations is listed as a psychological cause that results in 'changes that occur in men's attitudes of mind, so that, on a constant basis of fact, they do not form constant judgement'. In similar fashion, Keynes's (1964, p. 315) 'animal spirits' which were responsible for 'sudden and violent changes' in investment, were driven by changes in tastes and preferences of consumers along with their long-term expectations of future economic activity.[11]

A primary channel by which this causal role is manifested is in consumer purchases of household durables such as automobiles and refrigerators, and, to some extent, real estate.[12] This approach differs from traditional macroeconomic theory which suggests that consumer spending might be primarily influenced only by conventional economic variables such as relative prices and income. However, more recent research (Katona, 1975) pertaining to psychological consumption theory also includes confidence and expectations pertaining to future income and employment in the determinants of consumption expenditure.

The traditional and psychological views of consumption have been reconciled to some degree since the late 1970s by reinterpreting consumer confidence within the context of the life-cycle theory of consumption (Juster and Wachtel, 1972; Mishkin, 1978). The life-cycle theory (Modigliani and Brumberg, 1954) describes current consumption to be a function of perceived lifetime income, which includes current and expected future labour income as well as household wealth.

One possible mechanism for tying the two schools of consumption together and, perhaps, endowing confidence in the forecasting abilities of role 2, is that a household's expectations and perceptions of total lifetime resources are partly psychological. Katona and his co-workers found that since households were unable to accurately predict their incomes into the future, they attached greater weight to their present financial status. Therefore, their general attitudes regarding their present financial condition were found to predict their near-term expenditures on consumer durables more accurately than their expectations of future income.[13] Accordingly, consumer sentiment indexes might indeed be useful in forecasting total consumption expenditures and GDP as suggested in role 2, by virtue of the contemporaneous effects of consumer expenditures on durables and real estate.

The third role (which is related to the causal role) assigned to consumer sentiment, is that of a catalyst magnifying – or offsetting – the effect of shocks impacting on the business cycle. In his summary of the 'psychological theories' of business cycles which include those of Pigou and Keynes, Haberler (1939, p. 145) concludes that 'optimism and pessimism are regarded as causal factors which tend to induce or intensify the rise and fall of investment which are characteristic of the upswing and the downswing'. This role is captured in the Data Resources Inc. (DRI) model, for example, where variables such as oil prices, interest rates and employment influence consumer spending by virtue of the enhancing catalytic effect of consumer sentiment (Eckstein, 1983; Kelly, 1990). Therefore, fluctuations in explanatory variables that are not simultaneously accompanied by fluctuations in sentiment, might have a disproportionately lower effect on overall economic activity.[14]

The importance of role 4 cannot be denied. Regardless of whether the confidence indexes are useful as forecasters of aggregate economic activity, they nevertheless contain information on consumers' forecasts of future macroeconomic variables. Therefore, according to role 4, irrespective of the consumers' macroeconomic knowledge or interpretation, their individual forecasts, no matter how erroneous, still affect their spending and consumption patterns.

Finally, measures of sentiment may include information about the economy that has not yet been reflected in nationally compiled macroeconomic statistics. This is captured by role 5 where the sentiment index is a reflection of data and information endemic to the consumer that is not, as yet, in the public domain.

In fact, surveys of consumer sentiment are widely accepted among policy makers as summary statistics that add to the information content of forecasts of future economic activity. The US Department of Commerce, for example, includes the Michigan index in its composite index of eleven leading indicators. In this role, the confidence surveys add to, as well as proxy for, summary statistics of economic activity even though consumer sentiment might not be attributed with direct causal macroeconomic effects.

However, some economists remain divided regarding the usefulness of this index as an independent or stand-alone summary statistic. Critics of this fifth role of consumer sentiment (Garner, 1991; Fuhrer, 1993, for example) cite low correlation coefficients for both the US confidence indexes with respect to durable goods purchases to refute claims that sentiment indexes by themselves are capable of embodying current and expected future economic activity. Others, such as Leeper (1991), find that while innovations – or unanticipated changes in sentiment resulting from strong exogenous influences such as the Gulf War – do help to predict unanticipated changes in output and employment, the inclusion of a small set of readily available macroeconomic data renders the sentiment indexes redundant.

On the other hand, Throop (1991b) finds evidence that swings in sentiment do indeed produce systematic lagged effects in consumer spending on durables. Furthermore, he finds that the most accurate forecasts of spending on durables can be obtained by focusing on the current conditions component of the sentiment index (or the economic variables most closely related to this component of confidence) of either index in a stock-adjustment model of consumer purchases.

A more recent study by Fuhrer (1993) keeps the debate alive, however, by claiming that apart from some idiosyncratic information, the variation in the Michigan index can be explained by fluctuations in readily available macroeconomic data. Furthermore, he finds that the independent information in consumer sentiment, as well as the information pertaining to contemporaneous observations, only reduces the forecast error in consumption growth by at most 5 per cent. However, he does find statistically significant and reliable evidence of the sentiment's predictive ability from 1963 to 1993.

The following two chapters present research that further explores the potential importance of consumer confidence to macroeconomic stabilisation in the industrialised economies of the 1990s. We incorporate consumer and producer sentiment in the design and implementation of stabilisation policies in a manner significantly different from the previous approaches described above. The focus here is on an endogenous component of consumer and producer confidence that is allowed to be not just a function of the time path of past, present and future economic activity but also of past, present and expected future fiscal and monetary policies. In the following chapters we do not treat sentiment as some exogenously determined causal variable or catalyst, or as a forecasting tool (a summary statistic) to provide us with some composite 'photograph' of current and future economic activity. Instead, we allow for the endogenised sentiment to influence the business cycle by providing an additional conduit for effective monetary and fiscal stabilisation policies, of which it is a function.

The difference in definition between 'confidence/sentiment' and 'expectations' was discussed in the Introduction to the book. Simply, we define 'expectations' to mean 'rational expectations' in the sense of Muth (1961) which are mathematical conditional forecasts based on all available information. These 'expectations' are narrower in nature than 'confidence/sentiment', which includes idiosyncratic respondent-specific information in the current time period in addition to the conditional mathematical forecasts. Thus, in the present context, we see 'confidence' as capturing additional information not yet readily available in contemporaneous aggregate data.

Let us now turn to some possible theoretical implications of fiscal/monetary stabilisation when endogenised confidence variables are included in the macroanalysis.

Chapter 8

Consumer confidence and the optimal timing of effective monetary stabilisation

*(with Giles Mellon)**

Given the important role ascribed to confidence in the first two parts of this book, it certainly seems that the recent renewed interest in consumer and investor confidence has sound historical justification. This chapter extends the overview of consumer confidence presented in Chapter 7 to include the results of theoretical research on the possible role of confidence in macroeconomic stabilisation. In the model presented below we demonstrate the potential gains that might be achieved today through policies that explicitly target consumer confidence.

At present, the consequences (theoretical and empirical) of fiscal and monetary stabilisation policies remain controversial. While active demand-side stabilisation stimulates GDP and employment in the familiar Keynesian paradigm, the more recent rational expectations paradigm instead finds such stabilisation to result only in greater inflation with no real improvement in GDP and employment. Here output is 'neutral' to demand-side stabilisation characterised by changes in the monetary and/or fiscal growth rates.

This rational expectations paradigm, coupled with the hypothesis of flexible prices, has generated significant research, as well as policy interest, focusing on the 'policy ineffectiveness' proposition. In this new classical macroeconomics (NCM), only unanticipated changes in fiscal and monetary policy rules influence real variables which are otherwise neutral to the discretionary systematic application of stabilisation policies.[1] However, a growing body of research has cast doubt on the validity of these 'policy ineffectiveness' propositions.[2] For example, studies in the early 1980s by Mishkin (1982a, b), Gordon (1982), and Makin (1982), among others, find evidence that systematic, as well as non-systematic, policies affect output.

Recent sluggish domestic economic growth in the United States,

Europe and Japan has revitalised research on effective macro-economic stabilisation. For example, Laumas (1991) finds real output to be non-neutral with respect to anticipated money growth as well as to anticipated and unanticipated fiscal policies. Kretzmer (1992) suggests that, while discretionary monetary policy has indeed become less successful in stabilising real output during the 1962–1991 period, it nevertheless has been more effective than discretionary fiscal policy.

The present chapter attempts to bridge the gap between the policy irrelevance proposition of the new classical economics and the traditional Keynesian arguments for effective discretionary monetary policy. We model a rational expectations economy with flexible prices, and one that is fully consistent with the new classical economics. However, consumer and producer confidence terms (which appear to have contributed significantly to the 1990–1991 US recession) are seen to play a key role in our model.[3] These confidence terms are endogenously determined and are time-dependent functions of the current and future states of GDP growth, as well as of current fiscal and monetary policies.[4]

In particular, special attention is devoted to the trend components of potential output and aggregate demand, which provide the basis for these endogenously determined producer and consumer confidence terms. Linear rational expectations models usually divide output into a steady-state trend component and a cyclical component. The trend (potential output) component is often relegated to secondary status by being simply exogenised, or approximated by a trend variable as in Lucas (1973) and Cozier (1986), or, in some cases, completely ignored (Barro, 1978b).

However, a number of studies have raised questions about both the theoretical and empirical validity of this secondary status that is generally accorded to potential output. Rasche and Tatom (1977), for instance, find that 80–90 per cent of output variance can be attributed to the potential output component. Furthermore, Nelson and Plosser (1982) demonstrate that macroeconomic time series are not necessarily stationary processes, which implies that customary detrending procedures may exaggerate the influence of the cyclical impulses.[5] In fact, Alexander (1990) develops a rational expectations model with imported energy and labour as substitutive factors of production to analyse policy effects on the trend as well as the cyclical components of real output. Empirical results for Germany indicate significant effects of fiscal policy on both inflation and output that can be attributed to the potential-output trend component.

For these reasons, the present model incorporates a trend component that is not simply exogenised but is, instead, taken to be a function of endogenously determined confidence terms that are stochastic functions of the policy environment as shown below.

The confidence terms themselves affect labour demand; abrupt changes in confidence result in shifts in labour demand, which in turn shift employment and output given that the labour market is held constantly in equilibrium. This equilibrium property is also shared with the real business cycle (RBC) literature. However, while the RBC models are driven by intertemporal substitution of labour caused by fluctuations in technology, the present model, instead, focuses on shifts in labour demand stemming from endogenous changes in consumer and producer confidence. In this sense, this model differs from the contemporary new classical, as well as the new Keynesian literature, by virtue of the endogeneity of the confidence terms which affect the potential output, or the 'trend' components.

MODEL

The model is set out below, with the variables (except interest rates and tax rates) expressed in logs.[6]

$$n_t^{\mathrm{d}} = k_0\, c_t - k_4\,(w_t - p_t) \tag{1}$$

$$n_t^{\mathrm{s}} = k_5\,(w_t - p_t) \tag{2}$$

$$m_t^{\mathrm{s}} = x_t\,(\underline{c} - c_t) + p_t + v_t^{\mathrm{m}} \tag{3}$$

$$m_t^{\mathrm{d}} = g y_t - h i_t \tag{4}$$

$$y_t^{\mathrm{d}} = b(1 - t_t)y_t - f i_t + k_6 c_t + v_t^{\mathrm{d}} \tag{5}$$

$$y_t^{\mathrm{s}} = k_7 n_t + v_t^{\mathrm{s}} \tag{6}$$

$$c_t = u_t^{0} y_t + u_t^{1} E_t y_{t+1} - k_2 t_t + v_t^{\mathrm{c}} \tag{7}$$

where n_t = units of labour; c_t = investor confidence; y_t = real national output; t_t = marginal tax rate; w_t = nominal wage; p_t = price of good; m_t = nominal money balances; i_t = nominal interest rate; and v_t^{m}, v_t^{d}, v_t^{s}, v_t^{c} are zero mean, and finite variance iid money, demand, supply and confidence shocks, respectively. $E_t(X)$ is the conditional expectation of variable X given period t information.

Equation (1) is the expression for labour demand which is assumed to be a function of the endogenous confidence term c_t, and the real wage. An increase in the endogenously determined confidence or a decline in the real wage is assumed to boost labour demand.

The endogenised confidence term is given by expression (7) with investor confidence being a weighted function of current output y_t, expected future output $E_t y_{t+1}$, tax rates t_t, real money growth m_t, and a confidence shock v_t^c.[7]

The time-dependent weights u_t^0 and u_t^1 are the elasticities of confidence with respect to the current and future states of the economy, respectively. Along the lines of Lucas's (1973) 'islands economy' experimentally tested in Chapter 3, individuals are assumed to have imperfect information. In the present model, this translates to their inability to separate a decrease in the rate of real output growth due to a temporary, market-specific slump in demand from a decrease in growth due to an economy-wide recession.[8] As the recession worsens and as individuals continue to signal-extract the relevant economy-wide information from the observed declines in prices and output, they weigh expectations of future (more uncertain) economic growth more heavily in formulating their current levels of confidence. That is, u_t^1 increases as the recession worsens, and, in the limit, approaches infinity. In (7) an increase in the marginal tax rate t_t is assumed to have a negative effect on confidence.

Equation (2) is the standard neoclassical expression for labour supply as a positive function of the real wage. Once again, information is assumed to be asymmetric in that labour demanders have access to a larger information set relative to labour suppliers, along the lines of Gray (1976) and Phelps and Taylor (1977).[9] This accounts for the asymmetry in the labour market – demanders of labour react more quickly to changes in confidence which are, in turn, driven by their expectations of the current and future state of economic growth as given by expression (7).

Equation (3) presents the nominal money supply rule. In this economy, the central bank is committed to target some long-term trend level of confidence denoted $\underline{c}$, with the parameter x_t being the percentage to which fluctuations of confidence from the trend level are confined. Therefore, if endogenous confidence c_t in the current period were to drop below the trend $\underline{c}$, monetary growth would be loosened to close the difference $(\underline{c} - c_t)$ by x_t per cent.[10] If, however, the central bank were to abandon confidence targeting altogether, the parameter x_t would be set to zero and the monetary authority would then adopt a simple Friedman-like k per cent non-discretionary rule. Real money demand is given by the fairly standard expression (4) with g and h being the income and interest elasticities of money demand, respectively.

Domestic aggregate output demand is described by equation (5) with the right-hand-side comprised of the demand for the domestic good stemming from private consumption, private capital investment and demand influenced by the confidence term c_t. This is obtained from the consumption and investment functions:

$$\text{cons}_t = \underline{cons}_t + b(1 - t_t)y_t \tag{5a}$$

$$I_t = \underline{I}_t - fi_t \tag{5b}$$

where cons_t is current consumption and is a function of the trend component of consumption, $\underline{cons}_t$, which incorporates confidence, and disposable income $(1 - t_t)y_t$. Private capital investment, I_t, is a function of $\underline{I}_t$ representing trend investment (which incorporates confidence), as well as of domestic nominal interest rates, i_t. Along the lines of the investor confidence index described earlier, the two endogenous confidence terms reflect the current state of the economy and expectations of future output growth, and they are both captured by c_t in (5) which represents combined consumer and investor confidence.

Equation (6) is the standard production function necessary to close the model, with output simply a function of employment and a stochastic supply-side element.

SOLUTION TECHNIQUE AND RESULTS

The model described above can be simplified into three equations in quasi-reduced form with the endogenous variables being output, y_t, prices, p_t, and nominal wages, w_t. This system can be expressed as:

$$Ay_t^* = BE_t y_{t+1}^* + Dm_t^* + Ev_t^* \tag{8}$$

where the vectors $y_t^* = [y_t\, p_t\, w_t]$, $m_t^* = [t_t\, m_t]$, $v_t^* = [v_t^s\, v_t^d\, v_t^m]$, and $A - E$ are the corresponding coefficient matrices presented in Appendix A. Equation (8) is an expectational difference equation of the second order, which is solved using a vector-augmented version of the method of undetermined coefficients along the lines of Aoki and Canzoneri (1979).

Postulating the solution:

$$y_t^* = B_0 m_t^* + B_1 v_t^* \tag{9}$$

the next task is the solution for the values of the coefficients B_0 and B_1, where each B represents a matrix. Substituting (9) into (8) by appropriate manipulations and implementing the Weiner–Kolmogorov k-step-ahead linear least squares forecasting rule, the following results are obtained.

Results

The solution for output with respect to the vector of fiscal and monetary policy instruments t_t, and m_{t-1}, is found to be:

$$y_t = [(d_2 + 2a_1 d_5)m_t - (d_1 + 2a_1 d_4)t_t].[\mathrm{Det}]^{-1} \tag{10}$$

where the parameters a_1 and d_2–d_5 are substitutions made for notational convenience and are specified in Appendix A. [Det] is the determinant of the inversion matrix and is given by:

$$\mathrm{Det} = (u_t^1 + u_t^0)(k_0 - 2a_1\ (x_t + hk_6)) \tag{11}$$

where u_t^0 and u_t^1 are the time-dependent weights that individuals in this economy assign to the current and the expected future state of the economy in formulating their level of confidence c_t. The parameter x_t is the degree to which deviations in c_t from some long-term steady state are targeted by the central bank, as discussed earlier.

From result (10) we find that increases in discretionary monetary growth tend to stimulate output growth, while increases in the tax rate dampen growth in y_t. Output is found to accompany an increase in m_t due to the effect of monetary loosening on confidence and hence on labour demand.

However, the monetary stimulus is effective only as long as the weights u_t^0 or u_t^1 do not approach infinity. As individuals come to the realisation that the decline in the growth of wages and prices is not a temporary market-specific phenomenon, but, on the contrary, an economy-wide recession, they widen their planning horizon and assign greater weight to their expectations of future economic growth, u_t^1, in formulating their levels of confidence. Therefore, u_t^1 increases as the worsening recession becomes more apparent. Eventually, output y_t becomes neutral to monetary policy – dy_t/dm_t

approaches 0 as u_t^1 approaches infinity – and we obtain the familiar demand-side neutrality propositions of the New Classical Macroeconomics or the rational expectations paradigm.

Therefore, effective monetary stabilisation must be executed in the early stages of an economic downturn, before the decline in confidence levels becomes self-sustaining, and before expectations of slower growth dominate the composition of consumer and producer confidence c_t.

Furthermore, if u_t^1 lies below its limit, we find from (10) that the larger the degree of targeting x_t, the greater the sensitivity of output response with respect to fiscal and/or monetary stabilisation – dy_t/dg_t and dy_t/dm_t increase as x_t increases from 0 to 1. If the central bank does indeed embark on a policy of targeting current confidence to some trend level, it must do so by closing the gap between the two levels by 100 per cent, or, by setting $x_t = 1$, in order to maximise output stabilisation.

The solution of p_t is found to be:

$$p_t = [(a_1 - c - Dd_o)g_t + (Dd_1 + c - a_1)t_t + \{(a_1 - c)d_5 - Dd_2\}m_t].[\text{Det}]^{-1}, \tag{12}$$

where [Det] is as defined earlier, and the substitution $C = k_0 (u_t^0 + u_t^1)$ and $D = k_{10} - k_{11} (u_t^0 + u_t^1)$. Increases in the growth of discretionary government spending and the money supply are found to increase the inflation rate, while an increase in the marginal tax rate t_t is found to be deflationary since $(Dd_1 + c - a_1)$ is < 0.

Furthermore, as the recession worsens and confidence plummets, prices respond less to increases in g_t or m_t. In this case the dampening effect of the decline in confidence – or, the incipient leftward shift in aggregate demand – offsets the inflationary effect of attempted demand-side stabilisation. From (12), dp_t/dg_t and dp_t/dm_t < 0 as u_t^1 increases.

Additionally, the solutions of the output and prices with respect to the confidence, monetary, and supply shocks are found to be:

$$y_t = B_2 v_t^{\text{c}} + B_3 v_t^{\text{m}} + B_4 v_t^{\text{s}}, \tag{13}$$

$$p_t = B_5 v_t^{\text{c}} + B_6 v_t^{\text{m}} - B_7 v_t^{\text{s}}, \tag{14}$$

with B_2–B_7 defined in Appendix B. Output responds positively to all three shocks. Positive confidence shocks result in rightward shifts in aggregate supply. Conversely negative confidence shocks – the 1990 Iraqi invasion of Kuwait, for example – result in output being negatively affected. Similar results apply for the supply-side disturbances. Output responds positively to monetary shocks due to their effect on current prices (as obtained in (14)) and the resulting increase in current output supply by virtue of the intertemporal substitutability of leisure present in the Barro-type aggregate supply function (6).

Prices also respond positively to confidence and monetary shocks and negatively to supply-side disturbances due to the corresponding shifts in the aggregate supply.

We are now in a position to compare the discretionary monetary rule (where the central bank attempts to target the current confidence level to some long-term trend level of confidence) with a non-discretionary Friedman-like k per cent money growth rule. This latter rule is analysed by setting $x_t = 0$ in the money supply expression (3) and comparing the unconditional output and price variances for the two monetary rules, respectively:

$$S_y^2 = (B_2)^2 S_c^2 + (B_3)^2 S_m^2 + (B_4)^2 S_s^2, \tag{15}$$

$$S_p^2 = (B_5)^2 S_c^2 + (B_6)^2 S_m^2 + (B_7)^2 S_s^2. \tag{16}$$

Here S_y^2 and S_p^2 are the unconditional variances of output and prices for the discretionary rule, and S_c^2, S_m^2, S_s^2 are the variances of the confidence, monetary and supply-side shocks.

Setting x_t=0 in the B coefficients described Appendix B (namely, in the k_{11} term), the variances corresponding to the non-discretionary rule are found to be:

$$S_y^{n2} = (B_1^n)^2 S_c^2 + (B_2^n)^2 S_m^2 + (B_3^n)^2 S_s^2, \tag{17}$$

$$S_p^{n2} = (B_4^n)^2 S_c^2 + (B_5^n)^2 S_m^2 + (B_6^n)^2 S_s^2, \tag{18}$$

where the B_1^n–B_6^n terms represent substitutions for the B parameters with X_t=0.

From (15)–(18) we find that the non-discretionary money rule results in uniformly lower unconditional output and price variances – the parameters B_{1-6}^n are dominated by the corresponding parameters B_{1-6}. However, the stabilising effects of monetary stimuli are greater under discretionary money policy. The confidence-targeting money rule is found to have a greater effect on real output (compared to the rule setting $x_t = 0$) provided that the demand-side stabilisation is implemented in the early stages of recession – before the decline in consumer confidence becomes self-sustaining.

Therefore, the discretionary confidence-targeting money rule presents policy makers with a difficult tradeoff; the effective stimulation of a faltering economy in the early stages of a recession has to be traded-off against the increased unconditional output and price variances that such a policy would generate.

It should be noted that both discretionary as well as non-discretionary policies are neutral to real output as the recession worsens and u_t^1 approaches infinity; the discretionary rule is non-neutral to output only in the early stages of economic slowdown. The unconditional variances of output and prices, however, are not functions of the intensity or the duration of the economic recession – the variance terms are found to be independent of u_t^1. The intuition here is that fluctuations in output and prices are functions of the variances of contemporaneous confidence, monetary and supply-side shocks and not of confidence terms weighed heavily towards expectations of the next period's output by virtue of the u_t^1 term.

As a long-term rule, the non-discretionary constant monetary growth rule is clearly superior to the discretionary rule by virtue of its ability to minimise output and price variance. However, the discretionary monetary rule is indeed superior in the specialised case when the economy is in the early stages of a recession not fully recognised as such in the confidence terms of producers and consumers.

Therefore, effective monetary policy need not always be a choice of 'rules versus discretion' as traditionally presented in the literature. Instead, effective monetary policy might be characterised by 'rules with discretion', provided that discretion is exercised in a decisively timely fashion to shore up consumer confidence before it begins its inexorable descent.

APPENDIX A

The substitutions for a_1 and d_2–d_5 in the solution of real output with respect to the policy instruments, are as follows:

$$a_1 = (k_4 + k_5);\ d_2 = k_0 k_3;\ d_3 = (k_1 k_{11} + h);\ d_4 = k_{11} k_2;$$

$$d_5 = (k_{11} k_3 - 1);\ k_{10} = [h - h(1 - T_t) + k];\ k_{12} = (X_t + hk_6).$$

APPENDIX B

The substitutions B_2–B_7 are as follows:

$$B_2 = (k_0 + k_{11}a_1\ (1+a_2)).\{k_{10}a_1\ (1+a_2) - U_t^0(k_{11}a_1\ (1+a_2)+1) + a_1\}^{-1};$$

$$B_3 = a_1\ (1+a_1).\{k_{10}a_1\ (1+a_2) - U_t^0(k_{11}a_1\ (1+a_2)+1)+a_1\}^{-1};$$

$$B_4 = a_1\ .\{k_{10}a_1\ (1+a_2) - U_t^0(k_{11}a_1\ (1+a_2)+1)+a_1\}^{-1};$$

$$B_5 = (a_1 - k_0 U_t^0).\{k_{10}a_1\ (1+a_2) - U_t^0(k_{11}a_1\ (1+a_2)+1)+a_1\}^{-1};$$

$$B_6 = \{(k_{10} - k_{11} U_t^0)(-k_0) + k_{11}\ (a_1 - k_0 U_t^0).\{k_{10}a_1\ (1+a_2) - U_t^0(k_{11}a_1\ (1+a_2)+1)+a_1\}^{-1};$$

$$B_7 = (k_{11} U_t^0 - k_{10})a_1.\{k_{10}a_1\ (1+a_2) - U_t^0(k_{11}a_1\ (1+a_2)+1)+a_1\}^{-1}.$$

Chapter 9

Consumer confidence and domestic fiscal stabilisation

*(with Giles Mellon)**

This chapter re-examines the possible role of fiscal demand-side stabilisation on consumer confidence and real macreoeconomic growth. We extend the theoretical framework of Chapter 8 to include policies resembling the ill-fated 'jump-start' policies planned by the Clinton administration in early 1993 to revive GDP and employment in the United States. These proposed policies, that were essentially large fiscal 'infrastructure' outlays on mass transit, telecommunications, education and the environment, were pre-empted by (i) stronger-than-expected US economic growth in the first quarter of 1993, and (ii) a renewed government and public focus on shrinking the federal budget deficits by trimming government spending.

The theoretical basis for the stimulative effect of government spending on GDP is given by the familiar Keynesian paradigm that is well-articulated in most standard macroeconomic textbooks. Here (to sketch briefly), increases in government spending result in real increases in GDP and employment by virtue of 'multiplier effects' which result from (i) the marginal propensities to consume and save, and (ii) asymmetric adjustments in nominal wages and prices in imperfect labour markets.

In the Keynesian paradigm, the labour market is in a state of disequilibrium when not at 'full employment', and as prices increase due to fiscal (or monetary) stabilisation, nominal wages do not increase in proportion, resulting in a lowering of the real wage. This, in turn, increases labour demand, final employment and output.

More than thirty-five years ago, Phillips (1958) published his empirical observation of the above Keynesian phenomenon – he spotted what appeared to be a stable and negative relationship between inflation and unemployment in the United Kingdom between 1861 and 1957. This tradeoff implied that increases in the rate of inflation due to fiscal/monetary stabilisation would be accompanied by decreases in unemployment (and hence, increases in output).

This relationship continued to look stable and apparently incontrovertible for the UK as well as the US till the late 1960s. Theoretically and empirically, the 'Phillips curve' seemed to exist and to be exploitable. The 'tradeoff' represented the amount of inflation that governments would have to endure to bring about decreases in their rates of unemployment. Macroeconomic policy in this era was primarily concerned with the 'kind' of demand-side stabilisation – the fiscal/monetary 'mix' – with the basic theoretical paradigm of exploiting the tradeoff being basically unchallenged.

However, by the late 1960s, this Keynesian stabilisation paradigm came under sharp theoretical examination. According to *The Economist* (19 February 1994, p. 82):

> the simple Phillips curve faced two separate, but equally withering attacks: one from economic theory, the other from the real world. The theoretical attack was all the more impressive because it came first – at a time when the statistics appeared to say that the Phillips curve still worked.

In the 1960s, in separate articles, Milton Friedman (1968) and Edmund Phelps (1968) stressed that real wages, and not nominal wages, were the key long-term determinants of employment and output. Once workers (in the Keynesian economy discussed above) realised that when prices increased (due to fiscal/monetary stabilisation), their nominal wages did not increase in proportion, consequently leaving them 'worse off' in terms of real wages, they would bid for higher nominal wage increases to regain their original real wages. That is, they would move from having 'imperfect' or 'asymmetric' information to 'perfect' or 'symmetric' information.

As real wages would then return to their original levels, the demand for labour would also decline to its initial level, thus resulting in no permanent increases in real wages, employment and output. The only long-term residual effect of attempted demand-side stabilisation would be a new and higher permanent rate of inflation. The long-term Phillips relationship reflecting the unemployment–inflation tradeoff would cease to exist.

In fact, almost on cue, the Phillips curve relationship did indeed begin to unravel following the publication of these two papers. In the period 1970–1993, according to critics of demand-side stabilisation, there was no discernible relationship between unemployment and inflation in either the United Kingdom or the United States. Conventional Keynesian fiscal/monetary demand-side stabilisation seemed to produce no real long-term changes in employment or output, but only higher inflation, as predicted by Messrs Friedman and Phelps.

The labour market was now being theoretically (and empirically) characterised as comprised of individuals with symmetric information and having rational expectations, who would not confuse temporary increases in nominal wages with real wage increases. Workers would contract for nominal wage increases that would maintain their real wages constant, thus eliminating any changes in employment stemming from changes in the rate of inflation and nominal wage increases.

This paradigm of rational expectations with an accompanying full flexibility of wages and prices (resulting from the individual's ability to react fully to available information), is also referred to as the 'new classical macroeconomics' (NCM). Here only unanticipated changes in fiscal and monetary policy rules influence real variables which are otherwise neutral to the discretionary systematic fiscal/monetary stabilisation.[1]

In the previous chapter we briefly discussed how this policy ineffectiveness proposition was by no means incontrovertible. The growing body of research re-examining and challenging the theoretical and empirical validity of the 'policy ineffectiveness' propositions of the rational expectations paradigm has recently been aided by the dismal macroeconomic performance of the industrialised economies. As the Western economies experienced various stages of decline and sluggishness in real output growth in the early 1990s, this issue of macroeconomic stabilisation has generated renewed and greater research interest.

Dornbusch (1990) also makes a strong case against the new real business cycle (RBC) models that not only assume that all markets clear, but also posit that productivity shocks constitute the primary source of macroeconomic fluctuations.[2] His case study for Mexico highlights three areas in which the RBC model is inconsistent with the empirical evidence, namely, (i) the real exchange rate is not found to be independent of the nominal exchange rate regime, (ii) it is difficult to attribute the Mexican macroeconomic performance of the 1980s to a productivity shock, and (iii) the apparent importance of reversals, or 'U-turns' in Mexican fiscal policy which have no place in the RBC world.[3]

Meanwhile, Alexander (1990) develops a rational expectations model with imported energy and labour as substitutive factors of production to analyse the effects of fiscal policies on the trend as well as the cyclical components of real output. Empirical results for Germany indicate that there are significant fiscal policy effects on inflation and output stemming from the potential-output trend component.

Glick and Hutchison (1990), on the other hand, reaffirm the validity of the 'policy ineffectiveness' proposition with an empirical analysis of US data involving joint tests that capture the simultaneous interactive effects of anticipated and unanticipated fiscal and monetary policies. Their results support the short-run output neutrality proposition with respect to anticipated as well as unanticipated fiscal policy, but not with respect to short-run monetary policy. However, in the long run, all stabilisation policies, anticipated as well as unanticipated, are found to be output-neutral.

The present chapter attempts to extend the theoretical framework of Chapter 8 by providing a theoretical superstructure that might bridge the gap between the policy irrelevance proposition of the new classical economics and the discretionary fiscal stimulus of the new Keynesian school.[4]

The model is similar to that of Chapter 8. We model a rational expectations economy with flexible prices, no asymmetric or imperfect information, and one that is fully consistent with the new classical economics. Once again, consumer and producer confidence terms play a major role in our model, and are endogenously determined by virtue of the incorporation of the current and future state of GDP growth, as well as current fiscal policies. Additionally, the present model incorporates a trend component that is not simply exogenised but is itself a function of the confidence terms described earlier.

Along the lines of the labour market constructed in Chapter 8, these confidence terms also affect labour demand; abrupt changes in confidence result in shifts in labour demand, and hence in employment and output with the labour market constantly in equilibrium. The model of Chapters 8 and 9 differ from the contemporary new classical, as well as the new Keynesian literature, by virtue of the endogeneity of the confidence terms which affect the potential – or 'trend' – output.

MODEL

The model is set out below, with the variables (except interest rates and tax rates) expressed in logs.

$$n_t^d = k_0 E_t y_{t+1} + k_1 y_t - k_2 y_{t-1} + k_3 g_t - k_4 T_t - k_5(w_t - p_t), \quad (1)$$

$$n_t^s = k_6(w_t - p_t), \quad (2)$$

$$m_t^s = q_t m_{t-1} + p_t + v_t^m, \quad (3)$$

$$m_t^d = g y_t - h i_t, \quad (4)$$

$$y_t^d = k_7(E_t y_{t+1} + y_t - y_{t-1} - T_t) + b(1 - T_t)y_t - f i_t + g_t + v_t^d, \quad (5)$$

$$y_t^s = k_8 n_t + k_9 (p_t - E_t p_{t+1}) + v_t^s, \quad (6)$$

where n_t = units of labour; y_t = national output; g_t = discretionary government spending; T_t = marginal tax rate; w_t = nominal wage; p_t = price of good; m_t = nominal money stock; i_t = nominal interest rate; v_t^m, v_t^d, v_t^s = zero mean, and finite variance iid money, demand and supply shocks, respectively, and $E_t(X)$ = conditional expectation of variable X given period t information.

Equation (1) is the expression for labour demand which is obtained from the functional form of the demand for labour given by:

$$N_t^d = f_0 (Y_t/Y_{t-1}, E_t Y_{t+1}/Y_t, G_t, T_t) - f_1 (W_t/P_t), \quad (7)$$

with the variables (except T_t) now expressed in levels. This expression states that labour demand is a function of two terms, $(Y_t/Y_{t-1}, E_t Y_{t+1}/Y_t, G_t, T_t)$, and W_t/P_t. The former is the endogenised confidence term (discussed earlier) comprised of four components beginning with Y_t/Y_{t-1}, the ratio of current output to last period's output, which reflects the current state of economic growth.[6] The second component, $E_t Y_{t+1}/Y_t$, serves to incorporate expectations of future economic growth, while the last two components, G_t and T_t, are the two fiscal policy instruments that affect producer confidence.

A large infusion of discretionary government expenditures is assumed, at least in the short run, to boost producer confidence, while an increase in the marginal tax rate T_t has the opposite effect.[7] For example, an increase in government spending is assumed to improve the confidence term in labour demand (7) by contributing to productive job creation through, for example, infrastructure spending.[8]

This specification of including fiscal policy components in the confidence term of labour demand (and hence in the endogenised potential, or trend, output term) is similar to that discussed in Perloff and Wachter (1979) and later employed in labour demand by Alexander (1990). In the latter study, fiscal policy involving changes in taxes as well as in transfer payments is found to affect potential output through changes in the shift component of labour demand. Alexander treats the massive subsidy payments to German coal, steel and shipbuilding as incentives for 'marginal and extra-marginal' suppliers to stay in the market, thereby increasing labour demand.[9] The second term, (W_t/P_t), simply captures the negative relationship of labour demand with respect to the real wage.

Equation (2) is the standard neoclassical expression for labour supply as a positive function of the real wage. Equation (3) presents the money supply rule, with q_t being a feedback policy parameter. Money demand is given by equation (4) with g and h being the income and interest elasticities of money demand, respectively.

Domestic aggregate output demand is described by equation (5) which can be rewritten as:

$$y_t^d = \underline{y}_t + b(1 - T_t)y_t - fi_t + g_t + v_t^d, \tag{5a}$$

where the right-hand-side is comprised of the demand for the domestic good stemming from private consumption, private capital investment and government consumption. This is obtained from the consumption and investment functions:

$$c_t = \underline{c}_t + b(1 - T_t)y_t, \tag{5b}$$

$$I_t = \underline{I}_t - fi_t \tag{5c}$$

where consumption is a function of the consumer confidence component $\underline{c}_t$ and disposable income $(1 - T_t)y_t$, while private capital investment is a function of $\underline{I}_t$ representing investor confidence, as well as domestic nominal interest rates, i_t. Along the lines of the producer (employer) confidence index described earlier, the two endogenous confidence terms reflect the current state of the economy, expectations of future output growth, and the current tax rate, and they are both captured by $\underline{y}_t$ in (5a) which represents combined consumer and investor confidence. Therefore, this endogenised potential output term can be expressed in levels as:

$$\underline{Y}_t = f_3\ (Y_t/Y_{t-1},\ E_tY_{t+1}/Y_t, T_t). \tag{5d}$$

Therefore, the real aggregate demand in (5) is simply a log-linear version of (5a) which, in turn, is comprised of consumption, investment and government demand for output.

Real aggregate supply is represented by equation (6) which embodies the natural rate hypothesis and the intertemporal substitution of leisure as in Barro (1980), as well as nominal wage fixing along the lines of Fischer (1977). The conventional trend component is now a function of the rate of employment n_t, and deviations in aggregate supply are functions of the innovation in prices.

SOLUTION TECHNIQUE AND RESULTS

The model described above can be simplified into three equations in quasi-reduced form with the endogenous variables being output, y_t, prices, p_t, and nominal wages, w_t. This system can be expressed as:

$$Ay_t^* = BE_t y_{t+1}^* + Cy_{t-1}^* + Dg_t^* + Ev_t^*, \tag{7}$$

where the vectors $y_t^* = [y_t\ p_t\ w_t\ ]$, $g_t^* = [g_t\ T_t\ m_{t-1}]$, $v_t^* = [v_t^s\ v_t^d v_t^m]$, and $A - E$ are the corresponding 3×3 coefficient matrices, whose substitutions are presented in Appendix A. Equation (7) is an expectational difference equation of the second order, which is solved using a vector-augmented version of the method of undetermined coefficients along the lines of Aoki and Canzoneri (1979).

Postulating the solution:

$$y_t^* = B_0 g_t^* + B_1 v_t^*, \tag{8}$$

the next task is the solution for the values of the coefficients B_0 and B_1, where each B represents a 3×3 matrix. Substituting (8) into (7) by appropriate manipulations and implementing the Weiner–Kolmogorov k-step-ahead linear least squares forecasting rule, the following results are obtained.

Results

The solution for output with respect to the vector of fiscal and monetary policy instruments g_t, T_t and m_{t-1}, is found to be:

$$y_t = [k_3 g_t - k_4 T_t].(-k_8 k_{10}/\det)^{-1}, \tag{9}$$

where (det) is the matrix with the substitutions presented in Appendix B and is found to be negative.

From (9) we find that increases in discretionary government spending, as well as cuts in the marginal tax rates, increase the rate of growth of output. Here, discretionary fiscal policy increases real output by virtue of increases in investor and consumer confidence, as well as in labour demand; in effect, we obtain a rightward shift in a vertical AS curve. The absence of an offsetting crowding-out of capital investment (present in the conventional neoclassical framework) is attributed to the positive effect on capital investment stemming from an increase in the investor confidence term, which dominates the dampening effect of higher nominal interest rates associated with discretionary fiscal policy.

This scope for effective stabilisation is, however, confined to discretionary fiscal policy, as output growth is found to be neutral to discretionary monetary policy. The intuitive explanation of this form of monetary policy irrelevance will be provided after discussing the price and nominal wage results.

The reduced form solution of the rate of growth of the price level with respect to the vector of policy instruments is:

$$p_t = \{[-a_2 a_4 k_3 + d_2 B_2] g_t + [a_2 a_4 k_4 + B_2] T_t + B_2 m_{t-1}\}.[\det]^{-1}, \tag{10}$$

where B_2 is a substitution for the term $(k_5+k_6) - k_8 k_9(k_1+k_0-k_2)$ made for notational convenience, and a_2, a_4 and d_2 (and later, B_3 and B_4) are similar substitutions for the parameters of the matrix system (7) which are presented in Appendix B.

Result (10) provides us with the expected results of the inflation rate increasing with respect to the money growth and increases in the aggregate demand stemming from discretionary fiscal stabilisation.

The solution for the nominal wage is:

$$w_t = \{B_3 g_t - B_4 T_t + B_2 m_{t-1}\}[\det]^{-1} \tag{11}$$

Increases in the rate of growth of government spending (found to be inflationary from (10)) also serve to drive up the rate of growth of nominal wages, which is to be expected in the absence of imperfect information or binding long-term wage contracts, as in Taylor (1979) or Fischer (1977). Increases in tax rates, T_t, retard the rate of growth of nominal wages, which is again consistent with the deflationary effect of rising marginal tax rates obtained in (10).

Of particular interest is the percentage increase in nominal wages with respect to a unit percentage increase in monetary growth given by dw_t/dm_{t-1}. This is found to be identical to the percentage increase in the inflation rate stemming from unitary monetary creation, i.e. $dw_t/dm_{t-1} = dp_t/dm_{t-1} = B_2$. This implies that discretionary increases in money growth leave the real wage (w_t/p_t) unaffected, which in turn results in output stabilisation being neutral to discretionary monetary policy. Increases in money growth, therefore, do not affect the labour market and hence, the equilibrium rate of employment.[10] By virtue of the aggregate supply function described by (6), output supply is thereby insulated from any attempted monetary stabilisation, with the residual result only being increased inflation.[11]

Thus, our model reconciles the demand-side stimulus arising from an increase in discretionary fiscal policy with the rational expectations paradigm of the neutrality of real variables with respect to discretionary monetary stabilisation without the inclusion of features such as imperfect information, or rigidities stemming from long-term wage contracts.

In addition, the solutions for the endogenous variables y_t and p_t, with respect to the stochastic elements yield:

$$y_t = B_5 v_t^{\mathrm{s}} + B_6 v_t^{\mathrm{d}} + B_7 v_t^{\mathrm{m}}, \tag{12}$$

$$p_t = -B_8 v_t^{\mathrm{s}} + B_9 v_t^{\mathrm{d}} + B_{10} v_t^{\mathrm{m}}, \tag{13}$$

with $B_5 - B_8$ defined in Appendices B and C. Output responds positively to real supply shocks and demand shocks as well as to monetary shocks. The intuitive explanation of this result on the consequences of money shocks is that unanticipated monetary disturbances increase the current period price level (as obtained in (13)), and result in suppliers increasing their contemporaneous output supply by indulging in the intertemporal substitutability of leisure as per the Barro aggregate supply function (6). This result is consistent with the 'policy ineffectiveness' proposition; only innovations in money growth affect real output.

As current output is buffeted by real and nominal shocks it, in turn, affects the contemporaneous consumer and producer confidence terms. Therefore, a current period decline in y_t due to a negative shock in (12), for example, not only decreases current confidence, but, by virtue of the forward and backward looking behaviour embedded in these terms, affects next period's confidence as well. This mechanism, driven by the endogenised confidence terms, therefore permits propagation of disturbances over the business cycle, thereby capturing the serial correlation in output.

The solution for the rate of growth of the price level with respect to the shocks indicates that supply shocks are deflationary (due to the rightward shift in the aggregate supply), while demand as well as monetary disturbances exacerbate the inflation rate.

Finally, we explore the issue of procyclical vs countercyclical behaviour of prices. The real business cycle literature has challenged the stylised (and hitherto generally accepted) procyclical nature of prices described originally by Mitchell (1913). For example, Kydland and Prescott (1990), state that the assertion of procyclical (aggregate demand-driven) prices is false – a 'myth'. They find post-Korean War price data for the US to be, on the contrary, countercyclical in nature, thus lending credence to supply-side causes for the business cycle compatible with the real business cycle school of thought.

However, in a more recent study, Wolf (1991) attempts to reconcile the divergent views by concluding that postwar US data indicate a strong countercyclicality only in the post-1973, i.e. post oil shock, period, and not post-1953 as claimed by Kydland and Prescott. Furthermore, countercyclicality is not symmetric in both phases of the business cycle – it is found to be more pronounced in contractionary phases of output, as after the 1973–1974 and 1979–1980 oil shocks, relative to periods of strong growth.

For the present model, the covariances of prices and output, $\mathrm{Cov}[p_t, y_t]$, are found to be of indeterminate sign. In this economy, pro- or countercyclicality is a function of the magnitude of the responsiveness of both output and prices to the unconditional variances of the supply, demand and monetary shocks, given by B_5 – B_{10} , in results (12) and (13).

Prices are found to be countercyclical only when the following condition holds:

$$S_s^2 > (V_1/V_0)S_d^2 + (V_2/V_0)S_m^2, \tag{14}$$

where V_0–V_2 are substitutions presented in Appendix D, and S_s^2, S_d^2 and S_m^2 are the variances of the supply, demand and monetary shocks, respectively. This testable result is independent of the specification of the endogenised confidence terms, and is compatible with Wolf's finding that countercyclicality is only a post-1973 phenomenon. In other periods he finds prices to be procyclical, implying $S_s^2 < (V_1/V_0)S_d^2 + (V_2/V_0)S_m^2$ in terms of result (14), from 1945 to 1973, and stresses that for RBC models to be more realistic, demand-side shocks have to be given a greater role in explaining business cycles.[12]

In sum, it is entirely conceivable that the US postwar economy does indeed provide evidence of both procyclical, and (shorter episodes of) supply-shock-driven countercyclical behaviour, depending on the relative variances of the real and nominal disturbances of the sort described above.

SUMMARY AND CONCLUSION

This chapter shows that effectiveness of discretionary fiscal policy with respect to real output can be preserved in a theoretical analysis while maintaining the neutrality propositions of the neoclassical economics with respect to discretionary monetary policy. In this sense, we offer a reconciliation of the work of the New Keynesian school with that of the rational expectations 'policy irrelevance' school by introducing endogenised confidence terms.

Interestingly, the model refutes any notion of categoric pro- or countercyclicality of prices; rather the behaviour of prices over the business cycle is dependent on the relative magnitudes of the real and nominal shocks that buffet real output. This is in line with the varying impacts of the fiscal and monetary policies themselves that was shown in the different policy making environments examined both experimentally and empirically over the course of this book.

APPENDIX A

The substitutions are:

$$a_0 = k_1;\ a_1 = k_5 + k_1;\ a_2 = [(k_7 - 1) + k]h/f;\ a_3 = k_8 k_6 + k_9;\ a_4 = k_8 k_9;\ b_0 = k_0;\ b_1 = k_7 h/f = c_1;\ b_2 = k_9;\ c_o = k_2;\ d_0 = k_3;\ d_1 = k_4;\ d_2 = h/f = e_1.$$

APPENDIX B

The solutions of y_t, p_t and w_t are presented in terms of the above substitutions plus the additional substitutions given below:

$B_2 = (k_5+k_6) - k_8k_9(k_1+k_0-k_2)$; $B_3 = -k_3\ (1+a_2k_8k_9) - d_2a_1k_8k_6(k_1+k_0-k_2)$; $B_4 = k_4\ (1+a_2k_8k_6) + c_1\ (a_1-k_8k_6(k_1+k_0-k_2))$.

APPENDIX C

The substitutions for the coefficients of the stochastic terms in the solutions for y_t and p_t are:

$B_5 = -a_1/\text{Det}_1$; $B_6 = (a_1k_9h/f)/\text{Det}_1$; $B_7 = (a_4-k_1k_9)/\text{Det}_1$; $B_8 = [-a_1(a_2-b_1)]/\text{det}_1$; $B_9 = [a_1-a_4(a_0-c_0)].-h/f\text{Det}_1$; $B_{10} = \{[a_4(a_2-b_1) - (a_0-c_0)] + a_1\}/\text{det}_1$ and $\text{det}_1 = (a_0-c_0)a_4 + a_1a_4(a_2-b_1)-a_1[a_3(a_2-b_1) + 1] < 0$.

APPENDIX D

The substitutions for V_0-V_2 are:

$V_0 = a_1{}^2(a_2-b_1)$; $V_1 = (h/f)^2a_1k_9(a_1-a_4a_0+a_4c_0)$; $V_2 = (a_4-k_1k_9)[a_4(a_2-b_1)-a_0+c_0]$.

Notes

INTRODUCTION

1 The concept of 'rational expectations' propounded by Muth (1961) will be discussed in greater detail in Chapters 2 and 3, where the expectations formation mechanism of individuals will be experimentally tested under conditions of changing fiscal and monetary policies.
2 An overview of the alternative methods, and results, of deficit financing is presented in Chapter 1.
3 While US credibility – or at least what remains of it – was earned over a long period of relative price stability, New Zealand's experience in the post-1990 period suggests that credibility for anti-inflationary policy can be achieved relatively quickly if the policies in question are pursued rigorously and backed by appropriate institutional reform. The New Zealand parliament made price stability the sole objective of central bank policy under the Reserve Bank of New Zealand Act 1989, and this objective was given 'teeth' by the fact that, if the inflation targets were not met, the Governor of the Reserve Bank stood to lose his/her job. While initially confronted with extremely high real interest rates and rising unemployment, the government was able to prove its commitment to the new policies and Svensson (1993) finds evidence – based on financial market behaviour – that the inflation targets were credible by mid-1992. In a further show of confidence in the new targeting strategy, the duration of labour market contracts was seen to increase sharply after 1991 (see Fischer, 1993).
4 Specifically, Chapter 2 is an experimental test of the Ricardian equivalence theorem, revived by Barro (1974).
5 The experiment in Chapter 3 tests the Lucas (1973) 'islands' model of business cycles. This 'islands' approach described in Lucas's seminal work has had a very influential effect on research pertaining to the nature and causes of business cycles and the role of monetary policy.

1 FISCAL POLICY, CREDIBILITY AND INFLATION

* Portions of this chapter draw upon Burdekin (1995). The authors thank Sven Arndt, Cheryl Holsey, Tom Willett, King Banaian, Paul Burkett,

Mike Kuehlwein, Steve Lewarne and Pierre Siklos for helpful comments, and are grateful to Alan Herbert, editor of *Coins Magazine*, for drawing our attention to the circulation of Confederate currency during the post-First World War hyperinflations in Europe. The authors also wish to acknowledge King Banaian's help with the Central and Eastern European data.

1 See Keynes (1924, p. 46).
2 See Reynolds (1993, p. 662).
3 The US debt and deficit data are drawn from the 1994 *Economic Report of the President*, tables B-79 and B-87.
4 Subsequent developments appear to have validated these pessimistic expectations. While the Czech Republic enjoyed a small surplus for the first 9 months of 1993, the Slovak budget deficit grew to an estimated 4 per cent of GDP. The full-year Slovakian deficit was on course to exceed 6 per cent of GDP (*PlanEcon Report*, 1993h).
5 There was also just over 111 million gold marks worth of non-Reichsbank paper money issues (chiefly 'Notgeld' or emergency money issues that were authorised near the end of the hyperinflation) plus nearly 1,666 million gold marks in various domestic stable-value currency issues (see D'Abernon, 1927, p. 27). Even before the stabilisation achieved at the end of November 1923, the 'economy had already largely turned over to a foreign, hard-currency standard' (Holtfrerich, 1986, p. 313). (See, however, Chapter 5 on the relative stability in the demand for the Reichsbank's paper mark issues in the earlier part of the hyperinflation period.)
6 The original Ponzi scheme was a scam orchestrated after the First World War. Ponzi promised a high rate of interest but relied upon new subscriptions to pay the interest due to the earlier depositors. The end result was a jail sentence for Ponzi (Mayer *et al.*, 1993, p. 367*n*).
7 Sargent and Wallace (1981) suggest that, in order for fiscal policy to be sustainable, the real rate of interest on government debt must be below the real growth rate of the economy. This situation would be characterised by a declining debt/GDP ratio over time.
8 Under a Ricardian regime, however, deficits are temporary and the value of the bonds is fully offset by the implied stream of future taxes required to redeem these bonds (see Barro, 1974; and Chapter 2 of this volume).
9 For further analysis of the argument that, if issues of currency or bonds are considered 'backed' by future taxes, these issues need not be inflationary, see Smith (1985a,b), Bernholz (1988a), Calomiris (1988a) and Siklos (1990). Whether data from colonial America really support this 'backing theory' (as argued by Smith, op. cit.) remains a particular point of controversy, however (see McCallum, 1992).
10 Note that, while short-run inflation expectations may have been influenced by wartime price controls, such effects should not extend to the nominal rate of return on long-term bonds due to mature well after the controls (and the war) had ended (Toma, 1991, p. 464*n*). Evans (1985, p. 82) further argues that, with desired expenditures

apparently not increasing with the Second World War deficits, these deficits 'would probably not have produced high interest rates even if interest rates had not been pegged and prices had not been controlled'.

11 Although resales and debt settlements actually recouped £835,036 through 1 October 1864, leaving the Confederacy with a net loss of just £544,827 (Gentry, 1970, p. 164).

12 Sales at $12.50 per thousand of $145,600 in Confederate bonds were reported in Charleston, South Carolina, on 25 October 1882; and a further 2,000 bonds were sold in San Francisco, California, the following month (*New York Times*, 1882a,b). In Augusta, Georgia, there was even a suspicion 'that the General Government of the United States is now buying them up to destroy them and put an end to future sensation and speculation' (*Augusta Chronicle*, 1882).

13 Even stronger evidence of non-sustainability has been found for Italy, and the sustainability of the fiscal policies followed in other high-debt countries such as Belgium, Greece and Ireland is also in doubt (cf. Corsetti and Roubini, 1991). The increasing debt/GNP ratios in Belgium, Ireland and Italy since 1960 have also been accompanied by a decrease in average maturity levels that may have been necessary to reduce the government's incentive to inflate the debt away and, at the same time, make prospective bond-holders willing to hold the debt in the first place (Missale and Blanchard, 1994).

14 Statistical support for a strong effect of the budget deficit on inflation in one such high inflation country is provided by Choudhary and Parai (1991), using quarterly data for Peru over the 1973-1988 period. Consistent evidence of a link between deficits and inflation appears to arise only in more extreme cases, however (see De Haan and Zelhorst, 1990).

15 Heymann and Sanguinetti (1994, p. 87) emphasise that a drop in the measured deficit will not permit sustainable economic stabilisation unless 'the government attacks the "basic" inflationary forces deriving from the latent demands for spending and the nature of the tax system. This, in turn, may need the creation of new fiscal institutions or the strengthening of the existing ones'.

16 Brazil's own plans for fiscal reform and the replacement of the national currency with a new real value unit were announced on 7 December 1993 (Long, 1993).

17 Bresser Pereira and Dall'Acqua (1991, p. 35) also point out that, during the 1970s, the 'existence of easy foreign finance made it easier for Latin American countries practically to ignore budget deficits'. This was no longer the case in the 1980s, however, and these same countries then had to increasingly resort to money finance.

18 In Mexico, seignorage accounted for an average of 23.9 per cent of total government revenue over the 1971–1982 period – and similarly high averages of 17 per cent or more were recorded for Brazil, Chile, Colombia and Peru over this same interval (Cukierman *et al.*, 1992, p. 538).

19 These figures differ to some degree with the numbers reported by Lewarne (1993, p. 27) over this same time period. However, the relative

standings of the countries based on deficit and inflation performance are the same in each case.

20 The Ukrainian situation has been such as to make even the Russian case look relatively favourable. In consultation with the Ukrainian Embassy in Moscow, Lewarne (1993, p. 27) estimates that, in 1993, the Ukrainian budget deficit grew in excess of 35 per cent of the country's GDP – with inflation running between 7,000 and 10,000 per cent for the year.

21 Currency board arrangements also make much less sense for a large economy like Russia than for small open economies like Estonia and Hong Kong on optimum currency area grounds (see Willett *et al.*, 1993).

22 The government's incentive to put its house in order stems both from the high cost of the inflation tax (Banaian *et al.*, 1995) and the weak effects of fiscal expansion observed in high-debt countries (Dalamagas, 1992, 1993). In cases where additions to the deficit are non-sustainable and/or considered likely to produce greater resort to seignorage or foreign borrowing – or in the extreme case provoke default – it would in fact not be too surprising if such actions failed to boost economic activity. Indeed, Miller *et al.* (1990) examine how fears of default could rationally lead to perverse negative effects of deficit spending on private economic activity – but given the critical role of expectations in this process they refer to the outcome as 'psychological crowding out'.

2 BOND-FINANCED DEFICITS, TAXATION AND EXPECTATIONS

* The authors are indebted to Professor Robert J. Barro for his encouragement and suggestions pertaining to the experimental testing of his (1974) model, and to Professor Catherine Eckel and Professor Giles Mellon for their comments.

1 The Ricardian equivalence theorem is named after David Ricardo who articulated it in the early 1800s. Please refer to Ricardo (1951), Buchanan (1958) and Barro (1984). Ricardo himself had doubts regarding the empirical validity of his theorem, however, as pointed out in O'Driscoll (1977).

2 In the Keynesian model, government bonds are regarded as net wealth by consumers who are then induced to increase spending. Thus, in the Keynesian policy prescription, deficit spending can be used to smooth out cyclical variations in economic activity. See Motley (1987) for an excellent and succinct discussion of the effect of government debt on consumption.

3 This will be discussed in greater detail in the next section, which presents a version of Barro (1974), adapted to experimental testing.

4 This assumes that public and private savings are perfect substitutes. Empirical results on the effects of budget deficit on interest rates

largely support the Ricardian view. See Evans (1987), for a rigorous study incorporating the effects of current, past and expected future deficits on interest rates.

5 The Ricardian effect of deficits on national savings is well illustrated by the case of Israel during 1983–1987 described in Barro (1989); the evidence yields 'a roughly one-to-one offset between public and private savings that the Ricardian view predicts' (Barro, 1989, p. 50).

6 These are a few examples of formative research pertaining to equivalence. Evans (1991) is an excellent example of a recent theoretical piece that finds Ricardian equivalence to be a good approximation even when all households are not 'infinitely lived' as characterised by Barro's intergenerational transfers (bequests). Evans finds that if all households are not infinitely lived, many households have short horizons, and a significant portion of the wage income is obtained by 'liquidity-constrained' households, Ricardian equivalence is still a good approximation.

7 Furthermore, Bernheim (1989) argues that the econometric evidence is inconclusive. For theoretical justification of experimentation in economics *per se*, see Smith (1982), Lucas (1986) and Roth (1988).

8 This model is quite similar to the version of the original 1974 model presented in Barro (1984, chapter 15).

9 The equivalence results are found to hold even if some of Barro's simplifying assumptions such as 'no transfer payments', 'nonzero future deficits', and 'no monetisation', are dropped (see Barro, 1984, 1989, for good reviews).

10 As monetary variance increased, the Lucas experiment verified that producers on separate 'islands' would indeed increasingly attribute observed price changes to general inflation. But when tested in the opposite direction of decreasing monetary variance, the results were not consistent with the signal extraction parameters of the Lucas aggregate supply function. In spite of decreasing monetary variance, producers remained unconvinced of monetary reform.

11 Empirical evidence for Keynesian demand-side multipliers might be weak at best (see Barro, 1992, for an excellent brief overview). This chapter abstracts from the possible effects of stabilisation policy by assuming a vertical aggregate supply curve with income fixed at some $Y_0=500$. While different income groups might have led to greater variance in the 'bids' (discussed next), the average income, which is the relevant variable, would still remain fixed. Hence, one uniform income was adopted, primarily for experimental convenience.

12 The final 'destination' of government debt is not modelled in this experiment. Government debt issuance in this economy would have to be interpreted as funding transfer payments by virtue of the vertical aggregate supply curve implicit here. The author is grateful to Professor Robert Barro for his comments on this subject.

13 The 'bids' were submitted in writing on note-cards which allowed only the auctioneer (experimenter) to identify the bidder. This reduced potential game-theoretic implications that might have arisen from verbal bidding due to a strategic game between two or more bidders.

14 The average of the lowest ten bids was computed and the final rate announced, along with the ten winners of the auction, at the end of each period.
15 Dividing government borrowing into two components, namely, the 'primary' debt issued to finance new spending and debt issued to service past principal and interest payments, proved to be quite intractable in the trial runs of the experiment. Furthermore, it distracted from the emphasis on maintaining a total overall fixed level of government spending in the impending regime shift.
16 A total of three 'test' (trial) runs of the experiment were performed on a very small number of students (not part of the final experiment sample). From these runs it was evident that a post-experiment survey was necessary to enable the experiment director to obtain the intuition underlying the savings and interest rate results.
17 The number of phases and total time periods was dictated by binding time constraints, as the experiment had to be conducted in class and in the early stages of the semester.
18 The students had absolutely no knowledge of the existence of the different phases. The tax cuts were totally unanticipated and exaggerated to the polar case of zero lump-sum taxes primarily for experimental and expository convenience. The economic intuition for the construction of the three phases will be provided in the following section.
19 Household consumption C_t is simply income minus bond purchases and household savings. Since both B_t and S_t values are provided, the average C_t values and time paths have not been included due to space constraints.
20 There is no provision for private capital investment here. We focus only on the savings-driven interest-rate effects of the fiscal regime shift in this experiment.
21 See Langdana (1990) for a review of the literature on sustainability.

3 MONETARY CREDIBILITY AND NATIONAL OUTPUT

* The authors are most grateful to Professor Robert E. Lucas Jr. for comments and suggestions pertaining to the experimental testing of his 'islands' model. They also acknowledge valuable assistance from Phipps Arabie, Elizabeth Hoffman, Richard Hoffman, Giles Mellon, Mary Langdana and Christine Aliouche. This chapter is based on Langdana (1994). Financial support was provided by the Research Resources Committee of Rutgers-GSM.

1 The procyclicality of prices is defined here as a positive correlation between the rate of change in prices with respect to output. A good summary of the interwar US experience can be found in Mitchell (1951).
2 Please see the introductory chapter of Lucas (1981), as well as Lucas

(1977), for excellent reviews of the evolution of theories and models of business-cycle research.

3 Some formative RBC papers include Long and Plosser (1983) and Kydland and Prescott (1982, 1990).

4 For example, Kydland and Prescott (1990) find post-Korean War data for the US to be countercyclical, which supports the supply-side driven theory of the real business cycle. Recently, Wolf (1991) and Langdana and Mellon (1992), however, find no unambiguous empirical or theoretical evidence of consistent pro- or countercyclicality over successive business cycles (see Chapter 9 on this point).

5 By virtue of this construct, the information as perceived on the individual 'islands' will be different from that perceived by viewing the aggregate information on all the islands.

6 This is a simplified version of the aggregate supply function implemented in Lucas (1973) which also allows for serial correlation. The parameter k is Lucas's exogenously-given elasticity of output–supply with respect to relative prices, and is normalised to unity in this experiment, for convenience.

7 Please see Sargent (1979, chapter 10), for a discussion of the law of recursive projections and the signal-extraction problem.

8 In this experiment we hold T^2 fixed at 50 for convenience; the increase in overall 'noise' is solely due to increased monetary variance. The individual producers, however, do not have access to this information.

9 Stylised, theoretical figures explaining this deteriorating output–inflation tradeoff can be found in Parkin (1984, chapter 27).

10 In fact, both groups also have comparable GMAT scores. The only differences between the groups are (i) the 'Executive' programme meets during the day on alternate Fridays and Saturdays, while the regular 'Evening' programme meets in the evening during the early part of the week, and (ii) the 'Executive' group has been out of school for about 3–4 years longer (on average) than the 'Evening' group.

11 A post-course survey indicated that students overwhelmingly felt that the experiment contributed to a good 'hands-on' understanding of an imperfect information rational expectations model of the economy.

12 The 'Instructions to Participants' are given in the Appendix.

13 While producers acted as price takes facing horizontal demand curves and 'given' market clearing prices, they were, however, unable perfectly to sift out the inflationary and real components of the change in these observed prices by virtue of the unseen nominal and real shocks that constantly buffeted the demand and supply curves.

14 These specific percentages were arrived at simply due to the size constraints on the coding sheets which were used to facilitate the scanning, compiling and averaging of all the output decisions corresponding to each specific observed price.

15 A simple linear transformation of z was chosen to normalise all the real output changes to positive variables.

16 As noted earlier, we abstract from incorporating serial correlation by not carrying forward any inventory from past periods, as the main

focus here is on determining the changing output–inflation tradeoff, and exploring the issue of procyclicality.

17 The authors are grateful to Professor Robert E. Lucas Jr. for suggesting that the reverse direction of change in monetary variance – from the high-variance 'Argentina' case to the relatively low-variance 'US' case – also be tested. Ideally, it would indeed be interesting to test both groups in both directions of monetary variance. However, this was precluded by binding resource constraints such as the availability of assistants and time. Nevertheless, an agenda for a future experimentation (resources permitting), envisions a larger and lengthier experiment with both groups tested in both directions of monetary variance.

18 The reason that the values for R_j obtained here do not coincide with those obtained by substituting values of T^2 and S_j^2 into the expression for R_j is that we have suppressed the relative price elasticity of output, attributed by Lucas to the constant *k*. Here, solving for *k*, we find that *k* lies in the range 0.29 to 0.63.

19 The results for L2 have not been included here. The authors will be glad to send them upon request.

20 Please see Sargent (1993, chapter 3) for an excellent description of the drastic measures adopted by four European inflation-ravaged post-First World War economies in order to make their monetary reforms credible.

21 Once again, the authors are indebted to Professors Lucas and Elizabeth Hoffman for suggesting these interesting extensions for a possible future experiment.

4 PUBLIC CONFIDENCE AND PUBLIC FINANCE DURING THE AMERICAN CIVIL WAR

* The authors thank Sven Arndt, Cheryl Holsey, Mike Kuehlwein and Tom Willett for helpful comments, and would also like to acknowledge generous assistance rendered by Mike Musick of the National Archives in obtaining the Confederate financial data.

1 See Memminger (1862b).

2 Quoted in Morgan (1985, p. 117).

3 The Confederate Currency Reform Act of 17 February 1864 imposed a 33 per cent 'tax' on most Treasury notes not exchanged for bonds by 1 April 1864 (or 1 July 1864 in the case of notes held west of the Mississippi – see Pecquet, 1987). Although the Act was blamed 'for producing a scarcity' (Schwab, 1901, p. 147), Table 4.3 shows that there was actually a slight (temporary) increase in the real money supply between April and October of 1864.

4 In contrast to Lerner's (1955) findings – based on data less comprehensive than that employed by Godfrey (1978) – suggesting that the real money supply peaked in October 1861.

5 San Francisco effectively remained on a gold standard throughout the

Civil War, and peak inflation in wholesale prices was less than half that experienced in New York (Berry, 1984, pp. 144–145).

6 Lerner (1956, p. 174) also quotes Keynes in this context.

7 Furthermore, General Bragg's retreat from Kentucky following the Battle of Perryville on 8 October 1862 ended the threat of invasion in the west – a most disappointing end to an offensive operation that had seen Confederate armies win a victory at Lexington, Kentucky, and even threaten Cincinnati, Ohio.

8 An early harbinger of this may be found in the upsurge in Confederate inflation that seems to follow the battle at Manassas Junction on 21 July 1861 (or Bull Run as it was known in the North). Despite being a Confederate victory, the battle produced then-unprecedented casualties on both sides and gave the first real inklings of the scale of the conflict that would follow. Moreover, the South's failure to follow up that success reduced the Confederate chances for an early defeat of the North (see Burdekin and Langdana, 1992, chapter 3, on the apparent relationship between subsequent military developments and Confederate inflation performance).

9 For more details on Confederate fiscal and monetary policies, see Schwab (1901), Smith (1901), Lerner (1954), Todd (1954), Godfrey (1978), Ball (1991) and Burdekin and Langdana (1993).

10 The Confederate Treasury Reports, unlike those of the North, did not correspond to any fixed fiscal year. The intervals referred to here cover periods ranging from 9 months to 14 months, but have been selected with a view to providing at least some degree of comparability with the periods covered by the Northern Treasury Reports.

11 Excluding the North's lower deficit/expenditure ratio of 37 per cent in the fiscal year ending 30 June 1861 that was influenced by war expenditures only in the final three months or so.

12 Quoted in Todd (1954, p. 34).

13 The '*Trent*' was a British steamer carrying Confederate commissioners Mason and Slidell from Havana, Cuba, to Southampton, England. On 8 November 1861, a US warship intercepted the *Trent* and forcibly removed the Confederate commissioners, who were then imprisoned in the North. When news of this outrage was received in England on 27 November 1861, the British government sent a demand for the surrender of the prisoners and an apology. Intelligence of this threat was received in New York on 16 December 1861, and it was feared at the time that the Northern government's stated determination to retain the prisoners would lead to war. The matter was eventually resolved on 8 January 1862 – with the North agreeing to give up Mason and Slidell.

14 The blockade itself exacerbated the South's specie shortage. Had the blockade been less effective, the 'South would have received more imports at lower prices, exported more cotton, and reduced the outflow of gold and credit' (Ekelund and Thornton, 1992, p. 900).

15 Davis and Pecquet (1990, p. 142) point out that this was, perhaps, only a partial default 'in the sense that there was some chance that a victorious peace would be secured and gold payments resumed'.

16 The Treasury attempted to provide new backing for the Confederate

currency by offering to make bond payments with cotton under the Act of April 1863. Despite success in obtaining subscriptions for the 'cotton-backed' bonds sold in Europe under the Erlanger loan, domestic bond sales were disappointing, however. Of the $100 million of 6 per cent bonds authorised, only just over $8 million worth were disposed of – and those at a lower than expected 50 per cent premium over their face value in paper (Ball, 1991, p. 133).

17 Roll's (1972) finding that gold yields on Federal bonds were extremely sensitive to military events is echoed by Davis and Pecquet's (1990) analysis of the real rates of return on Confederate bonds.

5 DEFICIT FINANCE, EXPECTATIONS AND REAL MONEY BALANCES

* The estimation results included in this chapter were previously presented in Burdekin (1992). The authors thank Sven Arndt and Paul Burkett for helpful comments.

1 This statement was made in the course of an address by Dr Havenstein to the upper house of the German parliament, or Reichsrat, and is quoted in D'Abernon (1927, p. 3). Note that the 'milliards' referred to in the quote are a 'thousand million' – or a 'billion' in today's parlance. The 'thousand milliards' in turn are equivalent to a modern 'trillion'. In this book, we follow the convention of using 'billion' to refer to a 'thousand million'.

2 See Burdekin and Burkett (1992) for an analysis that explicitly incorporates the role of private sector pressure in exacerbating the accelerating monetisation of government and private debt by the Reichsbank.

3 It may be added that, in light of the tendency for money growth (and inflation) to accelerate within the month, the monthly data likely understates the government's ability to capture inflation tax revenue. Week-to-week (or even day-to-day) fluctuations in inflation provide scope for additional revenue gains that may not be fully captured in the monthly data series available for the empirical work.

4 The decree of 15 October established a new 'Rentenbank' that was to commence operations on 15 November 1923. The new 'rentenmark' was set equal to the pre-war gold mark and government credits were to be limited to 1.2 billion rentenmarks. The paper mark continued to circulate in the interim, however, and massive increases in the floating debt provided the basis for a final wave of currency depreciation in October–November 1923. The exchanges finally stabilised amidst moves to restore budgetary balance and the pegging of the paper mark at $US 4,200 billion on 20 November 1923. As this exchange rate was exactly 1,000 billion times higher than the pre-war rate, the paper mark/rentenmark exchange rate was itself fixed at 1,000 billion:1 (see D'Abernon, 1927; Holtfrerich, 1986, chapter 10).

5 The actual extent to which reparation demands contributed to the

German hyperinflation remains a subject of controversy. However, Holtfrerich (1986, p. 150) estimates that the percentage of total expenditures accounted for by expenditures under the Peace Treaty rose from 17.6 per cent in 1920, to 32.7 per cent in 1922, and to 69 per cent in 1923.

6 While government revenues from Reichsbank operations in the pre-war era accounted for only a small percentage of total revenue (ranging between 0.2 per cent and 2.7 per cent over the 1876–1908 period), Banaian (1992) finds that even here there were early indications of causality running from fiscal to monetary policy in Germany. Specifically, 'if the chief determinant of velocity was the discount rate, then the cointegration of velocity and tax rates indicates that in no small part monetary policy was debt service policy' (Banaian, 1992, p. 15).

7 For a critical evaluation of the related literature, and additional references, see Siklos (1990). Elsewhere, some direct evidence on the effects of the German deficits on inflation and exchange rate movements is provided in Burdekin and Langdana (1992, chapter 2).

8 See also Cagan (1991) on this point.

9 Although, given that disaggregated data on total deposits are not available until January 1921, non-government deposits for 1919–1920 are – as suggested by Webb (1985, p. 483) – estimated as 0.67 of total deposits (corresponding to the share they enjoyed in 1921). The basic data on both currency and deposits are obtained from Young (1925, pp. 526–529).

10 Although data on the forward discount is available through 1923:8, inclusion of the extreme tail-end observations would introduce data points for which the elasticity of money demand with respect to inflationary expectations – as based on the forward exchange market – was seen as rising above unity (Cukierman, 1988, p. 39). Other researchers also typically curtail the sample in mid-1923 owing to problems in treating the explosive properties of the latter observations, and Sargent and Wallace (1973), for example, use the same May 1923 end point.

11 For a demonstration that the limit distributions of the unit root test statistics are unaffected by the removal of seasonal means, see Dickey *et al.* (1986, appendix B). It should be added that further addition of a time trend was rejected by the data, while the subtraction of seasonal means makes a constant term redundant in this case.

12 The question of whether the real deficit is itself driven by inflation has been addressed by Webb (1986, p. 59), who concludes that 'an increase of the inflation rate was not significantly correlated with changes in the real value of the deficit'. This point is further corroborated in Webb (1989, chapter 2), with the evidence indicating that any lags in the collection of taxes were dominated by the changes in outlays.

13 The F-statistics for the specification in columns (1)–(6) of Table 5.5 are $F^9_{13}=0.75$; $F^9_{13}=0.78$; $F^9_{12}=1.05$; $F^9_{12}=0.99$; $F^9_{11}=1.04$; and $F^9_{11}=0.97$, respectively. The 10 per cent critical values range from 2.16 to 2.27. (While a few of the news variables do have significant t-statistics in the

individual regressions, there is a mixture of positive and negative signs and little apparent consistency in the indicated effects.)

14 This contrasts, of course, with the quite rapid stabilisation achieved by Germany after the paper mark exchange rate was pegged on 20 November 1923. However, in his well-known comparative analysis of the post-First World War stabilisations, Sargent (1993, p. 75) emphasises that the 'essential measures that ended hyperinflation in Germany, Austria, Hungary and Poland were, first, the creation of an independent central bank that was legally committed to refuse the government's demand for additional unsecured credit and, second, a simultaneous alteration in the fiscal policy regime'. In the German case, the percentage of expenditures that was tax-financed rose from 1 per cent in October 1923 to 46 per cent in December 1923, and reached 100 per cent in March 1924 (see D'Abernon, 1927, pp. 31–32).

6 DOES EXCHANGE RATE PEGGING FOSTER MONETARY CREDIBILITY?

* This chapter builds upon the empirical work published in Burdekin (1994). The authors are grateful to Sven Arndt, Paul Burkett, Cheryl Holsey, Pierre Siklos and Tom Willett for helpful comments.

1 See Lamont (1990, p. 15).

2 It may have been just as well that they gave up when they did. Shilling (1993, p. D2) compares the situation at the beginning of 1993 with that of the 1930s when 'most of the gold bloc held out for five years after the British devaluation of 1931, at great cost to their domestic economies'.

3 Indeed, the Reichsbank attempted to peg the exchange rate in early 1923 in the face of continued fiscal imbalance and debt monetisation, and was forced to abandon this policy within a few weeks.

4 While these findings may be influenced by different trends in the natural rate of unemployment, tests for rising natural rates among the ERM countries have, in fact, generally yielded only inconclusive results (cf. Egebo and Englander, 1992).

5 Owing to data limitations, sample periods for Belgium and Italy are curtailed at in the second quarter of 1989 and the third quarter 1989, respectively. The Netherlands estimation period is restricted to the second quarter of 1974–third quarter of 1989. Finally, the sample periods for Austria, Finland and Sweden end at the first quarter of 1988, fourth quarter of 1987, and second quarter of 1989, respectively.

6 Allowance for the interaction between domestic and foreign money growth implies that the net effect of domestic monetary base growth is sensitive to fluctuations in the average growth rates of US and German money. However, the similarity in the average values of USMB and GEMB before and after the 1979 and 1983 potential breakpoints mitigates against any effect that this might have on the power of the

tests set out below (see Burdekin, 1994, for further analysis of these interaction effects).

7 The basic equations for each country, with the dummy variables included, were estimated simultaneously by generalised least squares (GLS) using the iterative Zellner–Aitken procedure. The stationarity of the data was confirmed by applying the augmented Dickey–Fuller test for unit roots.

8 The coefficient values and standard errors reported in Tables A6.1–A6.6 refer to the sum of the lags on each right-hand-side variable. The standard errors on the coefficient sums are calculated using the heteroscedasticity-consistent covariance matrix available within the Time Series Processor (TSP) software package, and are derived from a Wald test of the restriction that the coefficient sum is insignificantly different from zero. Application of Durbin's *m*-test showed no evidence of serial correlation except in the single case of the Swedish inflation equation (the variables in this equation accordingly being rho-differenced prior to the estimation of the simultaneous equation system for that country).

9 The joint significance of these terms is assessed on the basis of a Wald test.

10 It should be added that the results for the individual equations further show that the limited evidence of post-1979 shifts revealed in the previous system-wide tests itself derives almost exclusively from the wage equations. The post-1979 dummy is negative and significant at the 5 per cent level or better in the wage equations for Belgium, Italy, Austria and Sweden, and is significant at the 10 per cent level for the Netherlands and Finland. As with the overall system-wide findings reported in Tables 6.3 and 6.4, the fact that the non-EMS countries reveal essentially the same pattern as the EMS countries makes it unclear whether or not the limited significance of the post-1979 dummy can really be attributed to an 'EMS effect' (see also Artis and Nachane, 1990; Artis and Ormerod, 1991).

11 This latter effect more than cancels out the positive coefficient on DY*D1979, leaving the net effect negative and significant at the 10 per cent level.

12 While the results for the non-EMS countries provide some evidence of post-1983 improvement in the Phillips curve tradeoffs, nowhere are the results as strong as for the French case discussed above (see Burdekin, 1994, for further analysis).

7 CONSUMER CONFIDENCE IN TODAY'S MACROECONOMY

1 In the United States, private and corporate debt as a percentage of GDP in the first quarter of 1990 was 130 per cent. In four earlier recessions – 1966, 1969, 1973, 1981 – characterised by similar credit crunches, this ratio was always less than 100 per cent.

2 This survey of consumer confidence is compiled at the University of

Michigan's Institute for Social Research. We will compare and contrast this index with that of the Conference Board later in this chapter.

3 In the United States, during May 1992, the Conference Board's measure of consumer confidence jumped 6.5 points to 71.6 on a scale of 100. Meanwhile, in the United Kingdom, better-than-expected industrial production figures for February, March and April 1992 followed three surveys that indicated marked improvements in business confidence.

4 Thanks to low interest rates in 1991–1992, households as well as businesses were able to shed their debt burdens somewhat. The ratio of consumer debt to disposable income in the United States fell from the peak of 21.7 per cent in 1987 to 19 per cent by May 1992. However, this was more than offset by the burgeoning federal government debt.

5 These data were obtained from the *Economic Report of the President*, 1994, table B-79.

6 The implications of the ERM were discussed in Part II.

7 'Investor confidence' and 'producer confidence' are used interchangeably in this volume.

8 Attempts to estimate consumption functions that include some form of consumer sentiment have produced mixed results. Some examples are Tobin (1959), Friend and Adams (1964), Fair (1971), Mishkin (1978), and Throop (1991a, b).

9 In the United States, the Conference Board Index reached its low point in January 1991 while the Michigan index bottomed out in October 1990. The monthly correlation coefficient of the two confidence indices is 0.75. Garner (1991) provides a comparison of these two indices and suggests guidelines for using them as forecasting tools.

10 Please see Leeper (1991) for a review of the three roles of consumer confidence along with an analysis of the predictive power of confidence indices relative to financial data.

11 Also see Keynes (1964, pp. 137–162), and Howitt and McAfee (1992).

12 The University of Michigan's confidence index, for example, is used in the Data Resources Incorporated (DRI) model of the US economy as a determinant of activity in the housing market.

13 See Throop (1991a,b, 1992) for a review of research on the factors affecting consumer sentiment and the mechanisms linking fluctuations in sentiment to economic activity via changes in spending on durable goods.

14 The minutes of the Federal Open Market Committee on 18 December 1990 seem to indicate that the Federal Reserve endorses the role of consumer sentiment as a catalyst by indicating that even if the Persian Gulf situation were settled 'the degree of confidence needed to induce substantial upturn in spending was not assured' (Board of Governors, 1991, pp. 7–8; Leeper, 1991).

8 CONSUMER CONFIDENCE AND THE OPTIMAL TIMING OF EFFECTIVE MONETARY STABILISATION

* The authors gratefully acknowledge comments and suggestions from Professors William Baumol, Alan Blinder and the participants of the Eastern Economic Association Conference, New York, 1992. Financial assistance was generously provided by the Rutgers New Jersey Center for Research in Financial Institutions, and the Rutgers GSM Research Resources Committee.

1 The origins of the discretionary policy ineffectiveness proposition of the new classical theory can be traced to Lucas (1972, 1973) and Sargent and Wallace (1975).

2 In addition, there exists the hyperinflation literature linking fiscal profligacy to endogenised money growth. (See Chapter 5 of this volume as well as Burdekin and Langdana, 1992, chapter 2.)

3 The record drop in the University of Michigan's consumer sentiment index between August and October 1990, as discussed in the previous chapter, led some analysts to label the US recession of 1990–1991 as being 'confidence-driven'.

4 In fact, this relates closely to Dunning (1991) where the government does indeed have the ability to affect competitiveness (and eventually aggregate output) by changing the 'economic climate' which, in turn, is accomplished by influencing changes in 'attitudes, values, and wealth creating ethos'.

5 This paper was instrumental in spawning the real business cycle (RBC) literature. Some formative RBC papers are King and Plosser (1984), Long and Plosser (1983), and Kydland and Prescott (1982).

6 The model implemented here is in contrast to the optimising 'real' models of macroeconomic policy analysis (see Sargent, 1987). These 'real' models differ from the present model in that the interactions between fiscal and monetary policies are of central importance in this economy incorporating both government outlays and money creation.

7 Perloff and Wachter (1979) and Alexander (1990) incorporate discretionary fiscal policy components in the specification of consumer confidence. In the latter study, fiscal policy involving changes in taxes as well as in transfer payments (subsidy payments to German coal, steel and shipbuilding, for example) causes changes in the shift component of labour demand which, in turn, affects potential output. The inclusion of such fiscal components in the endogenised consumer confidence term, however, renders the present model intractable.

8 Individuals here have rational expectations – they use all the information available to them in an efficient manner (as discussed in Chapter 7) to form conditional forecasts of the implications of the observed price levels.

9 The asymmetry between labour demand and labour supply is attributed to the greater sensitivity of demanders of labour to the current and expected future states of the economy and fiscal policies, relative to labour supply. The idea that labour supply adjusts relatively slowly to

changes in demand for labour has a long history in neoclassical economic history; see, for example, Marshall (1959).

10 The long-run trend of consumer confidence can be easily obtained from one of the two major measures of consumer confidence derived from large-scale surveys of US households – the University of Michigan's Index of Consumer Sentiment and the Conference Board's Consumer Confidence Index.

9 CONSUMER CONFIDENCE AND DOMESTIC FISCAL STABILISATION

* The authors are grateful to Professors William J. Baumol and Alan S. Blinder for comments and suggestions. The research was funded by a grant from the Research Resources Committee of Rutgers GSM.

1 A brief review of the policy ineffectiveness proposition can be found in the previous chapter.

2 Some formative RBC papers include King and Plosser (1984), Long and Plosser (1983), and Kydland and Prescott (1982, 1990). Also see Plosser (1989) and Mankiw (1989) for an excellent review and critique, respectively, of RBC models.

3 Dornbusch concludes that the Mexican macroeconomic performance from 1980 to 1987 would require a '*favorable* productivity shock of at least 20 percent' (p. 145), which is clearly a difficult proposition to sell.

4 The New Keynesian economics emerged in the late 1970s with significant early contributions by Fischer (1977) and Taylor (1979). Here, rigidities in nominal wage and price adjustments due to long-term contracting (discussed earlier in this chapter), for example, are found to void the policy irrelevance proposition in rational expectations economies.

5 As discussed in Chapter 7, the University of Michigan's Consumer Sentiment Index recorded the largest drop in any 3-month period in its 44-year history from August to October 1990.

6 An excellent review allowing this model to be contrasted with the RBC world in which labour demand (and hence employment and potential output) is shifted by technology shocks can be found in Hall and Taylor (1991, chapters 4 and 13).

7 The introduction of the money supply M_t in the confidence term of labour demand (1) (along with G_t) does not change our result of output neutrality with respect to a systematic anticipated change in money growth. Discretionary monetary policy is found to leave the real wage, and hence employment and output, unchanged, along the lines of the attempted monetary stabilisation in the final stages of the confidence-driven recession detailed in the previous chapter. The authors are grateful to Alan Blinder for his comments pertaining to the absence of money in the labour demand function.

8 We abstract here from the adverse effects on confidence that might stem from any movement into deficit as government spending

increases. The experiment in Chapter 2 suggested that only a sustainable sequence of deficits was likely to shore up agents' confidence. If this model were applied to the 1990s US case, therefore, the possibility of such negative responses would have to be explicitly taken into account.

9 We ignore efficiency losses, cost of deficits, etc.

10 Allowing labour demand to be independent of discretionary government spending by setting $k_3 = 0$ produces intriguing results; the real wage is not found to be independent of increases of g_t. This inconsistency is resolved with the caveat that k_3 be non-zero. If k_3 were indeed set equal to zero, then by definition, any increases in government spending – no matter how discretionary – would not be incorporated in individual's information sets, and would therefore have to be construed as non-discretionary demand-side shocks. When treated in this fashion we find that $dw_t/dv_t^d > dp_t/dv_t^d$, or the real wage does indeed 'blip' up with an increase in government outlays. Once again, the authors are indebted to Alan Blinder for the caveat that k_3 be non-zero.

11 This result is perfectly consistent with the discretionary monetary policy irrelevance of the new classical school (Glick and Hutchinson, 1990, is a good recent example). It should be noted, however, that any nominal wage–price adjustment rigidity due to, for example, long-term contracts or imperfect information, would produce real results. See Blinder and Choi (1990) for an interview survey examining wage-setter's reactions to macroeconomic theories of wage stickiness. Thus, the effectiveness of monetary policy becomes, in this context, a purely empirical question pertaining to the degree of imperfection in the labour market.

12 In fact, Prescott (1986) stresses that demand-side shocks must indeed play a greater role than that postulated in the early RBC models. More recently, King *et al.* (1991, p. 819) find that the inclusion of nominal variables in a large class of RBC models indicates that permanent productivity shocks 'typically explain less than half of the business-cycle variability in output, consumption, and investment'.

Bibliography

Akaike, H. (1974) 'A new look at statistical model identification', *IEEE Transactions on Automatic Control*, AC-19: 716–723.

Alexander, V. (1990) 'Fiscal policy and potential output in a model with rational expectations', *Weltwirtschaftliches Archiv*, 126: 432–455.

Aoki, M. and Canzoneri, M. (1979) 'Reduced forms of rational expectations models', *Quarterly Journal of Economics*, 93: 59–71.

Artis, M.J. and Nachane, D. (1990) 'Wages and prices in Europe: a test of the German leadership hypothesis', *Weltwirtschaftliches Archiv*, 126: 59–77.

Artis, M.J. and Ormerod, P. (1991) 'Is there an "EMS" effect in European labour markets?', Discussion Paper No. 598, Centre for Economic Policy Research, London.

Augusta Chronicle (1882) 'Confederate bonds: another boom in past due coupons and old securities', 19 September.

Balderston, T. (1989) 'War finance and inflation in Britain and Germany, 1914–1918', *Economic History Review*, 42: 222–244.

Balderston, T. (1991) 'German banking between the wars: the crisis of the credit banks', *Business History Review*, 65: 554–605.

Ball, D.B. (1991) *Financial Failure and Confederate Defeat*, Urbana, IL: University of Illinois Press.

Banaian, K. (1992) 'Tax smoothing, discount rates, velocity, and the gold standard in prewar Germany', mimeo, St. Cloud State University.

Banaian, K. (1995) 'Inflation and optimal seignorage in the CIS and Eastern Europe', in T.D. Willett, R.C.K. Burdekin, R.J. Sweeney and C. Wihlborg (eds), *Establishing Monetary Stability in Emerging Market Economies*, Boulder, CO: Westview Press, forthcoming.

Banaian, K., Burdekin, R.C.K. and Willett, T.D. (1995) 'On the political economy of central bank independence', in K.D. Hoover and S.M. Sheffrin (eds), *Monetarism and the Methodology of Economics: Essays in Honor of Thomas Mayer*, Brookfield, VT: Edward Elgar.

Barro, R.J. (1974) 'Are government bonds net wealth?', *Journal of Political Economy*, 82: 1095–1117.

Barro, R.J. (1978a) *The Impact of Social Security on Private Saving: Evidence from the US Time Series*, Washington, DC: American Enterprise Institute for Public Policy Research.

Barro, R.J. (1978b) 'Unanticipated money, output, and the price level in the United States', *Journal of Political Economy*, 86: 549–580.

Barro, R.J. (1980) 'A capital market in an equilibrium business cycle model', *Econometrica*, 48: 1393–1417.

Barro, R.J. (1984) *Macroeconomics*, New York: John Wiley.

Barro, R.J. (1989) 'The Ricardian approach to budget deficits', *Journal of Economic Perspectives*, 3: 37–54.

Barro, R.J. (1992) 'Keynes is still dead', *Wall Street Journal*, 29 October.

Belongia, M.T. and Chrystal, K.A. (1990) 'The pitfalls of exchange rate targeting: a case study from the United Kingdom', *Federal Reserve Bank of St. Louis Review*, 72: 15–24.

Bernheim, B.D. (1989) 'A neoclassical perspective on budget deficits', *Journal of Economic Perspectives*, 3: 55–72.

Bernholz, P. (1988a) 'Inflation, monetary regime and the financial asset theory of money', *Kyklos*, 41: 5–34.

Bernholz, P. (1988b) 'Hyperinflation and currency reform in Bolivia: studied from a general perspective', *Journal of Institutional and Theoretical Economics*, 144: 747–771.

Berry, T.S. (1984) *Early California: Gold, Prices, Trade*, Bostwick Paper No. 4, Richmond, VA: The Bostwick Press.

Bigelow, J. (1888) *France and the Confederate Navy, 1862–1868: An International Episode*, New York: Harper & Brothers.

Bivens, M. (1994) 'Two Baltic nations look west and east for their fortunes', *Los Angeles Times*, 15 March.

Blinder, A.S. and Choi, D.H. (1990) 'A shred of evidence on theories of wage stickiness', *Quarterly Journal of Economics*, 105: 1003–1015.

Blinder, A.S. and Deaton, A.S. (1985) 'The time series consumption function revisited', *Brookings Papers on Economic Activity*, No. 2: 465–521.

Board of Governors of the Federal Reserve System (1991) *Record of Policy Actions of the Federal Open Market Committee Meeting Held on December 18, 1990*, Washington, DC.

Bofinger, P. (1993) 'The output decline in Central and Eastern Europe: a classical explanation', Discussion Paper No. 784, Centre for Economic Policy Research, London.

Bresser Pereira, L. and Dall'Acqua, F. (1991) 'Economic populism versus Keynes: reinterpreting budget deficit in Latin America', *Journal of Post Keynesian Economics*, 14: 29–38.

Buchanan, J.M. (1958) *Public Principles of Public Debt*, Homewood, IL: Irwin.

Burdekin, R.C.K. (1989) 'International transmission of US macroeconomic policy and the inflation record of Western Europe', *Journal of International Money and Finance*, 8: 401–423.

Burdekin, R.C.K. (1992) 'Government budget deficits and real money balances in Germany, 1920–1923', *Economic Notes*, 21: 258–264.

Burdekin, R.C.K. (1994) 'Inflation, output and wages in Europe, 1971–1989: did membership in the European Monetary System matter?', Rivista Internazionale di Scienze Economiche e Commerciali, 41: 827–852.

Burdekin, R.C.K. (1995a) 'Budget deficits and inflation: the importance of budgetary controls for monetary stability', in T.D. Willett, R.C.K.

Burdekin, R.J. Sweeney and C. Wihlborg (eds), *Establishing Monetary Stability in Emerging Market Economies*, Boulder, CO: Westview Press, forthcoming.

Burdekin, R.C.K. and Burkett, P. (1992) 'Money, credit, and wages in hyperinflation: post-World War I Germany', *Economic Inquiry*, 30: 479–495 [reprinted in P.L. Siklos (ed.), *Great Inflations of the Twentieth Century: Theories, Policies and Evidence*, Brookfield, VT: Edward Elgar, forthcoming].

Burdekin, R.C.K. and Burkett, P. (1995) *Distributional Conflict and Inflation: Theoretical and Historical Perspectives*, London: Macmillan, forthcoming.

Burdekin, R.C.K. and Laney, L.O. (1988) 'Fiscal policymaking and the central bank institutional constraint', *Kyklos*, 41: 647–662.

Burdekin, R.C.K. and Langdana, F.K. (1992) *Budget Deficits and Economic Performance*, London: Routledge.

Burdekin, R.C.K. and Langdana, F.K. (1993) 'War finance in the Southern Confederacy, 1861–1865', *Explorations in Economic History*, 30: 352–376.

Burdekin, R.C.K.; Westbrook, J.R. and Willett, T.D. (1994) 'Exchange rate pegging as a disinflation strategy: evidence from the European Monetary System', in P.L. Siklos (ed.) *Varieties of Monetary Reform: Lessons and Experiences on the Road to Monetary Union*, Dordrecht, Netherlands: Kluwer Academic Publishers.

Burdekin, R.C.K.; Westbrook, J.R. and Willett, T.D. (1995) 'The political economy of discretionary monetary policy: a public choice analysis of proposals for reform', in R.H. Timberlake and K. Dowd (eds), *Money and the Nation State*, Oakland, CA: The Independent Institute, forthcoming.

Buyske, G. (1993) 'Estonia, monetary model for Russia', *Wall Street Journal*, 29 June.

Cadsby, C.B. and Frank, M. (1991) 'Experimental tests of Ricardian equivalence', *Economic Inquiry*, 29: 645–664.

Cagan, P. (1956) 'The monetary dynamics of hyperinflation', in M. Friedman (ed.), *Studies in the Quantity Theory of Money*, Chicago, IL: University of Chicago Press.

Cagan, P. (1991) 'Expectations in the German hyperinflation revisited', *Journal of International Money and Finance*, 10: 552–560.

Calomiris, C.W. (1988a) 'Institutional failure, monetary scarcity, and the depreciation of the continental', *Journal of Economic History*, 48: 47–68.

Calomiris, C.W. (1988b) 'Price and exchange rate determination during the greenback suspension', *Oxford Economic Papers*, 40: 719–750.

Calomiris, C.W. (1991) 'The motives of US debt-management policy, 1790–1880: efficient discrimination and time consistency', *Research in Economic History*, 13: 67–105.

Capers, H.D. (1893) *The Life and Times of C.G. Memminger*, Richmond, VA: Everett Waddey.

Choudhary, M.A.S. and Parai, A.K. (1991) 'Budget deficit and inflation: the Peruvian experience', *Applied Economics*, 23: 1117–1121.

Collins, S.M. (1988) 'Inflation and the European Monetary System', in F. Giavazzi, S. Micossi and M. Miller (eds), *The European Monetary System*, Cambridge: Cambridge University Press.

Collins, S.M. and Giavazzi, F. (1992) 'Attitudes towards inflation and the viability of fixed exchange rates: evidence from the EMS', Working Paper No. 4057, National Bureau of Economic Research, Cambridge, MA.

Corsetti, G. and Roubini, N. (1991) 'Fiscal deficits, public debt, and government solvency: evidence from OECD countries', *Journal of the Japanese and International Economies*, 5: 354–380.

Cozier, B.V. (1986) 'A model of output fluctuations in a small specialized economy', *Journal of Money, Credit, and Banking*, 18: 179–190.

Cukierman, A. (1988) 'Rapid inflation – deliberate policy or miscalculation?', in K. Brunner and A.H. Meltzer (eds), *Money, Cycles, and Exchange Rates: Essays in Honor of Allan H. Meltzer*, Amsterdam: North-Holland.

Cukierman, A.; Edwards, S. and Tabellini, G. (1992) 'Seignorage and political instability', *American Economic Review*, 82: 537–555.

D'Abernon, Right Hon. Viscount (1927) 'German currency: its collapse and recovery, 1920–26', *Journal of the Royal Statistical Society*, 90: 1–40.

Dalamagas, B.A. (1992) 'How rival are the Ricardian Equivalence Proposition and the fiscal policy potency view?', *Scottish Journal of Political Economy*, 39: 457–476.

Dalamagas, B. (1993) 'Fiscal illusion and the level of indebtedness: an international comparison', *South African Journal of Economics*, 61: 45–58.

Davidson, R.; Godfrey, L. and MacKinnon, J.G. (1985) 'A simplified version of the differencing test', *International Economic Review*, 26: 639–647.

Davis, G.K. and Pecquet, G.M. (1990) 'Interest rates in the Civil War South', *Journal of Economic History*, 50: 133–148.

De Grauwe, P. (1989) 'Disinflation in the EMS and in the non-EMS countries. What have we learned?', *Empirica*, 16: 161–176.

De Haan, J. and Zelhorst, D. (1990) 'The impact of government deficits on money growth in developing countries', *Journal of International Money and Finance*, 9: 455–469.

Dewey, D.R. (1934) *Financial History of the United States*, 12th edition, New York: Longmans, Green & Company.

Dickey, D.A.; Bell, W.R. and Miller, R.B. (1986) 'Unit roots in time series models: tests and implications', *American Statistician*, 40: 12–26.

Dornbusch, R. (1990) 'The new classical macroeconomics and stabilization policy', *American Economic Review*, Papers and Proceedings, 80: 143–147.

Dornbusch, R. and Fischer, S. (1993) 'Moderate inflation', *World Bank Economic Review*, 7: 1–44.

Dornbusch, R.; Sturzenegger, F. and Wolf, R. (1990) 'Extreme inflation: dynamics and stabilization', *Brookings Papers on Economic Activity*, No. 2: 1–84.

Dunning, J. (1991) 'Governments, economic organizations, and international competitiveness', in L.G. Mattsson and B. Stymne (eds), *Corporate and Industry Strategies in Europe*, Amsterdam: Elsevier Science Publishers.

Eaton, C. (1954) *A History of the Southern Confederacy*, New York: Macmillan.

Eckstein, O. (1983) *The DRI Model of the United States Economy*, New York: McGraw-Hill.

Economic Report of the President (1994), Washington, DC: US Government Printing Office.

The Economist (1994) 'Schools brief: a cruise around the Phillips curve', 19 February.

Edwards, S. (1993) 'Exchange rates as nominal anchors', *Weltwirtschaftliches Archiv*, 129: 1–32.

Edwards, S. and Tabellini, G. (1991) 'Fiscal policies and inflation in developing countries', *Journal of International Money and Finance*, 10: S16–S48.

Egebo, T. and Englander, A.S. (1992) 'Institutional commitments and policy credibility: a critical survey and empirical evidence from the ERM', *OECD Economic Studies*, 18: 45–84.

Ekelund, R.B., Jr. and Thornton, M. (1992) 'The Union blockade and demoralization of the South: relative prices in the Confederacy', *Social Science Quarterly*, 73: 890–902.

Evans, P. (1985) 'Do large deficits produce high interest rates?', *American Economic Review*, 75: 68–87.

Evans, P. (1987) 'Interest rates and expected future budget deficits in the United States', *Journal of Political Economy*, 95: 34–58.

Evans, P. (1991) 'Is Ricardian equivalence a good approximation?', *Economic Inquiry*, 29: 626–644.

Fair, R.C. (1971) *A Short-Run Forecasting Model of the United States Economy*, Lexington, MA: Heath Lexington Books.

Farley, J.U. and Hinich, M.J. (1970) 'A test for a shifting slope coefficient in a linear model', *Journal of the American Statistical Association*, 65: 1320–1329.

Feldman, G.D. (1993) *The Great Disorder: Politics, Economics, and Society in the German Inflation, 1914–1924*, New York: Oxford University Press.

Feldstein, M. (1982) 'Government deficits and aggregate demand', *Journal of Monetary Economics*, 9: 1–20.

Fernández, R.B. (1991) 'What have populists learned from hyperinflation?', in R. Dornbusch and S. Edwards (eds.), *The Macroeconomics of Populism in Latin America*, Chicago, IL: University of Chicago Press.

Fischer, A.M. (1993) 'Inflation targeting: the New Zealand and Canadian cases', *Cato Journal*, 13: 1–27.

Fischer, S. (1977) 'Long-term contracts, rational expectations, and the optimal money supply rule', *Journal of Political Economy*, 85: 191–206.

Fratianni, M. and von Hagen, J. (1992) *The European Monetary System and European Monetary Union*, Boulder, CO: Westview Press.

Frenkel, J.A. (1977) 'The forward exchange rate, expectations, and the demand for money: the German hyperinflation', *American Economic Review*, 67: 653–670.

Friedman, M. (1968) 'The role of monetary policy', *American Economic Review*, 58: 1–17.

Friedman, M. (1971) 'Government revenue from inflation', *Journal of Political Economy*, 79: 846–856.

Friedman, M. (1977) 'Nobel lecture: inflation and unemployment', *Journal of Political Economy*, 85: 451–472.

Friedman, M. and Schwartz, A.J. (1963) *A Monetary History of the United States, 1867–1960*, Princeton, NJ: Princeton University Press.

Friend, I. and Adams, F.G. (1964) 'The predictive ability of consumer attitudes, stock prices, and non-attitudinal variables', *Journal of the American Statistical Association*, 59: 987–1005.

Fuhrer, J.C. (1993) 'What role does consumer sentiment play in the US macroeconomy?', *New England Economic Review*, January/February: 32–44.

Fuller, W.A. (1976) *Introduction to Statistical Time Series*, New York: John Wiley.

Garner, C.A. (1991) 'Forecasting consumer spending: should economists pay attention to consumer confidence surveys?', Federal Reserve Bank of Kansas City, *Economic Review*, 76: 57–71.

Gáspár, P. (1993) 'The fiscal consequences of economic transition in Eastern-European economies', Working Paper, Institute for World Economics, Budapest, Hungary.

Gentry, J.F. (1970) 'A Confederate success in Europe: the Erlanger loan', *Journal of Southern History*, 36: 157–188.

Giavazzi, F. and Giovannini, A. (1989) *Limiting Exchange Rate Flexibility: The European Monetary System*, Cambridge, MA: MIT Press.

Giavazzi, F. and Pagano, M. (1988) 'The advantage of tying one's hands: EMS discipline and central bank credibility', *European Economic Review*, 32: 1055–1082.

Giovannini, A. (1990) 'European monetary reform: progress and prospects', *Brookings Papers on Economic Activity*, No. 2: 217–291.

Glick, R. and Hutchison, M. (1990) 'New results in support of the fiscal policy ineffectiveness proposition', *Journal of Money, Credit, and Banking*, 22: 288–394.

Godfrey, J.M. (1978) *Monetary Expansion in the Confederacy*, New York: Arno Press.

Goldberg, C. (1992) 'As "dollarization" grows, Russians disdain the ruble', *Los Angeles Times*, 27 November.

Goldberg, L.S. (1992) 'Moscow black markets and official markets for foreign exchange: how much flexibility in flexible rates?', Working Paper No. 4040, National Bureau of Economic Research, Cambridge, MA.

Goldberg, L.S.; Ickes, B. and Ryterman, R. (1993) 'Departures from the ruble area: the political economy of adopting independent currencies', paper presented at the Conference on 'Markets, States and Democracy: The Transformation of Communist Regimes in Eastern Europe and the Former Soviet Union', University of California at Berkeley.

Gordon, R.J. (1982) 'Price inertia and policy ineffectiveness in the United States, 1890–1980', *Journal of Political Economy*, 90: 1087–1117.

Granger, C.W.J. (1986) 'Developments in the study of cointegrated economic variables', *Oxford Bulletin of Economics and Statistics*, 48: 213–228.

Gray, J.A. (1976) 'Wage indexation: a macroeconomic approach', *Journal of Monetary Economics*, 2: 221–235.

Guinnane, T.W.; Rosen, H.S. and Willard, K.L. (1993) 'Turning points in the Civil War: views from the greenback market', mimeo, Yale University and Princeton University.

Haberler, G. von (1939) *Prosperity and Depression: A Theoretical Analysis of Cyclical Movements*, Geneva: League of Nations.

Hakkio, C.S. and Rush, M. (1991) 'Is the budget deficit "too large?"', *Economic Inquiry*, 29: 429–445.

Hall, K.G. (1993) 'Experts laud Mexico's proposal for autonomous central bank', *Journal of Commerce and Commercial*, Pacific Edition, 19 May.

Hall, R.E. and Taylor, J.B. (1991) *Macroeconomics*, 3rd edition, New York: W.W. Norton.
Hammond, B. (1961) 'The North's empty purse, 1861–1862', *American Historical Review*, 67: 1–18.
Hanke, S.H.; Jonung, L. and Schuler, K. (1993) *Russian Currency and Finance: A Currency Board Approach to Reform*, London: Routledge.
Hausman, J.A. (1978) 'Specification tests in econometrics', *Econometrica*, 46: 1251–1271.
Herz, B. and Röger, W. (1992) 'The EMS is a greater Deutschmark area', *European Economic Review*, 36: 1413–1425.
Heymann, D. and Sanguinetti, P. (1994) 'Fiscal inconsistencies and high inflation', *Journal of Development Economics*, 43: 85–104.
Hochreiter, E. (1995) 'Central banking in economies in transition', in T.D. Willett, R.C.K. Burdekin, R.J. Sweeney and C. Wihlborg (eds), *Establishing Monetary Stability in Emerging Market Economies*, Boulder, CO: Westview Press, forthcoming.
Hochreiter, E. and Winckler, G. (1994) 'Signaling a hard currency strategy: the case of Austria', *Kredit und Kapital*, 27: in press.
Holtfrerich, C.-L. (1986) *The German Inflation 1914–1923: Causes and Effects in International Perspective*, Berlin: Walter de Gruyter.
Hoover, K.D. and Sheffrin, S.M. (1992) 'Causation, spending, and taxes: sand in the sandbox or tax collector for the welfare state?', *American Economic Review*, 82: 225–248.
Howitt, P. and McAfee, R.P. (1992) 'Animal spirits', *American Economic Review*, 82: 493–507.
Jacobs, R.L. (1977) 'Hyperinflation and the supply of money', *Journal of Money, Credit, and Banking*, 9: 287–303.
Jones, J.D. and Joulfaian, D. (1991) 'Federal government expenditures and revenues in the early years of the American Republic: evidence from 1792 to 1860', *Journal of Macroeconomics*, 13: 133–155.
Juster, F.T. and Wachtel, P. (1972) 'Anticipatory and objective models of durable goods demand', *American Economic Review*, 62: 564–579.
Katona, G. (1942) *War Without Inflation: The Psychological Approach to Problems of War Economy*, New York: Columbia University Press.
Katona, G. (1975) *Psychological Economics*, Amsterdam: Elsevier Scientific Publishing Company.
Katona, G. and Mueller, E. (1953) *Consumer Attitudes and Demand, 1950–1952*, Ann Arbor, MI: University of Michigan Press.
Katsimbris, G.M. and Miller, S.M. (1993) 'Interest rate linkages within the European Monetary System: further analysis', *Journal of Money, Credit, and Banking*, 25: 771–779.
Keil, M.W. (1993) 'A model of speculative efficiency with "news" error components', *Applied Economics*, 25: 1293–1300.
Kelly, D. (1990) 'The plunge in confidence will hit spending – but how hard?', *DRI/McGraw-Hill US Review*, September: 17–21.
Keynes, J.M. (1924) *Monetary Reform*, New York: Harcourt, Brace and Company.
Keynes, J.M. (1964) *The General Theory of Employment, Interest, and Money*, New York: Harcourt Brace Jovanovich.

Kiguel, M.A. and Liviatan, N. (1991) 'The inflation-stabilization cycles in Argentina and Brazil', in M. Bruno, S. Fischer, E. Helpman and N. Liviatan (eds), *Lessons of Economic Stabilization and Its Aftermath*, Cambridge, MA: MIT Press.

King, R.G. and Plosser, C.I. (1984) 'Money, credit, and prices in a real business cycle', *American Economic Review*, 74: 363–380.

King, R.G.; Plosser, C.I.; Stock, J.H. and Watson, M.W. (1991) 'Stochastic trends and economic fluctuations', *American Economic Review*, 81: 819–840.

Kormendi, R.C. and Meguire, P. (1990) 'Government debt, government spending, and private sector behavior: reply and update', *American Economic Review*, 80: 604–617.

Kretzmer, P.E. (1992) 'Monetary vs. fiscal policy: new evidence on an old debate', Federal Reserve Bank of Kansas City, *Economic Review*, 77: 21–30.

Kydland, F.E. and Prescott, E.C. (1982) 'Time to build and aggregate fluctuations', *Econometrica*, 50: 1345–1370.

Kydland, F.E. and Prescott, E.C. (1990) 'Business cycles: real facts and a monetary myth', *Federal Reserve Bank of Minneapolis Quarterly Review*, 14: 3–18.

Lamont, N. (1990) 'Devalue? We cannot bow to the siren voices', *The Mail on Sunday*, 30 December.

Langdana, F.K. (1990) *Sustaining Budget Deficits in Open Economies*, London: Routledge.

Langdana, F.K. (1994) 'An experimental verification of the Lucas "islands" approach to business cycles', *Journal of Economic Behavior and Organization*, 25: 271–280.

Langdana, F.K. and Mellon, G. (1992) 'Fiscal and monetary stabilization in a confidence-driven rational expectations economy', mimeo, Graduate School of Management, Rutgers University-Newark.

Lastrapes, W.D. and Koray, F. (1990) 'International transmission of aggregate shocks under fixed and flexible exchange rate regimes: United Kingdom, France, and Germany, 1959 to 1985', *Journal of International Money and Finance*, 9: 402–423.

Laumas, G.S. (1991) 'Impact of monetary and fiscal policies on real output', *Eastern Economic Journal*, 17: 157–163.

Leeper, E.M. (1991) 'Consumer attitudes and business cycles', Working Paper No. 91-11, Federal Reserve Bank of Atlanta.

Lerner, E.M. (1954) 'The monetary and fiscal programs of the Confederate government, 1861–65', *Journal of Political Economy*, 62: 506–522.

Lerner, E.M. (1955) 'Money, prices, and wages in the Confederacy, 1861–65', *Journal of Political Economy*, 63: 20–40.

Lerner, E.M. (1956) 'Inflation in the Confederacy, 1861–65', in M. Friedman (ed.), *Studies in the Quantity Theory of Money*, Chicago, IL: University of Chicago Press.

Lewarne, S. (1993) *Assessment and Analysis of the Macroeconomic, Financial, and Fiscal Sector Environment in the Kyrgyz Republic*, report submitted to the United States Agency for International Development, Almaty, Kazakhstan.

Lewarne, S. (1995) 'The Russian central bank and the conduct of monetary policy', in T.D. Willett, R.C.K. Burdekin, R.J. Sweeney and C. Wihlborg (eds), *Establishing Monetary Stability in Emerging Market Economies*, Boulder, CO: Westview Press, forthcoming.

Livermore, T.L. (1900) *Numbers and Losses in the Civil War in America*, Boston, MA: Houghton Mifflin.

Long, J.B. and Plosser, C.I. (1983) 'Real business cycles', *Journal of Political Economy*, 91: 1345–1370.

Long, W.R. (1993) 'Brazil announces plan to slash inflation, cut spending', *Los Angeles Times*, 8 December.

Lucas, R.E., Jr. (1972) 'Expectations and the neutrality of money', *Journal of Economic Theory*, 4: 103–124.

Lucas, R.E., Jr. (1973) 'Some international evidence on output-inflation tradeoffs', *American Economic Review*, 63: 326–334.

Lucas, R.E., Jr. (1977) 'Understanding business cycles', in K. Brunner and A.H. Meltzer (eds), *Stabilization of the Domestic and International Economy*, Amsterdam: North-Holland.

Lucas, R.E., Jr. (1981) *Studies in Business-Cycle Theory*, Cambridge, MA: MIT Press.

Lucas, R.E., Jr. (1986) 'Adaptive behavior and economic theory', *Journal of Business*, 59: S401–S426.

McCallum, B.T. (1992) 'Money and prices in colonial America: a new test of competing theories', *Journal of Political Economy*, 100: 143–161.

Maddala, G.S. (1977) *Econometrics*, New York: McGraw-Hill.

Makin, J.H. (1982) 'Anticipated money, inflation uncertainty, and real economic activity', *Review of Economics and Statistics*, 64: 126–134.

Manchester Guardian Commercial (1922) 'An internal gold loan: Germany's new path to stabilisation', 26 October.

Mankiw, N.G. (1989) 'Real business cycles: a new Keynesian perspective', *Journal of Economic Perspectives*, 3: 79–90.

Marshall, A. (1959) *Principles of Economics*, 7th edition, London: Macmillan.

Mastropasqua, C.; Micossi, S. and Rinaldi, R. (1988) 'Interventions, sterilisation and monetary policy in European Monetary System countries, 1979–87', in F. Giavazzi, S. Micossi and M. Miller (eds), *The European Monetary System*, Cambridge: Cambridge University Press.

Mayer, T.; Duesenberry, J.S. and Aliber, R.Z. (1993) *Money, Banking, and the Economy*, 5th edition, New York: W.W. Norton.

Memminger, C.G. (1861a) 'Treasury Report of May 10, 1861', Montgomery, AL (reprinted in Capers, 1893).

Memminger, C.G. (1861b) 'Treasury Report of November 20, 1861', Richmond, VA (reprinted in Capers, 1893).

Memminger, C.G. (1862a) 'Treasury Report of March 14, 1862', Richmond, VA (reprinted in Capers, 1893).

Memminger, C.G. (1862b) 'Treasury Report of August 18, 1862', Richmond, VA (located in the *Confederate Archives*).

Memminger, C.G. (1863a) 'Treasury Report of January 10, 1863', Richmond, VA (reprinted in Capers, 1893).

Memminger, C.G. (1863b) 'Treasury Report of December 7, 1863', Richmond, VA (reprinted in Capers, 1893).

Memminger, C.G. (1864a) 'Treasury Report of May 2, 1864', Richmond, VA (reprinted in Capers, 1893).

Memminger, C.G. (1864b) 'Letter of May 20, 1864 to Senator R.M.T. Hunter' (reprinted in the *Charleston Daily Courier*, 30 May 1864).
Miller, M.; Skidelsky, R. and Weller, P. (1990) 'Fear of deficit financing – is it rational?', in R. Dornbusch and M. Draghi (eds), *Public Debt Management: Theory and History*, Cambridge: Cambridge University Press.
Mishkin, F.S. (1978) 'Consumer sentiment and spending on durable goods', *Brookings Papers on Economic Activity*, No. 1: 217–231.
Mishkin, F.S. (1982a) 'Does anticipated monetary policy matter? An econometric investigation', *Journal of Political Economy*, 90: 22–51.
Mishkin, F.S. (1982b) 'Does anticipated aggregate demand policy matter? Further econometric results', *American Economic Review*, 72: 788–802.
Missale, A. and Blanchard, O.J. (1994) 'The debt burden and debt maturity', *American Economic Review*, 84: 309–319.
Mitchell, W.C (1903) *A History of the Greenbacks, With Special Reference to the Economic Consequences of their Issue: 1862–65*, Chicago, IL: University of Chicago Press.
Mitchell, W.C. (1913) *Business Cycles*, Berkeley, CA: University of California Press.
Mitchell, W.C. (1951) *What Happens During Business Cycles*, New York: National Bureau of Economic Research.
Modigliani, F. and Brumberg, R.E. (1954) 'Utility analysis and the consumption function', in K.K. Kurihara (ed.), *Post-Keynesian Economics*, New Brunswick, NJ: Rutgers University Press.
Modigliani, F. and Sterling, A.G. (1990) 'Government debt, government spending, and private sector behavior: a further comment', *American Economic Review*, 80: 600–603.
Morgan, J.F. (1985) *Graybacks and Gold: Confederate Monetary Policy*, Pensacola, FL: Perdido Bay Press.
Motley, B. (1987) 'Ricardo or Keynes, does the government debt affect consumption?', Federal Reserve Bank of San Francisco, *Economic Review*, Winter: 47–62.
Muth, J.F. (1961) 'Rational expectations and the theory of price movements,' *Econometrica*, 29: 315–335.
Nelson, C.R. and Plosser, C.I. (1982) 'Trends and random walks in macroeconomic time series', *Journal of Monetary Economics*, 10: 139–162.
Newcomb, S. (1865) *A Critical Examination of our Financial Policy during the Southern Rebellion*, New York: D. Appleton and Company.
New York Times (1882a) 'Rebel bonds sold in Charleston', 29 October.
New York Times (1882b) 'Sales of Confederate bonds', 11 November.
The Numismatist (1920) 'Confederate paper money in Berlin', September: 411.
The Numismatist (1921) 'Russians victimized with Confederate notes', February: 53–54.
O'Driscoll, G.P. (1977) 'The Ricardian nonequivalence theorem', *Journal of Political Economy*, 85: 207–210.
Parkin, M. (1984) *Macroeconomics*, Englewood Cliffs, NJ: Prentice-Hall.
Pazos, F. (1990) 'Runaway inflation: experiences and options', *CEPAL Review*, 42: 115–130.
Pecquet, G.M. (1987) 'Money in the Trans-Mississippi Confederacy and the

Confederate Currency Reform Act of 1864', *Explorations in Economic History*, 24: 218–243.
Perloff, J.M. and Wachter, M.J. (1979) 'A production function-nonaccelerating inflation approach to potential output', in K. Brunner and A.H. Meltzer (eds), *Three Aspects of Policy Making: Knowledge, Data, and Institutions*, Amsterdam: North-Holland.
Phelps, E.S. (1968) 'Money wage dynamics and labor market equilibrium', *Journal of Political Economy*, 76: 678–711.
Phelps, E.S. and Taylor, J.B. (1977) 'Stabilizing powers of monetary policy under rational expectations', *Journal of Political Economy*, 85: 163–190.
Phillips, A.W. (1958) 'The relation between unemployment and the rate of change of money wage rates in the United Kingdom, 1861–1957', *Economica*, 25: 283–299.
Phillips, G.D.A. and McCabe, B.P. (1983) 'The independence of tests for structural change in regression models', *Economics Letters*, 12: 283–287.
Pigou, A.C. (1927) *Industrial Fluctuations*, London: Macmillan.
PlanEcon Report (1993a) Washington, DC, 10 March.
PlanEcon Report (1993b) Washington, DC, 22 March.
PlanEcon Report (1993c) Washington, DC, 5 April.
PlanEcon Report (1993d) Washington, DC, 20 April.
PlanEcon Report (1993e) Washington, DC, 30 April.
PlanEcon Report (1993f) Washington, DC, 23 July.
PlanEcon Report (1993g) Washington, DC, 17 September.
PlanEcon Report (1993h) Washington, DC, 10 December.
Plosser, C.I. (1989) 'Understanding real business cycles', *Journal of Economic Perspectives*, 3: 51–77.
Poterba, J.M. and Summers, L.H. (1987) 'Finite lifetimes and the effects of budget deficits on national saving', *Journal of Monetary Economics*, 20: 369–391.
Prescott, E.C. (1986) 'Response to a skeptic', *Federal Reserve Bank of Minneapolis Quarterly Review*, 10: 28–33.
Ramsdell, C.W. (1944) *Behind the Lines in the Southern Confederacy*, Baton Rouge, LA: Louisiana State University Press.
Rasche, R.H. and Tatom, J.A. (1977) 'Energy resources and potential GNP', *Federal Reserve Bank of St. Louis Review*, 59: 10–24.
Reid, B.G. (1985) 'Aggregate consumption and deficit financing: an attempt to separate permanent from transitory effects', *Economic Inquiry*, 23: 475–486.
Reserve Bank of New Zealand (1993) *Monetary Policy Statement, December 1993*, Wellington, NZ.
Reynolds, A. (1993) 'Monetary reform in Russia: the case for gold', *Cato Journal*, 12: 657–676.
Ricardo, D. (1951) 'Funding system', in P. Sraffa (ed.), *The Works and Correspondence of David Ricardo*, Volume IV, Cambridge: Cambridge University Press.
Roll, R. (1972) 'Interest rates and price expectations during the Civil War', *Journal of Economic History*, 32: 476–498.
Rosett, C. (1994) 'Russia expands use of treasury bills to cover government's deficit spending', *Wall Street Journal*, 21 June.

Roth, A.E. (1988) 'Laboratory experimentation in economics: a methodological review', *Economic Journal*, 98: 974–1031.
Roubini, N. (1991) 'Economic and political determinants of budget deficits in developing countries', *Journal of International Money and Finance*, 10: S49–S72.
Sargent, T.J. (1979) *Macroeconomic Theory*, New York: Academic Press.
Sargent, T.J. (1987) *Dynamic Macroeconomic Theory*, Cambridge, MA: Harvard University Press.
Sargent, T.J. (1993) *Rational Expectations and Inflation*, 2nd edition, New York: Harper Collins.
Sargent, T.J. and Wallace, N. (1973) 'Rational expectations and the dynamics of hyperinflation', *International Economic Review*, 14: 328–350.
Sargent, T.J. and Wallace, N. (1975) '"Rational" expectations, the optimal monetary instrument, and the optimal money supply rule', *Journal of Political Economy*, 83: 241–254.
Sargent, T.J. and Wallace, N. (1981) 'Some unpleasant monetarist arithmetic', *Federal Reserve Bank of Minneapolis Quarterly Review*, 5: 1–17.
Schwab, J.C. (1901) *The Confederate States of America, 1861–1865: A Financial and Industrial History of the South During the Civil War*, New York: Charles Scribner's Sons.
Schwert, G.W. (1987) 'Effects of model specification on tests for unit roots in macroeconomic data', *Journal of Monetary Economics*, 20: 73–103.
Seater, J.J. and Mariano, R.S. (1985) 'New tests of the life cycle and tax discounting hypotheses', *Journal of Monetary Economics*, 15: 195–215.
Sheehan, R.G. (1992) 'US influences on foreign monetary policy', *Journal of Money, Credit, and Banking*, 24: 447–464.
Shilling, A.G. (1993) 'Gold standard breakdown offers a lesson for the EC', *Los Angeles Times*, 31 January.
Siklos, P.L. (1990) 'Hyperinflations: their origins, development and termination', *Journal of Economic Surveys*, 4: 225–248.
Siklos, P.L. (1994) 'Central bank independence in the transitional economies: a preliminary investigation of Hungary, Poland, the Czech and Slovak Republics', in I. Székely and J. Bonin (eds), *Development and Reform of the Financial System in Central and Eastern Europe*, Brookfield, VT: Edward Elgar.
Smith, B.D. (1985a) 'American colonial monetary regimes: the failure of the quantity theory and some evidence in favour of an alternate view', *Canadian Journal of Economics*, 18: 531–565.
Smith, B.D. (1985b) 'Some colonial evidence on two theories of money: Maryland and the Carolinas', *Journal of Political Economy*, 93: 1178–1211.
Smith, E.A. (1901) *The History of the Confederate Treasury*, Harrisburg, PA: Harrisburg Publishing Company.
Smith, V.L. (1982) 'Microeconomic systems as an experimental science', *American Economic Review*, 72: 923–955.
Soellner, F. (1991) 'The inflation tax and its political dimension in developing countries', *Konjunkturpolitik*, 37: 228–241.
Studenski, P. and Krooss, H.E. (1952) *Financial History of the United States: Fiscal, Monetary, Banking, and Tariff, including Financial Administration and State and Local Finance*, New York: McGraw-Hill.

Svensson, L.E.O. (1993) 'The simplest test of inflation target credibility', Working Paper No. 4604, National Bureau of Economic Research, Cambridge, MA.

Sweeney, R.J. (1988) *Wealth Effects and Monetary Theory*, New York: Basil Blackwell.

Tallman, E.W. (1993) 'Inflation: how long has this been going on?', *Federal Reserve Bank of Atlanta Economic Review*, 78: 1–12.

Tanner, J.E. (1979) 'An empirical investigation of tax discounting: a comment', *Journal of Money, Credit, and Banking*, 11: 214–218.

Taylor, J.B. (1979) 'Staggered wage setting in a macro model', *American Economic Review*, Papers and Proceedings, 69: 108–113.

Thornton, D.L. (1990) 'Do government deficits matter?', *Federal Reserve Bank of St. Louis Review*, 72: 25–39.

Throop, A.W. (1991a) 'Consumer sentiment and the economic downturn', *Federal Reserve Bank of San Francisco, Weekly Letter*, 1 March.

Throop, A.W. (1991b) 'Consumer confidence and the outlook for consumer spending', *Federal Reserve Bank of San Francisco, Weekly Letter*, 19 July.

Throop, A.W. (1992) 'Consumer sentiment: its causes and effects', *Federal Reserve Bank of San Francisco, Economic Review*, No. 1: 35–59.

Thursby, J.G. and Schmidt, P. (1977) 'Some properties of tests for specification error in a linear regression model', *Journal of the American Statistical Association*, 72: 635–641.

Tobin, J. (1959) 'On the predictive value of consumer intentions and attitudes', *Review of Economics and Statistics*, 41: 1–11.

Todd, R.C. (1954) *Confederate Finance*, Athens, GA: University of Georgia Press.

Toma, M. (1991) 'World War II, interest rates, and fiscal policy commitments', *Journal of Macroeconomics*, 13: 459–477.

Trehan, B. and Walsh, C. (1988) 'Common trends, the government's budget constraint, and revenue smoothing', *Journal of Economic Dynamics and Control*, 12: 425–444.

Trenholm, G.A. (1864) 'Treasury Report of November 7, 1864', Richmond, Virginia (located in the *Confederate Archives*).

Végh, C.A. (1992) 'Stopping high inflation: an analytical overview', *International Monetary Fund Staff Papers*, 39: 626–695.

von Hagen, J. and Fratianni, M. (1990) 'German dominance in the EMS: evidence from interest rates', *Journal of International Money and Finance*, 9: 358–375.

Webb, S.B. (1985) 'Government debt and inflationary expectations as determinants of the money supply in Germany: 1919–1923', *Journal of Money, Credit, and Banking*, 17: 479–492.

Webb, S.B. (1986) 'Government revenue and spending in Germany, 1919 to 1923', in G.D. Feldman, C.-L. Holtfrerich, G.A. Ritter and P.-C. Witt (eds), *The Adaptation to Inflation*, Berlin: Walter de Gruyter.

Webb, S.B. (1989) *Hyperinflation and Stabilization in Weimar Germany*, New York: Oxford University Press.

Webb, S.B. (1992) 'Four ends of the big inflation in Germany after World War I', in B. Eichengreen (ed.), *Monetary Regime Transformations*, Brookfield, VT: Edward Elgar.

Weber, A.A. (1991) 'Reputation and credibility in the European Monetary System', *Economic Policy*, 12: 58–102.
Wells, G. (1990) 'Economic reform and macroeconomic policy in New Zealand', *Australian Economic Review*, No. 92: 45–60.
Westbrook, J.R. (1993) *The Effects of Exchange Rate Pegging on the Credibility of Stabilization Programs: An Empirical Investigation of the European Monetary System*, Unpublished PhD Dissertation, Claremont Graduate School.
Willett, T.D.; Al-Marhubi, F. and Dahel, R. (1993) 'Currency policies for Eastern Europe and the commonwealth countries: an optimum currency area approach', paper presented at the annual meetings of the Allied Social Science Associations, Anaheim, CA.
Wolf, H.C. (1991) 'Procyclical prices: a demi-myth?', *Federal Reserve Bank of Minneapolis Quarterly Review*, 15: 25–28.
Woolley, J.T. (1992) 'Policy credibility and European monetary institutions', in A.M. Sbragia (ed.), *Euro-Politics: Institutions and Policymaking in the 'New' European Community*, Washington, DC: Brookings Institution.
Young, J.P. (1925) *European Currency and Finance*, Volume I, Washington, DC: US Government Printing Office.

Index

For Product Safety Concerns and Information please contact our EU
representative GPSR@taylorandfrancis.com
Taylor & Francis Verlag GmbH, Kaufingerstraße 24, 80331 München, Germany

www.ingramcontent.com/pod-product-compliance
Ingram Content Group UK Ltd.
Pitfield, Milton Keynes, MK11 3LW, UK
UKHW022110190926
475702UK00013B/1363
* 9 7 8 1 1 3 8 8 6 5 8 0 8 *